AF566675

ALTERNATIVE ECONOMICS

Economic Thought of Mahatma Gandhi

ALTERNATIVE ECONOMICS

Economic Thought of Mahatma Gandhi

SECOND REVISED EDITION

DR. JAI NARAIN SHARMA
Professor and Hon. Director, Gandhi Bhawan
Department of Gandhian Studies
Panjab University, Chandigarh

Foreword by

HON'BLE SHRI T.N. CHATURVEDI
Governor of Karnataka

DEEP & DEEP PUBLICATIONS PVT. LTD.
F-159, Rajouri Garden, New Delhi - 110 027

ALTERNATIVE ECONOMICS
Economic Thought of Mahatma Gandhi

SECOND REVISED EDITION

ISBN 978-81-8450-423-1

Printed in India at MAYUR ENTERPRISES
WZ Plot No. 3, Gujjar Market, Tihar Village, New Delhi - 110 018

Published by DEEP & DEEP PUBLICATIONS PVT. LTD.
F-159, Rajouri Garden, New Delhi - 110 027 • Phone : 25435369, 25440916
E-mail : ddpubs@gmail.com • ddpubs@yahoo.com
Showroom :
2/13, Ansari Road, Daryaganj, New Delhi - 110 002 • Telefax : 23245122

Dedicated to

The Sacred Memory of

my Father

(Late) Pandit Sadhu Ram Vaikaranachariya

(1913-2005)

Contents

RAJ BHAVAN
BANGALORE

Foreword

Gandhi and his ideas continue to be enigmatic and yet of continuing interest and debate. He was not a system builder, nor a professional economist. But the insights as they arise from his writings and speeches lead to some conceptualization and visualization of Gandhi's vision of an economy and polity indeed, of society as such. It is so because of Gandhi's intuitive and inward look, pulse on the psychology of the people, the imperative of the situation and convincing as well as smooth, effortless identification with the common people and their hopes and fears, aims and aspirations. The quest among economists, social scientists, environmentalists and concerned citizens all over the world for an alternative model of development has led to renewed and wide ranging interest in Gandhi's ideas and views in matters economic.

The inadequacy or near-failure of various models of economic and political development in India has been a cause of frustration and bewilderment to the intellectual class, most particularly to those who have grown either in the traditions of 19th Century Liberalism, Fabian Socialism, or under the strong influence of Marxian thought and movements. Some of these intellectuals now feel the need for a more indigenous model, which can simultaneously meet the challenges of the modern world and make use of the best aspects of Indian traditions through which alone people can genuinely be involved in and enthused for political and economic development. Many Indian intellectuals are now prone to accepting the Gandhian alternative. Dr. Jai Narain Sharma is one of the social scientists who has taken up the study of Gandhian studies seriously.

The mixed system of planning in India by democratic persuasion, combined with a broad framework of direction, did not fully come up to people's expectations. Many critics felt that it was elitist. It led to great disparities of wealth and pushed more people into poverty. Some thinkers, other than sentimental Gandhians think that had we adopted the Gandhian model from the very beginning, many problems could have been avoided. However, the past is past, and we must learn from it so as not to repeat it. Instead, we should plan for a better future. That is how the feeling has grown that it is the greatest compulsion of our time to return to Gandhi.

Going along the path that he had chalked out for himself, Gandhi arrived at a social philosophy which could be characterized as a synthesis between the needs, urges and aspirations of the individual and the society of which the individual is an inseparable and indivisible part. He called it Sarvodaya—the well-being of all. While it is the duty and responsibility of society to plan for the fullest possible development of the best in every individual, it is equally necessary that the individual renders back unto society what he, in fact, owes to society. Thus, there has to be a balancing of rights and obligations between the individual and society. Society will be but an abstract concept, if we do not think in terms of the individuals who form it. An individual is equally an abstract, without a society to live in. Gandhi, therefore, gave the greatest importance to the flowering of the individual in a properly ordered society, and not merely to organizations and systems. He was of the opinion that this will provide the optimization of the potential of the individual and of society. It will lead to social cohesion and harmony. A chain is only as strong as its weakest link and a system is good and efficient only to the extent of the goodness and efficiency of the individuals working in it. Gandhi applied these principles to all human organizations and systems, economic, political and social.

Man, the individual, is at the core of the Gandhian system of thought. The objective is the moral and spiritual development of man. Man has consciousness, his capacity for self-consciousness, and his in-built capacity to judge between good and evil, between what will help him in his evolution to higher levels of being and what will obstruct his path. This gives him a leverage, not only to aspire after higher levels, but to endeavour to attain the same. Gandhi believed in self-effort and the path he outlined lay through ethical, moral and spiritual discipline. The keynote of Gandhian ethics is love, which largely means near-identity of interest with every sentient being; this love has to be expressed in the form of service and sacrifice.

Gandhi saw that there was much evil, injustice and exploitation in human relationships and public affairs. He was determined that all these must go. He wanted to devise ways and means which would be consistent with the principles he laid down for himself as being the best—non-violence or ahimsa. He was as heroic in fighting evil and injustice in the world outside as in conquering the evil and weakness in his own mind. The means he adopted satisfied his double criteria of moral excellence, namely that they should be based in truth and that they should be pure, moral and constructive. For him there was no conflict between ends and means.

The average leader of men, especially in a democratic society, has to continually adapt himself to his environment and choose what he considers the lesser evil. Some adaptation is inevitable. But as that process goes on, occasions arise when that very adaptation imperils his basic ideal and objectives. The amazing thing about Gandhi was that he adhered, in all its fullness, to his ideals, his conception of truth and yet, he did succeed in moulding and moving a large of human beings, with differing temperaments and backgrounds. He was not inflexible. He had remarkable intellectual resilience. He was very much alive to the necessities of the moment and adapted himself to changing circumstances. But all these adaptations were about secondary matters. In regard to basic postulates, he was inflexible and firm as a rock. There was no compromise for him with what he considered to be evil. His personal charisma was rooted in his selflessness, earnestness, social sensitivity and transparent integrity in approach to life and mission.

In the context of the wide parameters of Gandhiji's thought and action, Dr. Jai Narain Sharma has tried to focus on the varied aspects of Gandhi's economic thinking and has tried to develop a total picture of the Gandhian socio-economic order. It is not essential for anyone to agree with his prognosis, logic or even conclusions in all their details. But nobody can deny that his is a stimulating study based on extensive study and the author's own reflections and experience.

I welcome this study by Dr. Jai Narain Sharma. He makes out a strong case to produce indigenous solutions for the problems and needs of India's teeming millions, while, at the same time, keeping their minds open to whatever fresh ideas and ideals, ways and means, are available from anywhere in the world.

I express my thanks to the learned author for asking me to contribute a small foreword to his work. It was a rewarding experience to go through this book. Dr. Sharma is a serious scholar in the area of Gandhian studies. I hope that he will continue his pursuits further in his chosen field of interest. I wish him all the best in his future endeavours. The present exploration by him in Gandhiji's economic ideas and ideals certainly make a useful addition to the growing literature on Mahatma Gandhi.

T.N. Chaturvedi

T.N. CHATURVEDI

Preface

The science of economics is in crisis and it has begun to question its own philosophical assumptions and methods. The century old reign of positivist economics, which included famous models and their numerous versions such as Neo-classical, Keynesian and Marxian has lost track of its philosophical assumptions. Communism has become out of date. It has been virtually disowned by its own promoters. To speak for it, is fighting a lost battle. Capitalism has developed serious contradictions both economic and socio-cultural. The recent developments in the world bear testimony to it. Major economists of the world agree that they had not anticipated the crisis. Those who celebrated the economic miracle earlier are undoubtedly the ones who are most perplexed. The debilitating impact of panics in the markets, the moral hazard created by guarantees, the asset bubbles that result from crony capitalism as well as the effects of competitive devaluation, etc. were not unknown to the world. What is then, that prevented economists from using their knowledge to anticipate the crisis?

Various models of the world order are being suggested for the future but almost all of them are extensions of a set of analytical theories and ideologies based on a single paradigm be capitalist, socialist or any other, and aim at the survival of the existing international world economy which is of marginal signifies for the welfare of the majority of the people. For the third world all them are only of academic interest. These models conceal the real interests of the dominant groups who are pitted against others living in poverty, illiteracy and squalor. Most of the people are sinking into misery while a few are enjoying a life of luxury. Looking at the state of world economy, global inequalities, poverty, corruption and insensitivities of multi-nationals, one gets the impression that the economists are the highest paid legitimisers of this state of affairs.

There are rich nations and poor nations but the world order divided into nation-states also conceals the alliance between the ruling class or elites of most nation-states, which leaves billions of people in the cold. F.H. Cardose and E. Faletto in their work, *Dependence and Development in Latin America* saw this relationship clearly when they wrote about the relationship between national and international forces as forming a complex whole whose structural links are not based on mere external forms of exploitation and coercion, but are rooted in coincidence of interests between local dominant classes and international ones and, on the other side, are challenged by local dominated groups and classes.

That is why distinction between North and South—a divide between privileged and the under-privileged is of much greater significance. The latter are increasingly pushed out of global decision-making, with a few crumbs and weapons thrown for their consumption. Professor J.D. Sethi has rightly termed this phenomena as International Economic Darwinism (IED), which is a set of relations between nations and peoples on the principle of survival of the fittest except that nations or peoples do not disappear, if only because it is neither in the interest of the fittest nor in their power to make unfit completely disappear. They are obliged to make the least fit survive, but only marginally or as destitute living in ghettos. Modern Darwinism assumes that people and nations will generally remain intact. The North-South distinction is derived from this Darwinism, showing that under all assumptions made so far, no matter how the present order is reordered, it will allow the weaker and more unfit to survive but not to participate in and certainly not to decide about the global order.

This crisis can be analyzed in a historical perspective. More than two centuries ago, when modern economics started developing, it was called a dismal science. There were two reasons for this. One, economics was separated from ethics, two, the economic situation, which was translated into economic laws, was one of unrelieved misery on one hand and garish riches on the other. Then, a century later, economics became a matter of great optimism as it opened up tremendous vistas for the production of goods and services. Paradoxically, as life became more and more complex, holistic analysis gave way to compartmentalization and specialism which increasingly rested on pure economic analysis. That gave rise to the 'Economic Man' in whose name the economists played games with one another in terms of fancy theories unconcerned with the problem of relationship between facts and values. Whenever the question of value was brought in, the economists rejected it as belonging to some other field of analysis. But this concealed a death trap for this subject and hence begins a search for an alternative paradigm. It is in this context that the study of Economic philosophy of Mahatma Gandhi has become relevant and urgent.

Before one attempts to pronounce any judgement on the Gandhian economic system, it is obvious that one must know what the Gandhian economics is. Unfortunately, this is by no means easy, Gandhi was not an economist or a social scientist as for instance Marx was. He did not present his economic ideas in any systematic form though he wrote voluminously and steadily particularly in the columns of *Young India* and *Harijan*. He certainly did not have the time. I doubt whether he had the academic discipline needed for this purpose. Things have been made more difficult by his followers or professed followers. Much of his writings, particularly in the columns of *Young India* and *Harijan* was in response to *ad hoc* questions. Naturally, his answers were also often *ad hoc* to be read in the specific context of the question. This has led to a variety of interpretations of what he said and meant.

It seems, therefore, to understand the Gandhian economics, one must go back to Gandhi. This is what I propose to do. This will require me to quote rather extensively from Gandhi's writings with a request to the readers to bear with me. It is right and fair that, while we discuss things in the name of some one like Gandhi, we should check what he himself said and wrote about it.

The Mahatma regarded economics as a moral science and

laid tremendous emphasis on the ethical aspect of the problem. Economics that hurts the moral well-being of an individual or a nation is immoral and therefore, sinful. Its goal is not pure material benefits but advancement of humanity on its road to progress by strengthening the character and the development of personality of each individual engaged in such activity. No one's gain should be anybody's loss, financial, physical, moral or spiritual. This is the first brick upon which the edifice of his entire economic philosophy stands. He denounced the concept of 'Economic Man' because the mind of this industrialized robot suffers an almost complete black out when it comes to freedom and responsibilities of a human person and it will not easily be quickened into a realization of what has happened to it. We will have to learn or relearn, how to feed, clothe and house ourselves so that the entire process is creative, cooperative and satisfying. The aggressive instinct has, superseded the instinct to express and create, whence every human and social function has been vitiated, from the feeding and culture of the soil to the feeding and culture of man. Perhaps that is why Gandhi formulated his economic principles in the context of his design of an ideal social order: a non-violent, non-exploitative, humanistic and egalitarian society. He approached human problems from an integral outlook of life in which economics, ethics, philosophy and religion were synthesized. Since he was sensitive to the feeling and needs of masses, he could never stand apart from his people. Satisfaction of needs and moral elevation of individuals were not anti-thetical for him.

With this perspective in mind the present book has been written. It is an updated, enlarged and revised edition of my earlier work, 'Economic Thought of Mahatma Gandhi' first published in 1991 and then in 2003.

I am conscious that I am embarking upon rather an ambitious adventure, and I am equally conscious of my own limitations in doing so. But of late, I have found so much material both in the writings of Mahatma Gandhi and other Scholars that I am tempted to say publically what I have been ruminating in my mind during the last thirty years.

I simply can not write anything, much less see it published without considerable help from outside. I can not name them all. But I shall be failing in my duty if I do not record my deep sense of gratitude to my teacher Professor S.L. Malhotra for his constant encouragement and constructive criticism which culminated in the completion of the present work and my profound regard to my father Pt. Sadhu Ram Vaikaranachariya who was always a source of inspiration to me.

I also owe my sincere gratitude to Professor R.P. Mishra, former Vice-Chancellor, Allahabad University, Allahabad; Professor Naresh Dadich, Vice-Chancellor, Vardhman Mahavir Open University, Kota, Rajasthan; Professor S.K. Sharma, SVC Panjab University, Chandigarh; Professor D. Gopal, Co-ordinator, Gandhian Studies Programme, IGNOU, New Delhi; Pt. Onkar Chand, President, Servants of People Society, Lajpat Rai Bhawan, Chandigarh; Professor R.N. Pal, former Pro-Vice-Chancellor, Punjabi University, Patiala; Professor B.R. Dugar, Head Department of Non-Violence and Peace, Jain Vishva Bharathi University, Ladnun, Rajasthan; Professor R.S. Yadav, Chairman, Department of Political Science, Kurukshetra University, Kurukshetra; Professor K.S. Bharati, Head, Department of Gandhian Thought, Nagpur University, Nagpur; Professor Narendra Dogra, Director, Academic Staff College, Punjabi University, Patiala; Professor Anurag Gangal, Chairman, Department of Political Science, Jammu University, Jammu; Professor Rajendra Chauhan, Department of Political Science, H.P. University, Shimla; Professor K.C. Agnihotri, Director, Himachal Pardesh University Regional Center, Dharamshala; Professor R.P. Duvedi, Head, Department of Gandhian Thought, Mahatma Gandhi Kashi Vidhyapith, Varanasi; Professor Sanjeev Sharma, Chairman, Department of Political Science, C.C.S. Meerut University, Meerut and Dr. A.D. Mishra, National Gandhi Museum, New Delhi.

Dr. M.L. Sharma and Dr. Ashu Pasricha, my colleagues in the department deserve my sincere thanks for their untiring support and cooperation. I am equally grateful to Principal Raj Gopal Sharma for his expert comments on Isopanishad, Dr. Brij Sharma, I.F.S., on Ecology, and Er. Anil Sharma, I.E.S. on Technology.

Further as always, my wife Dr. (Mrs.) Rashmi Sharma took the brunt of burden of my work, having to share time with a manuscript, which as every author knows is a sacrifice indeed and to my publisher Sh. G.S. Bhatia for speedy and flawless publication of the book.

Above all, I feel elevated in acknowledging my sincere regards to His Excellency Shri T.N. Chaturvedi, a scholar of International repute and the Governor of Karnataka for taking pains to go through the manuscript and writing a Foreword of this volume.

In the end I wish to record that the author is anxious to express a sincere hope that other of his colleagues, profiting by what may be useful, avoiding what may be erroneous, supplying what may be defective in his labours, may be by then stimulated to undertake and execute a better treatise upon the same subject. Till they do so, should bear with me.

JAI NARAIN SHARMA

1

Evolution of Gandhi's Economic Thought

Economists are properly studied without undue reference to their personalities. Biographies of Adam Smith, Alfred Marshall, Karl Marx, J.M. Keynes, etc. may all throw some light upon their theories but need not affect our appraisals of them. No doubt, it is sometimes useful to know about the declared purposes or practical intentions of the abstract theorists. For example, awareness of Karl Marx's complex personality may be relevant to our grasp of his theories. But when we turn to Mahatma Gandhi's economic philosophy, we find it peculiarly difficult to ignore his personality and his activities.

For a proper appreciation of the ideas of Gandhi on any subject, it is necessary to bear in mind two things. First, he was not an economist in the conventional sense of the term. As Achariya J.B. Kripalani puts it, "If ever there was a planner without elaborate blue prints Gandhi was one".[1] Unlike other economists, he did not study Economics academically. It was not in his nature too. He did not assign himself the task of setting up an academic discipline. He did not present his economic ideas in any systematic form and at one place; they have to be culled from innumerable passages occurring in his articles, interviews, speeches and answers to the questions, etc. He was not a theorist; he was primarily an actionist—a Karamyogi. He himself admitted "I am not built for academic writings. Action is my domain. What I understand according to my lights to be my duty and what comes my way I do".[2] He did not spin his theories in the cloistered atmosphere of his study, they grew and developed in the crucible of experience, in the course of his attempt to wrest freedom for his country and to solve the various practical problems as and when they emerged in the course of his long struggle against foreign domination. It could not have been otherwise in the situation he was placed in. The solution he offered for the alleviation of the economic ills did not derive out of any rigid doctrinaire approach. His solutions were rooted in necessity. Thus, Gandhian economics was primarily a response, to use a Toynbeen expression, 'to the challenges that poverty ridden India flung at a particular phase in the process of the development of Indian history'.[3] For a person in the position which Gandhi occupied it was incumbent that he took the most pressing economic problems and issues into account and offered his own solutions. And from these solutions and experiences, there emerged a definite economic theory.

Second, his genius was more spiritual and moral than intellectual. His whole life was cast in the spiritual and moral mould of which truth and non-violence were the fundamental tenets. His economics has to be studied from the view point of his own moral and spiritual principles and ideals. One must try to understand the language that Gandhi used. It was not the language used by specialists. It was the language of the market place which common man uses and understands.

In considering Gandhian economics, or, for that matter any socio-economic philosophy, the scientific procedure as suggested by Professor N.K. Bose[4] should be followed. The scientific procedure is to understand and assess the doctrines in terms of the conditions that give rise to them. Gandhi's economic ideas, can, therefore be best understood in the light of physical and social conditions. Throughout the ages India was known for its riches. It was known as 'Golden Sparrow'. The source of its riches was not agriculture; in those days its produce could not be exported. Its wealth was derived from its industry, carried on in almost every home and village. The product of this industry found a ready market throughout the then known world. It was the lucrative trade with India that induced the seamen of the maritime countries of Europe to find a sea route to India. The trade with India was at first the monopoly of the Portuguese merchants. But soon other nations in Europe participated in it. Ultimately the British succeeded in creating themselves a vast empire.

In England the Industrial Revolution began in the later part of the 18th century. The British rulers progressively started destroying Indian handicrafts in favour of their own manufacturers. All the raw material was taken from India and products finished in England were shipped to India and found a ready market here. Deprived of their industry more and more of growing population of India had to rely for all its requirements on their income from land. The size of the farm holdings, went on diminishing, till most of them became uneconomic. The question before Gandhi was how to find useful and remunerative work for this vast population. His mental horizon was bound by the economics of colonial rules.[5] The problem of the problems that confronted India during the British Raj—was POVERTY and Gandhi reacted sharply to the crushing effect and demoralizing influence of grinding poverty of the masses of the country. This obvious fact should not be lost sight of in any study, worth the name, of the economic doctrines he propounded. Along with the objective background the ethos has to be taken into consideration. Failing this approach, pre-possessed feelings and subjective inclinations may blind our vision and lead as far away from an intelligent appreciation of the subject.

It seems, therefore, that to understand what the Gandhian Economic system, one must go back to Gandhi. This is what one should do. This will require one to quote rather extensively from Gandhi. This is also right and fair that while one discusses things in the name of someone like Gandhi, he should check what the Mahatma himself said and wrote about it. The only point to remember here is that there is no finality in the Gandhian concepts. This is largely so because his concepts are not absolute but relative. He himself kept on modifying, elaborating and enriching his own concepts on the basis of his experiences. He himself admitted, "I would like to say to the diligent readers of my writings and to others who are interested in them that I am not at all concerned with appearing to be consistent. In my search after Truth, I have discarded many ideas and learnt many new things. Old as I am in age, I have no feeling that I have ceased to grow inwardly, or that my growth will stop at the dissolution of the flesh. What I am concerned with is my readiness to obey the call of Truth, my God, from moment to moment, and, therefore, when anybody finds inconsistency between any two writings of mine, if he has still faith in my sanity, he would do well to choose the later of the two on the same subject."[6]

At an other place he confessed that he grew 'from truth to truth';[7] in other words, his earlier utterances need to be understood in the light of his later ones, not *vice versa*. Not having had the time and training for the systematic development of his thought Gandhi's ideas are in the main of an existential kind. They grew as he grew up.

He was not a man who embodied his ideas in a systematic treatise. Apart from his two well known works—An 'Autobiography' or 'The Story of My Experiments With Truth' and 'Satyagraha in South Africa'—the only other considerable work which attempt to set forth his ideas in anything approaching a systematic manner is 'Hind Swaraj'. All the rest of his truly voluminous writings are to be found scattered in his journalistic articles, his letters and memoranda and such of his speeches as have been recorded faithfully or of which the texts are available—are now available in the 100 volumes publication project, "The Collected Works of Mahatma Gandhi". A detailed account of different factors that shaped the economic ideas of Gandhi can make the picture more clear. But the evolution of his economic thought has to be viewed in the development of the Indian National Movement.

Firstly, the family in which he was born, the society that he confronted, the cultural values and traditional norms that he inherited all these factors left their impression on the mind of Mahatma. In Political Science, there is a proverb that "political cultures are changed and maintained in the family."

If the family of a child belongs to one particular political party, there is every likelihood that their children will become the members of the same political party when they grow up or for the time being the ideology of that particular party will have far reaching effects on the minds of their children. If the family changes its political ideology its effects can be traced on the mind of the children. The same proverb can be used here with slight modifications, "Economic cultures are changed and maintained in the family." Let us see what are the effect of his family on his economic thinking.

His was the truely Vaishnava Hindu family. His mother Pütali Bai was a deeply religious and pious lady. She belonged to Pranami Sect, which combined in it elements of Hinduism and Islam—known for its remarkable simplicity not worshipping images—but studying all scriptures—Koran and the sacred books of Vaishnavites. Many of friends of Karam Chand Gandhi, and some of his spiritual advisors were Jains and in their company, young Gandhi came to know the concept of ahimsa in depth. Religious background of the family was Vaishnavite but with a great tolerance for the other sects of Hinduism and other religions.

Since universal love has always played an important role in Hindu Dharma, it forms the basis of Gandhi's economic philosophy and as such his economics could never wringle out of this imprint of deep spiritual influence. The exalted life of self-abnigation of Buddha the aprigraha philosophy of Gita and the teachings of Mahavira also shaped his economic thinking. All these factors influenced Gandhi to regard economic as a moral science instead of a mere positive and analytical science, and that the renunciation of self-destroying competition and the endless wants will results in the abolition of engines of economic destruction. "Why should all of us possess property? Why should not we, after a certain time, dispossess ourselves of all property?" he asked. "For a Hindu it was the usual thing at a certain stage. Every good Hindu is expected, after having lived for household life for a certain period, to enter upon a life of non-possession of property. Why may we not revive the old traditions."[8] It was no doubt, without much conscious awareness that Gandhi absorbed these vital influences. He later wrote in his autobiography, "Children inherit the qualities of the parents, no less than their physical features. Environment does play an important part, but the original capital on which a child starts his life is inherited from his ancestors". This 'original capital' is later reflected in his economics where he maintained that economics and ethics are not separate entities.

The second influence that shaped Gandhi's economic thinking was his observation of the English Industrial scene in the last decade of the 19th century when he was a student in London. This find expression in his early book 'Hind Swaraj'. The book is, according to him, a faithful record of conversations he had with political workers. Some of the key passages in it read as follow:

> "Formerly, men worked in the open air only as much as they liked. Now thousands of workmen meet together and for the sake of maintenance work in factories or mines. Their condition is worse than that of beasts. They are obliged to work, at the risk of their lives, at most dangerous occupations, for the sake of millionaires. Formerly, men were made slaves under physical compulsion. Now they are enslaved by temptation of money and of the luxuries that money can buy".

At another place he writes, "Machinery is like a snakehole which may contain from one to a hundred snakes. Where there is machinery there are large cities, there are tram cars and railways; and there only does one see electric light. English villages do not boast of any of these things. Honest physician will tell you that where means of artificial locomotion have increased, the health of people has suffered. I remember that when in a European town there was a scarcity of money, the receipts of the tramway company, of the lawyers and of the doctors went down and people were less unhealthy I can not recall a single good point in connection with machinery".[9]

During industrial revolution exploitation was maximum and knew no bound. This was the worst phase of industrialism. The working conditions in the factories were worst. There was no limitation of the working hours. Children and women also used to work in the factories from morning till evening under conditions. There were no proper methods of wage fixation. On

Gandhi there was a negative impact of industrial revolution. He thought that all these problems and miseries of the labourers are due to this industrial civilization. He reacted strongly to it and this reaction is fully visible in the pages of his *Hind Swaraj* and later writings.

Gandhi was also greatly influenced by 'Unto This Last' of John Ruskin. This was Ruskin's first book that Gandhi read. About his reading habits he has made this refreshingly outspoken comment. "During the days of my education I had read practically nothing outside text books and after I launched into active life I had very little time for reading. I can not therefore claim much book knowledge. However, I believe that I have not lost much because of this enforced restraint. On the contrary, the limited reading may be said to have enabled me thoroughly to digest what I did read. Of these books, the one that brought about an instantaneous and practical transformation in my life was 'Unto This Last' I translated it later into Gujarati, entitling Sarvodaya."[10]

This book came in Gandhi's hands in curious circumstances. In 1903, he was leaving for Durban on a business trip. His friend Henry Polak came to see him off at the railway station (Johannesburg) and gave him this book to read during the journey. Gandhi read the book all through the journey. As he reached the last page, deeply reflecting all the while, he had come to a firm decision: he would change his entire outward life in accordance with the ideals set forth by John Ruskin. The decision was based on one solid reason: Gandhi found in this book, expressed in clear terms, the innermost echo of some of his own growing convictions.[11] That was why it held him with so much power and led him towards an entirely new order of life.

It was particularly Ruskin's ideas on political economy rather than anything else[12] that Gandhi assimilated into his own thinking and adopted from Ruskin without qualification the functional view of property. Ruskin's attack on the assumptions of political economy founded on an "ossifiant theory of progress" and on the industrial system is systematically set forth in his 'Unto This Last'. "Political economists assert", laments Ruskin. 'That social affections are to be looked upon as accidental and disturbing elements in human nature', but avarice and the desire for progress are constant elements. Let us eliminate the inconstants, and, considering the human element being merely as a covetous machine, examine by what laws of labour, purchase and sale, the greatest accumulative result in wealth is obtainable."[13] Ruskin with his strident call to mankind for equality and brotherhood had touched something that had been latent all this time in Gandhi himself.

Many years later, stressing what he owed to Great Britain, Gandhi wrote, "Great Britain gave me Ruskin, whose 'Unto This Last' transformed me overnight from a lawyer and city dweller into rustic living away from Durban on a farm three miles from the nearest railway station."[14] It was the work which had inspired him to found the Phoenix Settlement (1904) on principles of bread labour and the responsibility of the community organisation to provide for the physical welfare of the workers who were its members. The teachings of Unto This Last falls under three heads:

I. That the good of individual is contained in the good of all.
II. That a lawyer's work has the same value as the barber's in as much as all have the same right of earning their livelihood from their work.
III. That a life of labour, i.e., the life of tiller of the soil and handicraftsman, is the life worth-living.[15]

Gandhi remarked: "The first of these I knew, the second I had dimly realized. The third had never occurred to me. Unto This Last made it as clear as day light for me that the second and third were contained in the first. I arose with the dawn ready to reduce these principles to practice."[16]

Another great mind that influenced Gandhi was Leo Tolstoy. Gandhi had read Tolstoy long before he came across Ruskin's Unto This Last. But while the great Russian writer and philosopher affected his 'inner being' he was not yet ready for the tremendous impact that he was to experience later. Ruskin gave him the doctrine of manual labour. Tolstoy, in addition, led him to the avowal of complete non-violence. He was overwhelmed by Tolstoy's 'The Kingdom of God is Within You', with its strong denunciation of war and all violence, and sanction of resistance to a tyrannical state. No less powerful in its effect on Gandhi's mind was Tolstoy's 'Reason and Religion' which came out in 1894. Gandhi read several other works by the great writers, including Gospels in Brief; What to Do; The First Step; and How Shall We Escape. But the book which influenced Gandhi's economic thinking was 'What Then Must We Do' in which Tolstoy revealed in moving language the abject destitution and exploitation of the humble people in Moscow[17] and pointed out that the sole method of spiritual resurrection in the context of rampant misery was the law of labour. Tolstoy denounced the sharp separation of physical and manual labour because he regarded it as a device for perpetuating the slavery of the workers.

The ancient Egyptian economy, the economy of the Roman Empire and feudal Middle Ages and even the company of the Church have been based on this separation.[18] In their support, the advocates of the ascendant classes claim that they have been assigned the job of governing and educating others by God. Even at the time of the French Revolution, he clergy claimed to educate the people, the nobility to govern them, and the government servants and the army to protect them. For these services, their means of livelihood were produced by the labourers in the field. Tolstoy regarded this whole system as unjustifiable because it results in the enslavement of the working population. The latter are eternally condemned to tyranny and oppression and other appropriate the fruits of the labour. He condemned Hegelianism, Malthusianism and Comteanism as apologies for this unnatural system. Hegel with his notion of the real and the rational appeared, to Tolstoy, as the justifier of the oppressive *status quo*.[19] Malthus with his notion of disproportion between the law of arithmetical progression with which the resources increase and the law of geometrical progression with which population increases, seemed to put the blame for poverty on an uncontrollable law of Nature.[20] Tolstoy on the other hand felt that poverty could be controlled by the practice of the Biblical law of sharing one's coat with one's poor neighbour. Comtean positivism with its theory of society as an organism was basically a false philosophy because unlike society lacks a common sensorium. Furthermore, it appeared as a support to the modern system of division of labour with its attendants evils of inequality and gross appression.[21] He categorically stated that we have no right to exploit the labour of others. Every one must work for producing his means of livelihood. Only thus can the immoral system wherein millions perform to support the luxurious living of a chosen few can be ended. The Division of Labour, which is one of the prime concepts of modern political economy was regarded by Tolstoy as a clever and wicked device to prevent the working of the divine law that every one must produce his own food. Bread labour is the sole antedote to rampant exploitation. He quoted the saying of a Chinese prophet. "If there is one idle person in the world then some one must be dying of hunger." That every person should do manual labour, Tolstoy regarded as a universal law. Only this law if followed, could eliminate the differences between the social classes.[22] Furthermore, he pointed out that intellectuals could get enthusiasm even for their scholarly work if they engaged in physical labour.

Gandhi not only preached but also practised this concept of bread labour in his South African days. The Phoenix Farm was originally based on the practice of this principle. He was sincere in his conviction that the theory of bread labour if adequately practised would go a long way in creating the moral and social atmosphere for the realization of full equality. He wrote, "Everyone should deem it a dishonour to eat a single meal without honest labour. If we could shed the aversion to labour and adapt ourselves to unexpected changes of fortune, we would go a long way towards the acquisition of fearlessness and thus towards an upliftment of our national character."[23]

Curiously, Gandhi's earliest reference to Tolstoy seems to have been made years ago, when he was a student in London and saw the Eiffel Tower in Paris. He expressed his agreement with Tolstoy's view that the tower was a monument of man's folly.

His next notable reference to Tolstoy appeared in 'Indian Opinion' in 1905. "It is believed that, in the Western world, at any rate there is no man so talented as Leo Tolstoy", he wrote. Along with the theory of Bread labour as his main contribution, he formulated the remaining teachings of Tolstoy as follows:

1. Men should not accumulate wealth.
2. No matter how much evil a person does to us, we should always do good to him. Such is the Commandment of God, and also His Law.
3. No one should take part in fighting.
4. It is sinful to wield political power, as it leads to many evils.
5. Man must pay more attention to his duties than to his rights.
6. Agriculture is man's true occupation. It is wrong to establish large cities, to employ hundreds of thousands in factories so that a few can exploit the poverty of the many.[24]

Another factor which shaped Gandhi's economic philosophy was his concept of Swaraj which has a far broader and deeper significance than English term like freedom or independence. While advocating Swaraj Gandhi had in mind, apart from termination of British political control, economic self-sufficiency, dissolution of the firm grip of western civilisation culture and values. India was of course, a dependency of Britain, and her political affairs being controlled from West Minster. But such a debacle has overtaken the nations at the trail of economic and cultural subjugation of India. The growing flair of Indians for material comforts, their loss of faith in time honoured Indian values like simple living and high thinking, and their burning zeal for the dazzling articles of mass consumption produced in the industrialized west brought to Indian shores ship-loads of foreign goods. Political power followed the flag, and political domination was only a matter of times. Accordingly Gandhi posed the issue. "The English have not taken India; we have given it to them. . . . . They came to country for purpose of trade. . . . They had not the slightest intention at that time of establishing a kingdom. Who assisted the Company's officers? Who was tempted at the sight of their silver? Who bought their goods? The English merchants were able to get a footing in India because we encouraged them . . . its object was to increase its commerce and make money. It accepted our assistance and increased the number of its warehouses. To protect the latter it employed an army which was utilized by us also. Is it not then useless to blame to English for what we did at that time."[25]

The political domination of the country by Britain led to economic subjugation and provided an opportunity to the ruling power to indulge in the act of exploiting India. Money was being derived out of India in a variety of ways and the beneficiaries were not only the government of Britain but also her citizens in private capacities, as industrial, commercial and financial magnets, or as civil servants. Hence, Gandhi realised that termination of British rule in India would free Indian economy from foreign control, put a halt to economic exploitation of India, prevent the draining out of resources from India to the metropolitan country, open the flood gate to India's economic prosperity and thus lead to economic Swaraj. Elaborating his notion of Puran Swaraj, Gandhi wrote, "It is full economic freedom for the toiling millions."[26] Gandhi was painfully aware of the poverty, hunger, misery, wants, destitution and deprivation of the masses. Hence, when Gandhi thought of Swaraj, he had primarily in his mind these problems of the millions of people. Accordingly, he wrote in *Young India,* "The Swaraj of my dream is the poor man's Swaraj."[27]

As a practical philosopher and a man of action, the Mahatma realised that mere withdrawal of British political power from India may not spell relief for the suffering millions. The British industrial, commercial and financial interests deeply entrenched in Indian economy and they had so successfully spread their tentacles into the economic system of the company that even after the withdrawal of British political patronage they will not only survive but would very successfully continue its policy of exploitation. Hence, he stressed that the pursuit of Swaraj must necessarily involve the acceptance of Swadeshi. "Much of the deep poverty of the masses", he argued, "is due to the ruinous departure from Swadeshi in the economic and industrial life. If not an article of commerce had been brought from outside India, she would be today a land flowing with milk and honey. But that was not to be. We were greedy and so was England."[28]

It is also held in certain quarters that Gandhi had used Swadeshi as a political weapon also. He was of the confirmed view that basically the English people are traders. If by one way or the other, the economic benefits which England is taking from us can be curtailed, the freedom for the country can be achieved easily. That is why he talked of Swaraj through Swadeshi. Henery Brailsford, a contemporary of Gandhi wrote in his 'Rebel India', "His (Gandhi's) methods were designed to make the continuance of British rule impossible, but even more to train the people of India in self-respect. These methods, accordingly form a series of steps, each more difficult but also more effective than the last."[29]

Regarding the revival of hand spinning—Brailsford commented, "This revival of a hopelessly uneconomic craft signified, first of all Gandhi's revolt against our mechanical civilization—for he is a rebel, reminiscent of Tolstoy rather than of Ruskin, against Western machines no less than the British flag. It was secondly a way of freeing India from her tribute to Lancashire."[30] Referring to Salt Satyagraha, Brailsford wrote, "One enters the zone of Sedition with the next method, the attempt to smash the government's salt monopoly. It is the kindergarten stage of revolution. One smiles at the notion that the king emperor can be unseated by boiling sea water in a kettle. Even this mild activity is however an attack on the revenue system, and it landed thousands of Indians in prison, including Gandhi himself. He knew his public. He staged his salt making as a quasi-religious pilgrimage. Its pathetic innocence helped the law abiding people to take the first plunge in to disobedience. Here, too, one could argue that he was helping the impoverished peasant, and the protectionist motives made itself felt. Why salt from Liverpool, if one can evaporate salt water by the sun's heat on the shores of Bombay or Bengal?"[31]

The effect of contemporary ideologies can also be traced on the economic ideas of the Mahatma. Actually he was not influenced by these ideologies, he reacted to them or in a sense it can be called negative influence. The main ideologies of his time were, Capitalism, Communism, Socialism, Nazism and Fascism.

Brutal exploitation of man under the system of Capitalism evoked Gandhi's protest and he condemned the system in no uncertain terms. His denunciation of acquisitive society stemmed out of his feelings and deep concern for the down-trodden humanity.[32] For him the only yardstick of judging any economic system was human welfare. To him accumulation of property is immoral and always involves violence. That is why he extended his ethical principles to the domain of property relations. In his own words, „I suggest that we are thieves in a way. If I take anything that I do not need for my own immediate use, and keep it, I thieve it from somebody else. I venture to suggest that it is the fundamental law of Nature, without exceptions, that Nature produces enough for our wants from day-to-day, and if any body took enough for himself and nothing more, there would be no pauperism in this world, there would be no man dying of starvation in this world. But so long as we got this inequality so long we are thieving."[33] The solutions he offered for the elimination of capitalism were guided by this ethical outlook.

Gandhi rejected the Communist solutions with the equal force because he believed them to be based on violence and tyranny. He did not accept the basic belief of Communists way of forcible and violent expropriation of private property and collective state ownership, yet he was moved by the sacrifices of master spirits as Lenin. 'Bolshevism is the necessary result of modern materialistic civilization. Its insensate worship of matter has given rise to a school which has been brought up to look upon materialistic advancement as the goal and which has lost all the touch with the final things of life.'[34] His attitude towards 'socialism' is not very specific. In 1916 he said, "I am no socialist and I do not want to dispossess those who have got possessions, but I do say those of us who want to see light out of darkness have to follow this rule. I do not want to dispossess any body. I should then be departing from the rule of Ahimsa."[35] But in 1924 he admitted the necessity of Nationalisation or State Control. Though that was a guarded approval of socialism, yet a clear advance from his early position is evident. In 1934, he declared himself a socialist. In his own words, "I call myself a socialist. I love the very word, but I will not preach the same socialism as most socialists do."[36] In 1940, he moved one more step ahead. "I had claimed that I was a socialist long before those I knew in India had avowed their creed. But my socialism was natural to me and not adopted from any book. It came out of my unshakable belief in non-violence."[37]

These statements have shown that Gandhi moved with the time and responded to these challenges in his own way. Here, we find a man growing, developing and moving and making the masses move with him for the realization of a new society, as he envisaged it, free from exploitation. He reacted very sharply against Nazism and Fascism which put more and more emphasis on state and glorify violence. Thus these traits of these ideologies strengthened his belief in non-violence in economic matters also.

All these factors taken together gave a definite shape and content to his economic ideas and the process of evolution went on with the passage of time.

After examining the factors which influenced his economic ideas, we are now in a better position to understand the fundamental principles or bases of his economic thought. These can be discussed as follow.

FUNDAMENTAL PRINCIPLES OF GANDHI'S ECONOMIC THOUGHT

A. Moral and Spiritual Approach to Economics

Gandhi formulated his economic ideas and principles in the context of his design, of an ideal social order; a non-violent, non-exploitative humanistic and egalitarian society. This social order embodied the fundamental philosophy of his life. He approached all facets of his social order—its economics, its politics from the philosophical premises—truth and non-violence—that governed his entire life. It was, therefore, impossible for him to produce an economics that would be ethically neutral. When economics is related to this way of life it becomes "Meta-Economics."[38] 'True economics', Gandhi said, 'never militates against the highest ethical standard, just as all true ethics to be worth its name must at the same time be also good economics. An economics which inculcates Mammon Worship and enable the strong to amass wealth at the expense of the weak, is a false and dismal science. It spells death, True economics on the other hand stands for social justice; it promotes the good of all equally including the weakest, and is indispensable for decent life."[39] He was not willing to draw any sharp distinction between economics and ethics. "I must confess that I do not draw a sharp or any distinction between economics and ethics. Economics that hurt the moral well-being of an individual or a nation are sinful. Thus the economics that permit one country to prey upon another are immoral."[40] Or "That economics is untrue which ignores or disregards moral value. The extension of the law of non-violence in economics means nothing less than the introduction of moral values as a factor to be considered in regulating international commerce.[41]

The fullest statement of his views about ultimate criterion in the economics phere is to be found in his 1916 speech at Muir College, Allahabad. In that speech he declared, "I venture to think that the scriptures of the world are far safer and sounder treatises on laws of economics than many modern text books. . . . He (Jesus) is himself the "greatest economist of his time."[42]

This emphasis of the ethical aspect distinguishes Gandhian economics from that of Smith, Marshall, Marx or Keynes. Take for example, in his Liquidity Preference Theory of Rate of interest,[43] Lord Keynes argued that rate of interest is determined by demand for the liquidity (cash) in the short period because the supply of liquidity by and large remains constant. He tells us various motives for the demand of money and then the sources for the supply of cash. But he does not tell us whether this particular rate of interest is 'reasonable' or not or what should be the actual rate of interest, which do not exploit any one.

Let us take another example, while discussing the price determination in Perfect Competition, Dr. Marshall[44] tells that price is determined by the demand and supply of any commodity. If the demand is greater and supply is less, then price will be high and *vice-versa.* But he does not tell us whether this price is reasonable or not? There is every possibility and some supplier might have created artificial scarcity to decrease the supply so that the price may increase, or the price determined in this way may be so high that it may be beyond the reach of a common man to purchase that particular good. Dr. Marshall is silent over such queries. This conventional economics is neutral towards the value judgments. This is merely the science of getting rich. But there are many different ways of getting rich. There was a time in Europe when people sought to acquire wealth by poisoning owners of large estates and appropriating their possessions. Now-a-days, merchants adulterate the food sold to the poor, for example, milk with borax, wheat flour with potato flour, coffee with chicory, butter with fats and so on. This is on the same level as getting rich by poisoning others. "Can we call this either an art or a science of getting rich?", asks Ruskin.[45]

He further argued that "let us now, however, assume that by getting rich, economists merely mean 'getting rich by robbing others'. They should point out that theirs' is a science of getting rich by legal or just means. It happens these days, that many things which are legal are not just. The only right way therefore, to acquire wealth is to do so justly. And if this is true, we must know what is just? It is not enough to live by the laws of demand and supply. Fish, wolves and rats subsist in that manner. Bigger fish prey on smaller ones, rats swallow insects and wolves devour even human beings. That for them is the law of nature, they know no better. God has endowed man with understanding, with a sense of justice. He must follow these and not think of growing rich by devouring others—by cheating others and reducing them to beggary.[46]

That is why men of wisdom have held that where Mammon is God, no one worships the true God. Wealth can not be reconciled with God. God lives only in the homes of poor. Perhaps that is why Gandhi equated God with Daridranarayan. "Daridranarayan is one of the millions of names by which humanity knows God who is unnameable and unfathomable by human understanding, and it means God of the poor, God appearing in the hearts of the poor."[47] Because, for the poor economic is spiritual, you can not make any other appeal to those starving millions. It will fall flat on them. But you take food to them and they will regard you as their God. They are incapable of any other thought."[48] While writing in *Young India,* he poured his heart, "It is good enough to talk of God whilst we are sitting here after a nice breakfast and looking forward to a nicer luncheon, but how am I to talk of God to the millions who have to go without two meals a day? To them God can only appear as bread and butter."[49]

The Mahatma does not ignore the divinity of man which is epitomised in the great maxim that 'a jiva is always shiva': a man is by and large, divine. And in this respect, it is difficult to distinguish between a man and a man. It is from this deep feeling of spirituality and divinity of man that Gandhi derived his ethico-economic theory of trusteeship and inheritance.

He wrote, "Every thing belonged to God and was from God. Therefore, it was *His people* as a whole, not for a particular individual. When an individual has more than his proportionate portion, he became a trustee of that portion for God's people."[50] That is why he talked of equality of distribution of national wealth.

He approached human problems from an integral outlook of life in which economics, ethics, psychology and religion were synthesized. He wanted economics to be reduced to the terms of religion and spirituality. But since he was sensitive to the feelings and needs of the masses, he could never stand apart from his people. As has been correctly observed by Frank Moraes, "To him the basic fact of economics is that man must eat. Freedom from want is the first article of his creed, and throughout his public life he has worked passionately to free his countrymen from the degradation of this poverty."[51] In his own words, "No one has ever suggested that grinding pauperism can lead to anything else than moral degradation. Every human being has a right to live and therefore, to find wherewithal to feed himself and where necessary to cloth and house himself."

Satisfaction of basic needs and moral elevation of individuals are not antithetical for him. And that is why he could adopt a spiritual and moral approach to economics.

B. Study of Man

Adam Smith, the father of modern economics in his magnum opus, 'An Enquiry into the Nature and Causes of Wealth of Nations' defined economics 'as a study of wealth.[52] Smith has paid his attention exclusively to wealth. Little attention was paid to man for whom wealth is really meant. Writers like Carlyle and Ruskin condemned this Mammon worship. They accused economics of selfishness and meanness and therefore called it a dismal science. Dr. Alfred Marshall removed this shortcoming to a great extent. According to him, "Economics is a study of man's action in the ordinary business of life; it enquires how he gets his income and how he uses it. Thus, it is on one hand a study of wealth and on the other, and more important side, a part of the study of man."[53] Dr. Marshall made it clear that although economics still studies wealth but it has a secondary place and the first place being given to man. It is for his sake and for the sake of welfare that wealth is studied. Thus, it becomes a study of material welfare.

Robbins offered a more acceptable definition of economics. In his words, "Economics study human behaviour as a relationship between end and scarce means which have alternative uses."[54] He raised three fundamental issues : (i) Human wants are unlimited; (ii) Means to satisfy them are limited; and (iii) Means have alternative uses. And because of these, there arises the need to study economics. It teaches us how to get maximum satisfaction from limited resources.

The centre of Gandhi's economic thought is man and not the material prosperity or scarcity. He aimed at the development, upliftment and enrichment of human life rather than a higher standard of living with scant respect for human and social values. He wanted to elevate modern economic philosophy from its materialistic base to a higher spiritual plane where human actions were motivated by social objective rather than individualistic and selfish consideration. But it does not mean that he did not give any importance to the economic conditions of man. He was of the confirmed view that economic development must proceed other developments. That is why he gave due importance to the economic activities of an individual. In a speech at Muir College Economic Society, Allahabad he clarified, "By economic progress, I take it, we mean material advancement without limit, and by real progress we mean moral progress which again is the same thing as progress of the permanent element in us. The subject may therefore be stated thus: Does not moral progress increase in the same proportion as material progress? I know that this is a wider position than the one before us. But I venture to think that we always mean large one even when we lay down the smaller."[55]

The economic activity of a man is concerned with the production of material goods their exchange, distribution and consumption. These activities are necessary not only for the existence of man but also for his happiness and progress. Man lives in a society and all these activities concern not only the individual in isolation but they create social relations. As a matter of fact, all wealth is socially produced. No Robinson Crusoe on a solitary island, he be a capitalist or a labour can produce wealth. He, therefore, held that socially produced wealth must be equally divided among all those who are instrument in producing it.

Gandhi had a total, integrated and an evolving approach at the centre of which was man's whole being in search of knowledge and truth. He rejected such categories as the 'pure economic man' or the 'pure political man'. All facets of man's life can be unified if one set of moral values is applied to them all. If the same moral values are not applied to all human activities the result will be conflict within the individual and in society. Take, for instance, the Marxist idea that the whole of human history is a record of the conflict between economic classes is a partial view. Man has many urges. The economic urge is one, however, basic it may be. It is true that an individual life would be bleak if he lacked the minimum requirements of a cultured life. But if economic competence is necessary for the happiness and progress of an individual and a group, freedom too is as necessary and so are moral and spiritual values. Christ truly said, "Man does not live by bread alone." But it is also a fact that he can not live without it either. Matter may be less important than the spirit; but in human beings the spirit manifests itself and works through the flesh. The economic activity can not dispense with moral values is a fact of life. Acharya Kripalani quotes a true story in his 'Gandhi: His Life and Thought'.[56]

A young lady went to a fashionable shop, she purchased a piece of cloth. The price demanded was four times what would have been reasonable. The lady paid the price and went away. The merchant afterwards discovered that she had left her purse behind. The purse contained jewellery worth a few thousands. The merchant was very much disturbed. He did not know her address. What was he to do with the purse? After a few days of enquiry he found out the address of the lady and took the purse to her. The lady smiled and said, "You charged me four times the value of the cloth. The excess price could be Rs. 20 or 25; and now you have restored to me my purse which contains jewellery worth a few thousands. How is that? The merchant too smiled and said: 'Madam the price that I charged you was according to my commercial morality. The restoration of the purse is my individual morality, I am not a thief.

Such incogruties are found in our every day life. But the old habits, traditions and conventions do not allow purely economic gains to come in the way of man's moral sensitivity and intellectual honesty.

The main purpose to study economics should be the whole happiness of man. Material advancement is only one ingredient in this. Along with it other elements such as moral, spiritual, psychological, etc. should also be taken into consideration. Then and only then a man can be truly happy which can lead to a perfect development of his personality.

C. Emphasis on Wantlessness

Economic theory deals with the laws and principles which govern the functioning of an economy. An economy exists because of three basic facts: (i) Human wants are unlimited; (ii) Means to satisfy them are limited; (iii) Means have alternative uses. Had the wants been limited or resources unlimited or both, then, there would have been no need to study economics. We can satisfy one want for all the times or all the wants for one time but we can not satisfy all the wants for all the times. Therefore, we must decide some way of selecting those wants which are to be satisfied first. In other words, we face the problem of allocating scarce resources so as to achieve the greatest possible satisfaction.

However, there is a paradoxical twist in Gandhian method of solving economic problem of unlimited wants and limited resources. It almost amounts to putting the energy in the reverse gears.[57] Instead of satisfying maximum wants with limited resources Gandhi advocated wantlessness. He was of the opinion that wants are the sources of pain. Instead of adding to the sum total of human happiness wants subtract from it to a good deal. In fact, he thinks that, maximization of satisfaction is rather completely inconsistent with the maximization of human wants. A want is a painful experience. That is evident from the fact that we wish to satisfy it and want to get rid of it as soon as possible. We would not have bothered to remove or satisfy it, had it not been painful. So the removal of want is removal of pain and procurement of pleasure. This pleasure is something as satisfaction or utility if one wants to get maximum pleasure, one should see to it that all pain is removed and no fresh pain is experienced in future. At least this is the ideal for any one wants to achieve maximum pleasure from his limited resourced.

Professor J.K. Mehta,[58] a distinguished economist, further elaborated this concept that to satisfy a want is to yield to it. To remove the pain caused by the presence of wants by satisfying them is, therefore, an undignified way of getting pleasure. Instead of obeying the orders of want we can ourselves order the want to quit. When we satisfy a want we make it quiet for the time being. When we order it to quit we do not merely make it quiet we kill it as it was. The process of killing of wants has been called elimination of wants. But wants can be killed by wants. That is why Professor Mehta suggests that stronger wants be employed to kill the weaker wants. When such a battle is fought all the inferior wants get ultimately killed and one is left with superior wants only. The better among these can, in their turn, be employed to kill the other wants. In this way we can ultimately reach a stage in which only one, the most superior want, would be left. It is only when this stage is reached that we can with impunity satisfy the wants. Once satisfied such wants never recurs. Thus, by the process of killing or eliminating wants, we ultimately reach the state of wantlessness—a stage in which perfect happiness is experienced.[59]

Gandhi approached the problem of wantlessness from another angle also. "We should not receive any single thing that we do not need", he wrote in 'From Yervada Mandir', "We are not always aware of our real needs and most of us improperly multiply our wants and thus unconsciously make thieves of ourselves. If we devote some thought to the subject, we shall find that we can get rid of quite a number of our wants. One who follows the observance of non-stealing will bring about a progressive reduction of his own wants. Much of the distressing poverty in this world has arisen out of breaches of the principle of non-stealing.[60] He further said that the profound truth upon which this observance is based is that God never creates more than what is strictly needed for the moment. Therefore, who ever appropriates more than the minimum that is really necessary for him is guilty of theft.[61] The propensity to accumulate commodities cramps the soul and degenerates into the morbid desire to make a fetish of external goods of life. The luxury of the ascendant classes therefore makes them morally deprived. The monopolization of the things needed by all, by a few men at the top, is unjust. Moreover, accumulation is condemnable because it is not possible to be practised by all. Accumulation by a few amounts to the dispossession of the many. Thus the alternative lies in renunciation. To him, renunciation is life. Accumulation spells death. But he classified, "This does not mean that if one has wealth, it should be thrown away and the wife and children should be turned out of doors. It simply means that one must give up attachment to these things and dedicate one's all to God and make use of His gifts to serve Him only."[62] He advised the moneyed men to earn their crores (honestly only, of course) but asked them to dedicate themselves to the service of all. For those who wish to follow this way, "The best and most effective mantra is (Enjoy thy wealth by renouncing it). Expanded it means: Earn your crores by all means. But understand that your wealth is not yours; it belongs to the people. Take what you require for your legitimate needs and use the remainder for society."[63]

Thus it is clear that he offered his doctrine of non-possession as an indictment of one of the most powerful drives in modern economic society the drive for multiplication of wants, fuelled by an insatiable propensity for superfluous or conspicious consumption. One may justify such consumption as an essential prerequisite for economic growth.[64] This argument is of course, based on economic grounds. To Gandhi, it was an economic as well as a moral issue.

D. Critique of Industrial Civilization

The advance of the industrial revolution in the West brought new hopes and fears. Some view that the harnessing of machine power bring in the New Jerusalem and man will have the blessings of freedom and abundance. Dr. S. Radhakrishanan has described these achievements in these musical words, "We have learnt to ride the waves of the wind, to harness the rivers for watering deserts, to master the earth and the creatures thereof and with the earth as our foot stool reach out to the stars.[65]

But Leo Tolstoy sounded a different note. In his 'What Must We Do Then?, he categorized the grave evils of machinery and industrial civilization. In his opinion, it was gravely disadvantageous for the workers. Gandhi's opinions regarding machinery and industrialism as stated in the *Hind Swaraj* are very similar to Tolstoy's denunciations.

In the South African period Gandhi was far more critical of the machine civilization than in the later period. He was trenchantly hostile to machines in the 'Hind Swaraj' and considered them to be a snake pit. "Machinery is like a snake-hole which may contain from one to a hundred snakes."[66] But even in that classic work he did not advocate the destruction of machines. But certainly, he categorically denied that the machine could produce any good. It led to the slavery of labour both male and female because it took away from them (the labourers) their traditional means of subsistence. It deprived them of the source of livelihood. It also led to the private monopoly because it resulted in the concentration of wealth in the hands of a small section of population. In reply to a question as to whether he was against all machinery, he said, "What I object to, is the craze for machinery, not machine as such. The craze is for what they call labour saving machines. Men go on saving labour till thousands are without work and thrown on the open streets to die of starvation. I want to save time and labour, not for a fraction of mankind, but for all, I want concentration of wealth, not in the hands of a few but in the hands of all. Today, Machinery merely helps a few to ride on the back of millions. The impetus behind it all is not the philanthropy to save labour, but greed. It is against this constitution of things that I am fighting with all my might.[67]

Hence with the passage of time, his attitude became more realistic. During the course of years there was a gradual transition from the exalted heights of utopians ideas of 'Hind Swaraj' to the more cautious realism of his articles in the 'Harijan' in late thirties and forties. "Mechanization is good when hands are too few for the work intended to be accomplished. It is an evil where there are more hands than required for the work, as is the case of India. The problem for us is not how to find leisure for the teeming millions inhabiting our villages. The problem is how to utlize their idle hours..,."[68]

Gandhi did not sacrifice his 'ideal position.' In a conversation with Ramachandran he clarified, "Ideally, however I would rule out all machinery, even this very body, which is not helpful to salvation and seek the absolute liberation of the body and soul. From this point of view I would reject all machinery, but machines will remain because like the body, they are inevitable."[69] But the social and economic reality cast its impress upon his mind, and he was no dogmatist to reject the inevitable. If there were to be established factories for producing essential commodities, he wanted them to be nationalized and not to be retained under private ownership, because that would result in the exploitation of the labourers. "At the same time", he wrote, "I believe that some key industries are necessary. I do not believe in arm-chair or armed socialism. I believe in action, according to my belief, without waiting for whole sale conversion. Hence, without having to enumerate key industries, I would have state ownership, where a large number of people have to work together. The ownership of the products of their labour, whether skilled or unskilled will vest in them through the state.[70]

Dr. Buddhadeva Bhattacharya draws our attention to a pertinent fact that charge of Gandhi was not against machine qua machine, but in so far as it stood for the enslavement of human beings.[71] This point needs to be stressed upon for many took him for the anti-machinist in the absolute sense of the term. Gandhi, it appears did not depart from this original position even at the last phase of his life, although the meaning of the term 'machinery' underwent some amount of modification for him. Professor N.K. Bose has also emphasized this point in his 'Studies in Gandhism'. "In 1908, the term evidently meant for him something more than the machinery itself, for he included in it the industrial system which went along with the use of power driven mills in India at that time. The distinction between industrialism and machinery had not yet been drawn by him. As a matter of facts his knowledge or experience of machines was very limited."[72] At this stage he did not know the distinction between the loom and spinning wheel. In *Hind Swaraj* he used the term loom to mean the wheel. He had not seen a handloom or a spinning wheel when he described it in *Hind Swaraj*, or even in 1915, when he returned to India from

South Africa. He accepted in his autobiography, "I do not remember to have seen a handloom or spinning wheel when in 1908, I described it in *Hind Swaraj* as the panacea for the growing pauperism of India. . . . Even in 1915 when I returned to India from South Africa, I had not actually seen a spinning Wheel. When the Satyagraha Ashram was founded at Sabarmati we introduced a few handlooms there."[73] Thus the term industrialism, machinery, mechanical civilization mean the same thing to him.

E. Bread Labour

Bread labour was both philosophy and economics to Gandhi. In a precise sense it means 'that to live man must work."[74] The work is to be done with physique not by mind. To borrow a terminology from economics Gandhi means by bread labour something like 'productive labour' as conceived by Adam Smith. Though strictly speaking Gandhi would have restricted the meaning of bread labour only to agricultural labour but being conscious of the impracticability probably due to the scarcity of primary factors of production—land, he allowed for undertaking other works as well. He said, "This labour (Bread labour) can truly be related to agriculture alone. But at present at any rate, every body is not in a position to take it. A person can therefore spin or weave, or take up carpentry or smithery instead of tilling the soil, always regarding agriculture however to be ideal."[75] According to Gandhi the violation of the bread labour is the root cause of the present economic disequilibrium. He considers it to be the natural law and therefore enjoins even Rabindra and Raman to do some manual labour. "It is a tragedy of the first, magnitude", he remarks, "that millions have ceased to use their hands as hands. Nature is revenging herself upon us with terrible effect for this criminal waste of the gift she has bestowed upon us as human beings."[76] Also, "We are destroying the matchless living machines, i.e. our own bodies, by leaving them to rust and trying to substitute lifeless machinery for them."[77] He extols labour so much that he conceived it as the medium of exchange. He observes "Under my system it is labour which is the current coin, not metal. Any person who can use his labour has that coin and is wealthy. He converts it into cloth, he converts his labour into grain. If he wants paraffin oil, which he cannot himself produce, he uses his surplus grain for getting the oil. It is exchange of labour on free, fair and equal terms hence it is no robbery, you may reject that this is a reversion to the primitive system of barter. But is not all international trade based on the barter system".[78] He regarded manual labour to be the yajna prescribed in the Bhagvadgita and while explaining the dignity of labour he used to quote several verses from Gita in support of himself.[79]

The following extract from 'From Yervada Mandir' will give us an idea of how the concept of Bread Labour gripped his mind:

> "The law, that to live man must work, first came home to me upon reading Tolstoy's writings on Bread Labour. But even before that I had began to pay homage to it after reading Ruskin 'Unto This Last'. The divine law that man must earn his bread by labouring with his own hands, was first stressed by a Russian writer named T.M. Bondaref. Tolstoy advertised it and gave it wider publicity. In my view the same principle has been set forth in the third chapter of Gita, where we are told, that he who eats without offering sacrifice eats stolen food."[80] Sacrifice here can only mean bread labour.

F. Sarvodaya

People in the West generally hold that the duty of man is to promote the happiness of the majority of mankind, and happiness is supposed to mean only physical happiness and economic prosperity. If the laws of morality are broken in the conquest of this happiness, it does not matter very much. Again, as the object sought to be attained is the happiness of the majority; they do not think there is any harm if this is secured by sacrificing a minority. The consequences of this line of thinking are writ large on the face of the Western world. This exclusive search for physical and economic well-being prosecuted in disregard of morality is contrary to divine law, as some wisemen in the West have also shown. One of these was John Ruskin who contends in 'Unto This Last' that man can be happy only if they obey the moral law. As already discussed Mahatma Gandhi was so much fascinated by 'Unto This Last' of

John Ruskin that he paraphrased it and later translated this paraphrase into Gujarati and named it Sarvodaya.

That is how the word 'Sarvodaya' came to be used. But now it is generic name given to the non-violent order which the Mahatma aimed at. This philosophy was propounded by him and later Vinoba Bhave and Jayaprakash Narayan tied to translate it into action. Revolutionary and path finding thinkers in history have usually been followed by mere interpreters, systematisers and analysts. There have been rare exceptions such as Rosa Luxemburg and Lenin in case of Marx, Vinoba and J.P. are such exceptions in the case of Gandhi. They not only elaborated and interpreted Gandhian thought, particularly in terms of conditions and problems of independent India and of the world since Gandhi, but also experimented and innovated thereby saving it from becoming pontifical and authoritative and preserving its creative adventurousness.

Sarvodaya stands for the emancipation, the uplift and elevation of all, and that all living beings are participants in or portions (amsa) of a super-material reality. Hence the good of all living beings which necessarily implies the good of all humanity has to be positively fostered. It repudiates therefore, the limited gospel of the greatest good of the greatest number. It is certainly, not opposed to the concept of social and economic equality. Since all beings are reflections or manifestations of a supreme spiritual ultimate hence all have to be provided the opportunity for their greatest development and perfection.

The fundamental notion in the Sarvodaya philosophy is the primacy and ultimateness of the spirit. Gandhi's dominant concern was the realization of God as all pervasive truth. His political, economic and social endeavours and programmes were oriented towards progressive enlargement of the moral consciousness through the service of the Daridranarayana and the consequent intimate and intuitive realization of the primordial divine spirit. But in the theory of Sarvodaya, there is no negation of political and economic satisfactions and requirements. It does not negate the importance of material commodities. It would refuse, however, to regard them as the dominant goal of all human endeavours. Like Aristotle, Sarvodaya would like to use external goods for the satisfaction of the human spirit.

In politics, Sarvodaya accepts the sacrosanct character of the human spirit. It is hence, emphatic on the inculcation of the 'value' of freedom, equality, justice and fraternity It, therefore, opposed to the state machine. The state is not the terrestrial reflection of the merciful divine being but is a soulless mechanical instrument to effectuate the will of those who have the manipulating skill, dash, cunning and capacity to control the governmental structure. Gandhi pleaded the Swarajya—the inner rule of man over himself.

In economic field Sarvodaya pleads for: (a) the repudiation of the proprietary possession of the non-producers, (b) the establishment of proprietary possession of the producers, and (c) the neutralisation or the negation of ownership. It hopes to establish a society of producers or labourers. Bhoodan and Sampattidan are regarded as step towards the realisation of that kind of society. One of the great economic advantages that have been claimed for Bhoodan is that it effectuates the redistribution of land without the payment of any compensations. If Bhoodan and Gramdan are techniques of agrarian revolution based on moral force, Sampattidan is a significant path in the transformation of capitalism into the Sarvodaya society. For the realization of Sampattidan, man is, at first, to utilize one-sixth of his wealth for the sake of society. In the words of Jayaprakash Narayan, "The next step is that of 'Full Trusteeship'. Under trusteeship, commercial and industrial enterprises would belong to the society and there would be no employer and employee. The management and labour would have joint responsibility to run them not for themselves but for the good of the society as a whole."

Notes and References

1. J.B. Kripalani, "Gandhi: His Life and Thought" (Calcutta: Orient Longmans, 1961), p. 252.
2. *Harijan—A Journal of Applied Gandhism,* 1933-55 (New York: Garland Publishing Inc., 1973), 3.1.1946, p. 28.
3. Buddhadeva Bhattacharyya, "Evolution of the Political Philosophy of Mahatma Gandhi", (Calcutta: Calcutta Book House, 1969), p. 197.
4. N.K. Bose, "Studies in Gandhism" (Calcutta: Indian Associated Publishing Co., 1940), p. 52.
5. M.L. Dantwala, Seminar, 46, June 1963, p. 20.
6. *Harijan,* 29.4.1933, p. 2.

7. *Ibid.*, 28-9-1934, p. 260.
8. *Young India*, 23.3.1920, p. 4.
9. M.K. Gandhi, "Hind Swaraj or Indian Home Rule" (Ahmedabad; Navajivan Publishing House, 1982), pp. 36-96.
10. M.K. Gandhi, "An Autobiography or The Story of My Experiments with Truth" (Ahmedabad: Navajivan Publishing House, 1983), p. 250.
11. Bhabani Bhattacharyya, "Gandhi the Writer" (New Delhi: National Book Trust, 1969), p. 31.
12. Ruskin's influence on Gandhi was in no sense total. As John Bondurant puts it: "Gandhi did not share the more conservative views of Ruskin which held the common man inferior, erected an aristocratic hierarchy, and denied the masses any political control of Violence (Bombay; Oxford University Press, 1959), p. 65.
13. Unto This Last in Quennell Peter (ed.), Selected Writings of John Ruskin (London: The Farcon Press, 1952), p. 65
14. D.G. Tendulkar (ed.), "Mahatma", Vol. VI (New Delhi: The Publications Division, Ministry of Information and Broadcasting, Government of India, 1962), p. 177.
15. M.K. Gandhi, An Autobiography, *op. cit.*, p. 250.
16. *Ibid.*
17. Leo Tolstoy, 'What Then must We Do?' (translated by Aylmer Maude) (London: Oxford University Press, 1950), p. 3.
18. *Ibid.*, pp. 301-03
19. *Ibid.*, pp. 235-37
20. *Ibid.*
21. *Ibid.*, pp. 238-39.
22. *Ibid.*, pp. 303-21.
23. *Harijan*, 19.1.1947, p. 495.
24. "The Collected Works of Mahatma Gandhi", Vol. V, New Delhi, The Publications Division, Ministry of Information and Broadcasting, Government of India, 1961, pp. 56-57. Hereinafter as CWMG.
25. M.K. Gandhi, 'Hind Swaraj' *op. cit.*, pp. 56-57.
26. *Young India*, 1.5.1930, p. 149.
27. *Ibid.*, 26.3.1931, p. 46.
28. "Speeches and Writings of Gandhi" (Madras: G.A. Natesan & Co., 1933), pp. 336-44.
29. Henery Brailsford, "Rebel India" (London: Leonard Stein, 1931), p. 21.
30. *Ibid.*, p. 22.
31. *Ibid.*, p. 24.
32. Buddhadeva Bhattacharya, *op. cit.*, p. 220.
33. "Speeches and Writings of Gandhi", *op. cit.*, p. 384.
34. *CWMG*, Vol. VI, p. 168.
35. "Speeches and Writings of Gandhi", *op. cit.*, p. 324.
36. Tendulkar, *op. cit.*, Vol. VI, p. 171.
37. *Harijan*, 20-04-1940, p. 97.
38. Bepin Behari, "Gandhian Economic Philosophy" (Bombay: Vora & Co., 1963), p. 2.
39. *Harijan*, 20-10-1937, p. 292.
40. *Young India*, 13.10.1921, p. 325.
41. *Ibid.*, 26.10-1924, p. 421.
42. *CWMG*, Vol. XIII, pp. 311-17.

43. J.M. Keynes, "General Theory of Employment, Interest and Money" (London: Macmillan & Co., 1951), pp. 194-95.
44. Alfred Marshall, "Principles of Economics", (London: Macmillan & Co., 1949).
45. Unto Ruskin, 'This Last: A Paraphrase by M.K. Gandhi" (Ahmedabad: Navajivan Publishing House, 1989), pp. 18-35.
46. *Ibid.*
47. *Young India,* 4.4.1929, p. 110.
48. *Ibid.,* 5.5.1927, p. 142.
49. *Ibid.,* 15.10.1931, p. 310.
50. *Harijan,* 23.2.1947, p. 39.
51. Frank Moraes, 'Gandhi the Humanist' in Tendulkar, D.G. & Others (eds.), "Gandhiji—His Life and Work" (Bombay, Karnataka Publishing House, 1944), p. 24.
52. Adam Smith, "An Enquiry into the Causes of Wealth and Nations" (New York: The Modern Library, 1937).
53. Alfred Marshall, *op. cit.,* p. 1.
54. Lionel Robbins, "An Essay on the Nature and Significance of Economic Science" (London: Macmillan & Co. 1948), p. 16.
55. *CWMG, op. cit.,* Vol. XIII, pp. 311-12.
56. J.B. Kripalani, *op. cit.,* p. 367.
57. Jai Narain, Article : "The Doctrine of Wantlessness: A Gandhian Perspective", in *Gandhi Jyoti: Journal of Gandhian Thought,* May 1987, Year 4, No. 3, (Bhagalpur University, Bhagalpur), p. 2.
58. J.K. Mehta, "A Philosophical Interpretation of Economics" (London: George Allen & Unwin Ltd., 1962).
59. *Ibid.*
60. M.K. Gandhi, "From Yeravada Mandir", Ch. V, (Ahmedabad: Navjivan Publishing House, 1957).
61. *Harijan,* 10.10.1948, p. 271.
62. *Ibid.,* 28.4.1946, p. 111.
63. *Ibid.,* 1.2.1942, p. 20.
64. Jai Narain, *op. cit.,* p. 7.
65. S. Radhakrishnan, "Speeches and Writings", Third Series, (New Delhi: The Publications Division, Government of India, Ministry of Information and Broadcasting), July 1959-May 1962.
66. M.K. Gandhi, "Hind Swaraj", *op. cit.,* p. 96.
67. *Young India,* 13.11.1924, p. 378.
68. *Harijan,* 16.11.1934, p. 316.
69. Tendulkar, D.G. (ed.), "Mahatma", *op. cit.,* Vol. 2, p. 162.
70. *Harijan,* 1.9.1946, p. 285.
71. Buddhadev Bhattacharyya, *op. cit.,* pp. 206-07.
72. N.K. Bose, *op. cit.,* pp. 53-54.
73. M.K. Gandhi, "Autobiography", *op. cit.,* p. 407.
74. M.K. Gandhi, "From Yeravada Mandir", *op. cit.,* p. 35.
75. *Ibid.,* p. 37.
76. *Young India,* 17.2.1927, p. 52.
77. *Ibid.,* 3.1.1925.
78. *Harijan,* 2.11.1934, pp. 300-01.
79. *Young India,* 13.10.1921, p. 328.
80. M.K. Gandhi, "From Yeravada Mandir", *op. cit.,* pp. 36-37.

2

Alienation and Wantlessness

A person may be said to be confused, when he has the overlapping ideas regarding the single concept and cannot choose from these, according to the need of the situation. But the essence of the problem lies in the fact that he is unaware of his condition. As soon as he realizes that he is confused, he will not be at that time, in the former condition. This is a very simple problem but complexity arises when it is applied to man himself, when the individual does not know his own self, 'Who am I', the same centuries old question. Man is a rational and social animal and the social norms are created by him for proper adjustment in the society. Since these standards are made by man, it is expected that he should be able to govern over these rules and standards. Conversely, what happens, these social norms and standards are enforced by the society of which an individual is a part. When the individual indulges in this jargon created by himself like 'Spider Web', he is said to be alienated. The problem becomes abstract when one thinks about the whole society as alienated.

Before proceeding further, it is essential to understand clearly the meaning of the term, 'alienation'. If we see the etymology of this term, we find that the Latin origin of 'alienation' is 'alienatio'. This noun derives its meaning from the verb 'alienare' which means to make some thing other's or to take away. Further, 'alienare' is derived from 'alienus', i.e. belonging or pertaining to another and 'alienus' is derived ultimately from 'alius' (other or another).[1]

The term alienation has many different meanings in every day life, most of them can be regarded as a modification of this one broad meaning which is suggested by the etymology and morphology of the word—the meaning which alienation (or estrangement) is the act or result of the act, through which something or somebody, become (or has become) alien (or strange) to something, or somebody else.

This is a concept of considerable antiquity. Historians of philosophy trace the concept back to the writings of Plotinus[2] and the early Christian theology.

But the first philosophical elaboration of the concept is found in Hegel who maintains that whole of human history is the constant growth of man's knowledge of the Absolute, who through finite mind becomes self-aware and return to himself from his self-alienation in nature. However, finite mind also becomes alienated. It is an essential characteristic of finite mind (man) to produce things, to express itself in objects, to objectify itself in physical things, social institutions and cultural object; and every objectification is, of necessity, an instance of alienation: the produced objects become alien to the producer. Alienation in this sense can be overcome only in the sense of being adequately known. Again, it is the vocation of man as man to serve as the organ of the self-knowledge of the Absolute. To the extent that he does not perform this function he does not fulfil his human essence and is merely a self-alienated man.[3]

Ludwig Feuerbach accepted Hegel's view that man can be alienated from himself, but he rejected both the views that nature is a self-alienated form of Absolute Mind and the view that man is absolute mind in the process of dealienation. Man is not self-alienated God. On the contrary, God is self-alienated man; He is man's essence absolutised and estranged from man. And man is not alienated from himself when he refused to recognise nature as a self-alienated form of God; man is alienated from himself when he creates and puts above himself an imagined alien higher being and bows before that being as a slave. The dealienation of man consists in the abolition of that estranged picture of man which is God.[4]

The concept of alienation was fully elaborated by Karl Marx, in his early writings, especially in his "Economic and Philosophical Manuscript." He argued that the division of labour created vast accumulation of capital and personal wealth at one pole of society, an increase in the value of things achieved only at the cost of progressive devaluation of man as a human species. The source of this evil should be found in the capitalist system in which organization of labour has the effect of directly transforming man's labour into a saleable commodity. Marx thus says, "This fact implies that the object produced by labour, its products, now stands opposed to it as an alien being, as a power independent of the producer. The product of labour is labour which has been embodied in an object and turned in to a physical thing; this product is an objectification of labour."[5]

Hegel takes the two terms 'objectification and alienation' as synonymous. Marx for this reason critises Hegel for adding to the stock of confusion in view of the fact that the two are not interchangeable. "Objectification is the process through which man eternalizes himself in nature and society, for example by producing things as tools, a process whereby he becomes necessarily an object for others, within the structure of the social relations built upon the simplest form of economy. Alienation occurs only when man having externalized himself in nature and society, finds his activity, his essence operating on him as an external, alien and oppressive power."[6]

To Marx, alienation has four distinct dimensions—from nature, from himself, from fellow beings and from society. It is the system of capitalism that constitutes the total alienation of human labour, for capital dominates completely the worker as a labourer and also as a man. In his own words, "This system alienates man essentially from his own activity, from the product of his labour, thus turning labour's product into an alien object; the more he works, the more he finds himself dominated by the world of objects his own labour has created. The worker puts his life into the object, and his life then belongs no longer to himself but to the object. The greater his activity, ...the less his processes. What is embodied in the product of his labour is no longer his own. The greater this product is ... the more he is diminished."[7]

This idea of alienation finds its manifestation in the later works of Marx as well. In his master piece contribution to the critique of political economy he says: "We have seen that the growing accumulation of capital implies its growing concentration. Thus, grows the power of capital, the alienation of the condition of social production personified in the capitalist from the real producers. Capital comes more and more to the fore as a social power, whose agent is the capitalist. This social power no longer stands in any possible relations to that which the labour of a single individual can create. It becomes an alienated, independent social power which opposed to society as an object, and as an object that is the Capitalist's source of power."[8]

Marx also offers a solution to this problem. When will alienation come to an end? His answer is that the end of capitalism and its substitution by the socialist system will entail the era of human emancipation implying the advent of the state of disalienation. Obviously, Marxism has a definite goal—a free and whole man instead of a man like a fragmented creature. Like Rousseau, he desires that man must be returned to a non-alienated state, reunited with nature, his fellow—beings and his own personality. Obviously, 'disalienation' would come to take place in the final stage of 'communism' when division of labour would no longer allocate man to specific occupational roles but allow him, if he so wishes, "to hunt in the morning, fish in the afternoon, rear cattle in the evening, criticize after dinner ... without ever becoming a hunter, a fisherman, a shepherd or a critic."[9]

Unlike Marx, Gandhi did not give any systematic exposition of the concept of alienation. His social philosophy and particularly, his lifestyle, have positive elements that seem quite relevant in this context. His lifestyle bridged the gulf between the heart and the intellect, between the claims of humanism, self-determination and freedom, on one hand and those of social and political organization, on the other. It is here we can trace the roots of his concept of alienation.

Before coming to this question, it is better to start with the main problem which led Gandhi to think about alienation of man. The chief economic problem in India is mass poverty. Gandhi refused to accept the thought that the problem of poverty was a fact of nature and that unless external assistance or government action would be forthcoming, poverty would not be overcome. In order to overcome the twin evils of poverty and unemployment, Gandhi held that self-realization or dealienation is necessary.

He took in to account the dual aspect of life, i.e. material and spiritual. He considered both mind and body as of equal importance. He did not rule out the fact that all living things first strive for material existence. The idea of better life comes only after the material existence is secured or in other words before there can be good life or spiritual life, there must be life. In reply of Rabindera Nath Tagore's criticism of Non-Cooperation movement and Spinning Wheel he wrote, 'When all about me are dying for want of food, the only occupation permissible to me is to feed the hungry. . . . To a people famishing and idle, the only acceptable form in which God can dare appear is work and promise of food as wages."[10]

It is true that man does not live by bread alone but he can live only if he has bread. "The fundamental urge of life being material, man's striving for securing the material means of existence has supplied the fundamental motive force to all human development."[11] In order to exist in the world, physical labour is necessary but at the same time the value of intellectual labour cannot be ignored. Gandhi puts in this regard," I do not discount the value of intellectual labour, but no amount of it is any compensation for bodily labour which every one of us is born to give for the common good of all.[12]

Gandhi without consciously attempting at systematic theory explained the phenomena of poverty, unemployment and of economic distress of individual through alienation. He was of the opinion that the more nature was overpowered the more alienated man would become from nature. He simultaneously wanted to focus on the relationship between man and his natural environment which would end human exploitations, which in turn is the very cause of exploitation of nature. But to Gandhi the alienation of man is as much from the environment as from his true self. His true self is what man can discover through the search for truth following the path of non-violence. Man ceaselessly tries to get more and more money through any means. He desperately wants to improve his standard of living. Life has become very fast for him and he lives in fear and insecurity because of the demolition of joint family system. He lives with crime, fraud or assassination as in the West, or in a state of total fear as in the communist countries. Man indulges in heavy smoking, drinking and drugging to relieve tension and frustration which inturn further aggregate his problems. To him alienation meant fear, the craze for luxuries and exploitation of man by man.[13]

The term self-alienation seems to suggest some or all of the following points:

1. The division of the self into two conflicting parts was not carried out from outside but is the result of an action of the self.
2. The division into conflicting parts does not anihilate the unity of the self; despite the split, the self is nevertheless a self.
3. Self-alienation is not simply a split into two parts that are equally related to the self as a whole: the implication is that one part of the self has more right to represent the self as a whole, so that by becoming alien to it, the other part becomes alien to the self as a whole.[14]

Though Gandhi did not elaborate these technicalities of alienation but he had a full or total view of man, his spiritual, cultural and social aspects as such as his economic needs. This led him to advocate that machine must adjust man and not the other way round. He would not permit imbalance to be rested between increase in material production and man's spiritual and cultural needs. He was more concerned with the contradictions created by the way machinery was being used to debase man.

What Gandhi said in the simple words is now being increasingly stated in complex terms—is that in technological development, one must not merely take into account increasing productivity as the main factor but, along with it, one must pay attention to ecology and social relationships, as well as all that technology does to man's spiritual and cultural welfare. This does not necessarily mean limiting technological development. It implies rather a reorganization back to the principle that existed at the beginning of the scientific age, namely, that technology must be pressed into the service of man even though that principle was never put into action.[15]

This is how the situation for the alienation of man is created by technology. This approach can be reconciled with the French Existentialist Camus who says, "the society based on production is only productive and not creative."[16] The entrepreneur produces for the sale of production and tries to sell it to his maximum. Gandhi diagnosed this problem in his own characteristic way. The ideal before him was that the actual producer must not be alienated from his small means of production because the producer here is connected with a mode of production based on self-employment or an organization of economic activity by the producer himself. The absence of alienation of the producer from his means of production here stand for the marked contrast and with polarization between masters and producers which characterized classical feudalism and capitalism in the Western societies.

Further, here the self-employed producer is engaged in productive activity for the fulfilment of his basic needs and requirements, he is not motivated by his pursuit for wealth for the sake of wealth. To Gandhi, the alienation of producer from his production generates and intensifies violent conflict between masters, and actual producers who are reduced to the mere sellers of labour power. Violence here means exploitation or centralization of power and the dominance which retards the free expression and development of persons and institutions, especially of weak, who live at the base of weak, who live at the base of the society, namely, 'daridranarayan'. He wrote,

> "Economic equality is the master key to non-violent independence. Working for economic equality means abolishing the external conflict between labour and capital."[17] Though initially it may seem to be an utopia but it should be the goal of human life. If once the individual becomes conscious of it, the solution will automatically come.

The method for the attainment of the purpose is to let the people know the problem of their own. Gandhi knew that only enlightened and vigilant masses are an effective guarantee and proof against exploitation. "The present inequalities are merely due to the people's ignorance. With a growing knowledge, half their natural strength, the inequalities must disappear."[18]

The factor of enlightenment need not to be external to the individual but it is the internal conscience which is the supreme principle. Gandhi called conscience as a little voice within. He argued, "A little voice within us tells us 'you are on the right track, move neither to your left or right, but keep to the straight and narrow way'."[19]

Thus to follow the dictates of the inner voice is the main factor towards self-realization. Gandhi admits that such a process of self-realization is difficult to follow in the practical life situation. Before one is able to listen to that voice one has to go through a long and fairly severe course of training, and when it is the inner voice that speaks, it is unmistakable. Erickson has applied the theory of 'ego identity' for interpretation of this doctrine, "By 'ego identity' is meant the creative polarity of what other take one to be."[20] This personal identity means, not an awareness of the fact of existence, but a subjective awareness of inner sameness and continuity matched by the sameness and continuity of one's meaning to others. The individual who has achieved the sense of ego identity feels that he belongs to his group, as Erickson points out, "he knows where he is going." Both conscious and unconscious factors play a part in the process of discovering it.[21]

Gandhi attempted to achieve "an identity of the two identities," i.e. personal identity and the identity located in the core of his communal culture.

II

THE DOCTRINE OF WANTLESSNESS

Economic theory deals with the laws and principles which govern the functioning of an economy and its various parts. An economy exists because of two basic facts. Firstly, human wants are unlimited. Although differing degrees of acquisitiveness have been exhibited in different civilizations, it appears indisputable that human wants can be regarded as insatiable. At no time in our society has our economic system had sufficient resources to produce all that would be needed to satisfy everyone. Wants, have been and remain greater than the quantity of goods, available for the satisfaction of these wants. Secondly, means to satisfy wants are limited. The resources of a society consists not only of the free gifts of nature, such as land, forests and minerals, but also of human resources, both mental and physical, and of all sorts of man-made aids to further production, such as tools, machinery and buildings. If the resources like wants were unlimited, no economic problem would have arisen because in that case all wants could have been satisfied and there would have been no problem of choosing between the wants and allocating the resources between them.

Because our wants are unlimited and means to satisfy them are scarce, we can not satisfy our all the wants. We may be able to satisfy one want for all times or all the wants for one time but we cannot satisfy all the wants for all the times. We must decide some way of selecting those wants which are to be satisfied. Thus, a society is faced with the question of choice-choice among vast array of wants that are to be satisfied. We know that the resources have alternative uses. If it is decided to use more resources in one line of production, then resources must be withdrawn from the production of some other goods. Because of the scarcity of resources, we are confronted with the problem of choosing among the different channels of production to which resources are to be devoted. In other words, we have the problem of allocating scarce resources so as to achieve the greatest possible satisfaction.

Thus, it is evidently clear from the above discussion that the economic problems are due to unlimited wants and limited resources. Had there been limited wants or unlimited resources or both, then there would have been no economic problem or even the need to study Economics. In that state of affairs goods would have been free goods. But in actual life we can not obtain goods freely or without price, we have to pay price for them and do labour to obtain them.

It may be pointed out here that recently some economists in the industrially developed countries, especially U.S.A., have pointed out that the basic problem now confronting them, is the problem of 'affluence' rather than 'scarcity'. During the past century or two there has been a rapid economic growth in these countries which has brought unprecedented riches and prosperity for their citizens. As a result, the standard of living of the people there have gone up very high. It is said, they have won over the problem of scarcity and poverty, and are facing the problems created by affluence and growth; such as problems of mental tensions, optimum use of leisure, luxury, longevity, etc. Thus having achieved growth and affluence they are now thinking about what might be called, 'beyond economic growth'. The economist who has put forward this point of view is J.K. Galbraith, Professor of Harward University and former Ambassador of U.S.A. to India. He presented this view point in his revolutionary work, "The Affluent Society."

The use of the term, the Affluent Society looks strange, since economists have always been laying a great stress on the point that the basic economic problem a society has to encounter is the problem of scarcity, which is the mother of all economic problems that arise in a society.

It is true that U.S.A. and Western European countries have eliminated general poverty from their people, and, with the phenomenal progress of science and technology, have achieved unprecedented affluence and abundance of production of goods with which they have been able to satisfy their wants to a greater extent. But from this it should not be construed that the economic problem of scarcity of resources has ceased to exist in the so-called affluent world of U.S.A. and Western Europe. The term scarcity in Economics is used in a relative sense, that is, in the sense of scarcity of resources relative to the wants of people. With technological advancement no doubt that developed countries have greatly increased their resources and production but with growth and development new wants have also been created. The problem of economic scarcity could be said to have been won only if the resources would have been abundant in relation to wants which are multiplying during the process of growth. The problem of unlimited wants still exist in the affluent societies also.

Even otherwise, it is important to note that the two-third of the world is still lying in poverty. The abysmal poverty, hunger, disease, squalor and unemployment rule the land here. The problem of scarcity is present here in its full strength and the affluence for these people is still a far cry. They nourish unlimited wants, not to speak of desires. It is important to note here that there is a vast difference between desires and wants. Every desire is not a want. Human being, cherish unlimited desires in their hearts. To fulfil some of the desires, human beings do efforts and earn money. If they are still willing to spend that money to fulfil their desires, then these desires become wants. Thus the number of wants is several times less than the number of desires. When wants are unlimited, the number of desires can only be imagined. But we are taking the wants into consideration and not the desires.

Thus, because of the unlimited wants and limited resources human beings strive to get maximum satisfaction from what so ever they have.

However, there is a paradoxical twist in Gandhian method of solving this economic problem of unlimited wants and limited resources. It almost amounts to putting the energy in reverse gears instead of satisfying the maximum wants with limited resources. Gandhi advocated wantlessness. He was of the opinion that wants are the sources of pain. Instead of adding to the sum total of human happiness, wants subtracts from it a good deal. In fact, he thinks that maximization of satisfaction is rather completely inconsistent with the maximization of human wants. A want is a painful experience. This is evident from the fact that we wish to satisfy it and want rid of it as soon as possible. We would not have bothered to remove or satisfy it had it not been painful. So the removal of a want means removal of pain and procurement of pleasure. And this pleasure is the same thing as satisfaction or utility. If one wants to get maximum pleasure one should see to it that all pain is removed and no fresh pain is experienced in future. At least this is the ideal for any one who wants to achieve maximum pleasure from his limited resources.[22]

The absolute removal of pain by eliminating wants, seems impossible on the surface. But it is really not as impossible as thought by several scholars. This, of course is true that for a man who has a large number of wants to satisfy and, therefore, a large amount of pain to remove, the task of removing all pain becomes more difficult than for one who has less wants and hence a smaller amount of pain to be rid of. But this does not imply that complete removal of pain is necessarily impossible in each case. It rather implies a more hopeful state of affairs, that it becomes increasingly possible to remove all pain provided the wants and hence the pain corresponding to them decrease in their number and amount. The less wants we have, the less our pain, and hence the easier task of removing that pain and achieving maximum satisfaction. If therefore, maximum satisfaction is the object behind the behaviour of human being while he makes his choices for satisfying his wants, it would be more fully achieved us if his wants are few rather than if they are many. And thus we are led to the objective of controlling or simplifying wants for the purpose of attaining maximum satisfaction through human behaviour. Now since Economics studies human behaviour as concerned with the maximisation of satisfaction and since maximization of satisfaction is better achieved when wants are at the minimum rather than when they are not. This led Professor J.K. Mehta to define Economics as the study of human behaviour as concerned with the wantlessness.[23] And this minimization of wants can be rightly regarded as the ultimate objective of the science of economics.

Professor Mehta further elaborates his thesis that to satisfy a want is to yield to it, as it were. When we satisfy a want we obey the commanding voice of the wanting mind. When we go on satisfying wants as and when they arise all that we do is to pamper the wanting mind. One who yields to such a mind becomes virtually its slave. To remove the pain caused by the presence of wants by satisfying them is, therefore, an undignified way of getting pleasure. Instead of obeying the orders of a want we can ourselves order the want to quit. When we satisfy a want we make it quiet for the time being. When we order it to quit we do not merely make it quiet, we kill it as it were.

The process of killing wants has been called elimination of wants. But wants can be killed only by wants. Hence, stronger wants must be employed to kill the weaker and inferior wants. And when such a battle is fought all the inferior wants get ultimately killed and one is left with superior wants only. The better among these can, in their turn be employed to kill the other wants. In this way we can ultimately reach a stage in which only one, the most superior want would be left. It is only when this stage is reached that we can with impunity satisfy the wants. Once satisfied such want never recurs, the pleasure then obtained lasts as it were, forever. The state of happiness is reached—the state in which the mind remains absolutely free from the tormenting pressure of wants. The one final want, the satisfaction of which frees us from all wants, can be called the want of being wantless. By the process of killing or eliminating wants we thus ultimately reach the state of wantlessness—a state in which perfect happiness is experienced.[24]

Gandhi approached the problem of wantlessness from another angle also. "We should not receive any single thing that we do not need," he wrote in "From Yervada Mandir". We are not always aware of our real needs, and most of us improperly multiply our wants, and thus unconsciously make thieves of ourselves. If we devote some thought to the subject, we shall find that we can get rid of quite a number of our wants. One who follows the observance of non-stealing will bring about a progressive reduction of his own wants. Much of the distressing poverty in this world has arisen out of breaches of the principle of non-stealing. He further clarified that the profound truth upon which this observance is based is that God never creates more than what is strictly needed for the moment. Therefore, who ever appropriates more than the minimum, that is really necessary for him, is guilty of theft.[25] The propensity to accumulate commodities cramps the soul and degenerates into the morbid desire to make a fetish of external goods of life. The luxury of the ascendant classes, therefore, makes them morally deprived. The monopolization of the things needed by all, by a few men at the top, is unjust. Moreover, accumulation is condemnable because it is not possible to be practiced by all. Accumulation by a few amounts to the dispossession of the many. Thus the alternative lies in renunciation. To him, renunciation is life. Accumulation spells death. But he clarified. "This does not mean that, if one has wealth, it should be thrown away and his wife and children should be turned out of doors. It simply means that one must give up attachment to these things and dedicate one's all to God and make use of His gifts to serve Him only".[26] He advised the moneyed men to earn their crores (honestly only, of course) but asked them to dedicate themselves to the service of all. For those who wish to follow this way, "The best and most effective mantra is" (Enjoy thy wealth by renouncing it). Expanded it means: Earn your crores by all means. But understand that your wealth is not yours; it belongs to the people. Take what you require for your legitimate needs, and use the remainder for society.[27]

Thus, it is clear that he offered his doctrine of non-possession as an indictment of one of the most powerful drives in modem economic society; the drive for multiplication of wants, fuelled by an insatiable propensity for superfluous or conspicuous consumption. One may justify such consumption as an essential prerequisite for economic growth. This argument is, of course, based purely on economic grounds. To Gandhi, it was an economic issue as well as a moral issue. To him, Ethics and Economies are inseparable. "I must confess that I do not draw a sharp or any distinction between Ethics and Economics. The Economics that hurt the moral well-being of an individual or nation are immoral and, therefore, sinful."[28] But he realised that the perfect idea of wantlessness is unattainable because it demands total renunciation. His pragmatic mind would accept something short of perfect realization of the ideal; namely, a movement towards it through the process of gradual reduction of wants minimization of consumption.

The doctrine of non-possession, if it implied only voluntary reduction of wants, could be construed as a totally negative doctrine. But Gandhi expounded it as a positive doctrine. According to him, the doctrine of non-possession would teach that even one should limit his own wants and spend the rest for the welfare of others. He considered this as a desirable non-violent method of reducing inequality of income distribution and mal-distribution of wealth. In his own words: "Now let us consider how equal distribution can be brought about through non-violence. The first step towards it, is for him who has made this ideal part of his being to bring about the necessary changes in his personal life. He would reduce his wants to a minimum bearing in mind the poverty of India".[29] He was aware of other means of dealing with these problems of inequality of income distribution and mal-distribution of wealth but he discounted this because of his fear that other methods may include the coercive power of the state. Thus Gandhi put utmost reliance on the individual and his moral awakening to bring these radical changes in the distribution of income and wealth in the society through wantlessness.

Gandhi's insistence on minimizing wants has been attacked on several ground; 'Necessity is the mother of invention' is an old proverb often heard. It describes the way in which men's wants have brought into existence new wants and then these new wants have created fresh activities and wants, and these in turn have produced more new wants. All the discoveries of new lands, of new material, of new variety of food, clothing and houses, of new machinery, etc. are due to the working out of this proverb. And if the doctrine of wantlessness is followed then all progress will stop leading to economic stagnation and reversing the circle of human progress.

Again, more than two-third countries of the world are underdeveloped or developing. Majority of people in these countries are living on bare necessities. Their daily needs are hardly fulfilled. And to preach further reduction of wants to these persons is a sin. Their wants are already minimum. For a country like India where nearly 40% of the population is living below poverty line, the doctrine of wantlessness have no meaning. It is rather a mockery to teach them to reduce their wants.

Further, this doctrine may not take the form of Escapism: That we know that all our wants can not be satisfied. Instead of doing efforts to satisfy those wants, we may not take the shelter of wantlessness. This is against 'The Theory of Karma', which teaches us to work tirelessly. Then, the doctrine may be philosophically sound but it is almost impossible to practise it. If attempted to do, it will create several problems.

Thus, it is not necessary to go fully with Gandhi in reducing wants to follow a godly path. But it also remain true that anyone who wants to pursue serious interests in life, apart even from spiritual ends, finds it essential to regulate his wants severely: he chooses to forego many of his wishes. It is also patently wrong to say that human wants are insatiable.

Anthropological studies of tribal culture show that there is not inherent insatiability where wants are concerned. This is also proved today, by the fact that huge amounts are spent to persuade people to buy what they, in all likelihood would not buy otherwise. At best, then, it can be said that human want is malleable and can be manipulated to make it insatiable. The converse would also be true then. Wants could be reduced without loss.

Notes and References

1. Ernest Klein, "A Comprehensive Etymological Dictionary of English Usage,' Vol. I (New York: Elservier Publication Co., 1966), p. 49.
2. Plotinus (205-270) is considered as the founder of Neoplatonism. His doctrine of emanation assumed a procession from an ultimate indefinable source or principle to a multiplicity of finite beings: the undivided one unfolds into its various manifestations by a downward process linking the supersensible. Being with a hierarchy of lower spheres and ultimately with the world of nature and material existence, matter being the lowest stage of the universe and the antitheses to the one. Philip Merton, 'Plotinus' in The Encyclopedia of Philosophy, Vol. 6 (New York: Macmillan Publishing Company, 1972), pp. 351-59.
3. G.W.F. Hegel, "The Phenomenology of Mind" (Translated by J.B. Baillie), (London: George Allen & Unwin Ltd., 1955), pp. 11-45.
4. G. Petrovic, "Alienation" in The Encyclopedia of Philosophy, Vol. 1 (*op. cit.*), p. 77.
5. Karl Marx, Early Writings (Translated and edited by T.B. Bottomore) (London: C.A. Watts & Co. Ltd., 1963), p. 112.
6. Alen Swingewood, Marx and Modern Social Theory (London: Macmillan, 1975), p. 90.
7. Karl Marx, Early Writings, *op. cit.*, p. 124.
8. Karl Marx, Capital, Vol. III (Moscow: People Publishers), p. 259.
9. The German ideology, Edited by R. Pascel (New York: International Publisher Co., 1901, pp. 44-45.
10. *Young India,* 13.10.1921, p. 325.
11. C.G. Shah, Marxism, Gandhism, Stalinism (Bombay: Popular Prakashan, 1963), pp. 255-56.
12. M.K Gandhi, Socialism of My Conception (Bombay: Bhartiya Vidya Bhawan, 1960), p. 63.
13. J.D. Sethi, Gandhi Today (New Delhi: Vikas Publishing House Pvt. Ltd., 1970), p. 82.
14. G. Petrowic, Alienation, *op. cit.,* p. 78.
15. J.D. Sethi, Gandhi Today, *op. cit.,* 83.
16. Albert Camus, The Rebel (Harmondsworth: Penguin Books, 1967), p. 237.
17. M.K. Gandhi, Constructive Programme : Its Meaning and Place (Ahmedabad: Navajivan Publishing House, 1947), p. 20.

18. C. Rajagopalachary, and Kumarappa, J.C. (eds.), The Nation's Voice (Ahmedabad: Publishing House, 1958), p. 232.
19. *CWMG*, Vol. XIII, p. 311.
20. Erik, H. Erikson, Gandhi's Truth (New York: W.W. Norton, 1969), p. 265.
21. *Ibid*.
22. J.K. Galbraith, The Affluent Society (London: Hamish Hamilton, 1958).
23. J.K. Mehta, A Philosophical Interpretation of Economics (London: George Allen and Unwin Ltd., 1962), p. 67.
24. M.K. Gandhi, From Yervada Mandir (Ahmedabad: Navajivan Publishing House, 1962).
25. *Harijan*, 10-10-1948, p. 271.
26. *Ibid*., 28-4-1946, p. 111.
27. *Ibid*., 1-2-1942, p. 20.
28. *Young India*, 13.10.1921, p. 325.
29. 28-8-1940, p. 260.

3

On Industrialization

Technology has changed the world in which we live. The landing on the moon and the transplant of human heart are only the more spectacular of them but in countless ways, advances have been made which are likely to have a tremendous impact on man's life in the decades to come. Modern technology can produce so much wealth with so little effort that man can be set free for the first time in human history from the clutches of poverty and misery. It can straight way lead to the light of affluence. Dr. S. Radhakrishnan has described these achievements in these musical words: "We have learnt to ride the waves of the wind, to harness the rivers for watering deserts, to master the earth and the creatures thereof and with the earth as our footstool reach out to stars."[1]

Some argue that the modern technology as developed mainly in the West is even most desirable object for adoption by poor countries, which are poor because their productivity is low. It is often suggested that developing countries have even a special advantage in being late-comers as they can jump over the intermediate stages of technological development and can now go straight to the highest level of technology to produce affluence without exploitation. This idea of the great pump, they feel, from bullock cart to jet engine can remove several bottlenecks from the path of development of the third world.

In fact the very success of science and technology has generated to some extent a backlash. There is a great debate in the West among the economists and technologists about the dangers of unlimited application of modern technology for accelerating industrialisation leading to exploitation of natural resources and the anti-life impact of technology on human existence itself. There is a growing feeling among many that we are going too far and the vastly increased power that technology has placed in the hands of man has not been matched by his ability to use it wisely.

The 'Club of Rome'[2] thesis on this is a product of such debate. In a commentary on the Report, the Executive Committee of the Club expresses this view.

"We are convinced that realisation of the quantitative restraints of the world environment and of the tragic consequences of an overshoot is essential to the intimation of new form of thinking that will lead to a fundamental revision of human behaviour and by implication, of the entire fabric of present day society."

They go on to say:

> "We affirm finally that any deliberate attempt to reach a rational and enduring stage of equilibrium by planned measures rather than by chance or catastrophe, must ultimately be founded as a basic change of values and goals at individual, national and world level."

And they do not hesitate to use highly dramatic language, such as the following:

> "The concept of a society in a steady state of economic and ecological equilibrium may appear easy to grasp although the reality is so distant from our experience as to acquire a Copernican revolution of the mind. Translating the idea into deed, though, is a task filled with overwhelming difficulties and complexities. We can talk seriously about where to start only when the message of "The Limits of Growth", and its sense of extreme urgency, are accepted by

a large body of scientific, political and popular opinion in many countries. The transition in any case is likely to be painful and it will make extreme demands on human ingenuity and determination. As we have mentioned, only the conviction that there is no other avenue to survival can liberate the moral, intellectual and creative forces required to initiate this is precedented human undertaking."[3]

The new technology generated dangers on land, ocean and sky have added new dimensions to human life. Indeed it is now being suggested that with the present rate of use of natural resources, may mean the tragic end of scarce resources and consequently the technology itself, though paradoxically, the solution is still being sought in technology, itself.

Alvin Toffler, in his best seller, 'Future Shocks' has well described the inexorable price we are paying for the advanced technology which we are told is being developed for our benefit.

"Our technological powers increased but the side effects and potential hazards also escalate. We risk thermopollution of the oceans themselves, overheating them, destroying immeasurable quantities of marine life, perhaps even melting the ice caps. On land, we concentrate such large masses of population in such small urban-technological islands—that we threaten to use up air's oxygen faster than it can be replaced, conjuring up the possibility of the new saharas where the cities are now. Through such destruction of natural ecology, we may literally in the words of biologist Barry Commoner be destroying this planet as a suitable place for human habitation."[4]

Similarly, the major findings of the Global 2000 Report to the President of United States of America are:

"If the present trends continue, the world will be more crowded, more polluted, less stable ecologically, and more vulnerable to disruption than the world we live in now. Serious stresses involving population, resources and environment are clearly visible ahead. Despite greater material output, the world's people will be poorer in many ways than they are today". The average gross national product per capita is projected to rise substantially in some

> Low Developed Countries, (especially in Latin America) but in the greater population of South Asia it remains below $ 200 a year (in 1975 dollars). The large existing gap between the rich and the poor nations widens."[5]

The next crisis, deals not merely with "exploitation of natural resources and pollution" but with the mounting danger which present day modes of production and pattern of living, including excessive urbanisation, pose to the living nature around us, on the only Earth we have.[6] It is often asserted that there is a close link between economic growth and technological improvement; labour and capital becomes more productive, or production of the same goods becomes less costly with technology. At least half of the productive capacity in the developed world is attributed to technological change. But technology profoundly affects relations between man, nature and society. This relationship is varied and complex.

Our purpose here is to explore these notions, from a practical point of view. Our point of departure, must be the actual situation of an actually existing society, poor bound by all sorts of traditions, slow to change its way of life, yet in some way managing to live and survive. To take as one's point of departure certain general notions of "What science can do," or "The potentialities of automation," and such like, would involve us in the danger of utopianism. What is food to one man may be poison to another and the cases are known when men, nearly dying from thirst actually killed themselves by suddenly drinking an ample quantity of fresh water. In short, we are not concerned with the general and abstract question of whether science or industrialisation or modern technology is "a good thing," whether we are in favour of the machine or against it: We are concerned with the really vital and urgent question of the manner and the speed in which an actually given society can adopt new methods of production, higher level of technology, technical progress or whatever we like to call it.

The main contradiction in the world today is that whereas the economic and technological interdependence of countries is increasing, neither economic nor technological resources are global. Therefore, not only the technological gap between nations is increasing but transfer of technology has become a source of exploitation of poor nations and, ironically, for perpetuating the technological gap.

Let us take our own example. According to one report there have been 4000 foreign collaborations in India since independence. There must be something drastically wrong with our country because Japan with 25,000 collaborations has pushed its per capita income to $ 14,000 as compared to $ 260 in our country. Foreign multinationals in the name of transfer of technology are leaving India dry. Same is true about all other Third World countries who have allowed collaboration on their soil

It is a familiar sight in the developing countries to find somewhere, in the midst of great poverty, and a primitive way of life, a gleaning, steamlined new factory, created by foreign enterprise and producing consumer goods of just the kind that poor people need. Such a factory, as a factory may be in no way inferior to anything that could be found in the Western world, superbly equipped and well managed and attaining, with native labour, as high a level of productivity as might be attained in the country of its origin. When inspecting the factory one might think that he was in America. But he would not think so the moment he stepped outside. Not only there might be a huge barbed wire fence, heavily guarded, around the whole property but immediately outside the gate one might find a shanty town, full of slums of the most miserable kind teeming with thousands of people most of whom are unemployed and do not seem to have a chance of ever finding regular employment of any kind. The contrast is so striking that one might begin to wonder, not merely what this factory represent by itself but what it means to the society into which it has been planted.

The first question which Professor Schumacher asked, is this: "What is the chance of providing modern factory employment for all or most of these people who are hanging around the factory gates, hoping against hope?"[8] He, himself answers the questions by making some simple calculations.[9]

Let us look at the National Income statistics of an advanced country employing the level of technology which is represented by the factory in question, say the United Kingdom. Annual capital consumption per head of the working population, as covered by the depreciation allowances, amounts to roughly £ 100. From this we can deduce, without any pretension to statistical accuracy, that the average capital cost per work place would be some thing of the order of £ 1000. Now this sum of £ 1000 is roughly equal to the average annual (national) income per head of the working population (i.e., annual national income divided by the number of the working population). In other words, the creation of one working place and what goes with it, at the average level of technology currently represented by the British economy, would require one year's income (or output) of one man. Since this one year's income, at £ 1000, is rather high, Britain can offer a fairly high level of technology, that is, to say, a high capital investment for each workplace (and everything that has to go with it). The converse, of course, is equally true. The annual income is as high as it is, largely because of the great amount of capital equipment that has gone in to each work place. But we shall not see the decisive point if we focus our attention on the second statement, true as it is. For we are starting from a position when incomes are low and there is very little availability of capital; to dwell on the situation that would exist if great wealth had already been attained would merely deflect attention from reality.

It would seen to be obvious therefore, that a poor country such as India for example, could not afford a level of technology that required the investment of £ 1000 per workplace, representing not one but perhaps twenty or thirty years income of one (average) man. That is to say, even if certain islands of such a level of technology were created (as they have been created) in various parts of this country, there would seem to be no hope that this level of technology would generally establish itself throughout the country within a reasonable period of time.

These implications were not clear a few decades ago when the newly independent and developing countries allowed all kinds of technological inroads to be made into their economies from the developed world. These countries have now realized that what has come in the name of technology transfer is designed to quote Professor J.D. Sethi:

I. To exploit the resources of the poor countries for the benefit of the developed countries.
II. Create a dualism by isolating the sectors depending on Western technology from those dependent on and emerging from endowment of national resources.
III. Widen the already technological gap.
IV. Stunt the very process of growth by creating a new consumer-oriented industry and a class which consumes valuable resources.
V. Create a kind of technological imperialism which demoralized developing countries and makes them accept the superiority of Western civilization.[10]

It is true that the goods produced by such technology are superior and produced at a much lower cost than they can be and are being produced elsewhere in the country. These goods are very cheap and therefore in great demand. They are being sold all over the country. The locally produced goods become unsaleable. The traditional producers of similar goods in small towns and villages can not compete with them and are forced out of business. No amount of personal effort or ingenuity can ensure their survival. The rural populations are impoverished precisely because a large part of their non-agricultural production dies away. In their impoverishment, they lack the purchasing power to buy the very goods, the cheapness and superiority of which forced them to abandon their own productive efforts. But the process of the more efficient replacing the less efficient producer is considered to be the very essence of economic progress. Before reaching to some conclusions two more points raised by Professor Schumacher have to be clarified.[11]

If a low cost of producer replaces a high cost producer, this is progress indeed. 'But what are the costs asks Professor Schumacher. The very crux of sound economic teaching is given in the doctrine that the only socially relevant concept of cost is 'opportunity cost', also called 'alternative cost.' If the high cost producer has an opportunity of engaging in alternative production, the opportunity cost of the labour is nil. This means that there is a social gain only, the non-labour costs of the low cost producers are lower than the non-labour costs of the high costs producers, who is being displaced. Labour costs in this context are not confined to the labour actually employed in any particular establishment, but extend also to the native labour content of materials used in the manufacturing process, unless such materials themselves have a scarcity value due to natural causes.

In a country like ours in which the opportunity cost of labour is nil—high cost products produced by indigenous labour from indigenous materials are normally very much more advantageous than low cost products produced with the help of highly efficient machinery from special material which may themselves have been imported or else prepared by a further set of special machinery. It is of course unfortunate that prices, as actually charged, do not and can not reflect the basic fact that the opportunity costs of labour may be nil. Many of the paradoxes of economies result from precisely this divergence between private cost accounting and true special cost. That is why Khadi appears expensive, while mill cloth appears cheap. Yet as long as Khadi is produced by labour which would otherwise do nothing at all, it is, for the economy as a whole, the cheapest cloth of all—a fact very clearly appreciated by Gandhi.

The second point which Professor Schumacher raised is closely related to the first. It relates to the foreign cost, or import cost of the goods produced most efficiently at a high level of technology. For illustration, let us take the case of a fully automated factory which uses imported equipment and imported raw materials. The indigenous labour content of its products may be so small as to be negligible. As a technical achievement, such a factory may be the pride of the place. Its products, of course, are recorded as a part of the national income. Yet, economically speaking, these products are the same as imports; they only appear to be part of the national product; since all the costs—of capital equipment and of raw materials, perhaps even of top level management—are incurred abroad. The product itself is a foreign product, although it happens to come into existence on home territory. It is simply an optical illusion that these products were home-made and make a contribution to the national income. The income accrues where the work is done, and in the case under consideration the work is done abroad. Yet the factory may be highly profitable to its owner. Such profits do not indicate that the factory makes an yearly contribution to the national income; they are strictly analogous to the profits an import merchant makes when he buys cheap goods abroad and sells them dear at home.

Thus if an under-developed country goes straight to a higher level of technology, it normally finds, itself committed to the use of expensive foreign equipment and a large element of foreign raw materials (because the latest equipment is often extremely sensitive to the material it can use), and the result is that very little income is actually generated at home, while a great deal of income is generated abroad, giving rise to foreign exchange crises.

The same kind of problem can arise even if the equipment and the highly refined raw materials come from certain metropolitan areas. A high technology factory situated in a rural area may infact generate income not for the area where it is located but mainly for the area from which it obtains its equipment and raw materials. Its products, therefore may be economically speaking, mainly import from the metropolitan area, leading to no appreciable rise of incomes in the rural areas where the factory happens to be situated because income is generated where the actual work is being done, not where the products happen to make their appearance. If the existence of the 'high technology factor' in the rural area, through its apparently low-cost production, kills, off the locally established 'low technology' production of similar articles, the locality itself is actually impoverished.

Professor Schumacher points out some other complications also. The high technology units of production not merely produce goods at low costs; they are also able to pay relatively high salaries and wages. Whoever can obtain a job in such establishments thereby moves into an income group which is utterly out of reach for the great bulk of population which, whether they like it or not, must continue to work with only the barest minimum of capital by whatever method they know. The most enterprising individuals among the rural populations may be able to make their escape and gain one of those rare and apparently rewarding jobs. But this only means that the great majority are left behind in greater apathy and in a worse predicament than ever before. No wonder if the spirit of self-help dies altogether.

The upshot of this analysis can be stated quite simply and is in line with actual historical experience. Economic development is obviously impossible without the introduction of 'better methods', 'higher technology', 'improved technology'—or whatever we call it. But the degree of betterment and improvement must be such that great mass of producers, upon whom the survival of the country depends can so to speak—keep in touch with it. The steps must be small so that they produce stimulation and not discouragement. In terms of capital expenditure, the improved method, the higher technology, must be accessible to the majority of existing producers, even if only a minority will actually have the drive to reach out of it. Intellectually, the better method must equally be accessible to the average man. All development, like all learning, is a process of stretching. If we attempt to stretch too much, we get a rupture instead of a stretch, or we lose contract and nothing happens at all.[12]

The primary task of technology, is to lighten the burden of work man has to carry in order to stay alive and develop his potential. Whether technology perform this function or not is therefore, worthy for investigation. It obviously greatly reduces some kinds of work while it increases other kinds. Technology has been very successful in reducing skilful, productive work of human hands. It has deprived man the kind of work that he enjoys most, creative, useful work with hands and brains and gives him the plenty of work of a fragmented kind, most of which he does not enjoy at all. It has multiplied the number of people who are exceedingly busy doing kinds of work, which, if it is productive at all, is so only in an indirect or 'round about' way, and much of which would not be necessary at all, if technology were rather less modern. Thus, modern technology, the way it has developed, is developing and promises further to develop, is showing an increasingly inhuman face, and that we might do well to take stock and reconsider our goals.

Taking stock, "We can say, that we possess a vast accumulation of new knowledge, splendid scientific techniques to increase it further, and immense experience in its application. All this is truth of a kind. This truthful knowledge, as such, does not commit as to a technology of giantism, supersonic speed, violence, and the destruction of human work enjoyment."[13]

The poor of the world can not be helped by mass production, but by production by masses which mobilises the priceless resources which are possessed by all human beings. This technology, making use of the best of modern knowledge and experience is conducive to decentralisation. Compatible with the laws of ecology, gentle in its use of scarce resources and designed to serve the human persons, instead of making him the servant of machines. Professor Schumacher has named it 'Intermediate Technology' to signify that it is vastly superior to the primitive technology of bygone ages but at the same time much simpler, cheaper and freer than the super technology of the rich.

Thus, there is an urgent need to give a new direction to technology a direction that can lead it back to the real needs of man, and that also means; to the actual size of man. Man is small, and therefore, small is beautiful. To go for giantism is to go for self-destruction.[14]

It is, therefore, no exaggeration to say that because of this highly sophisticated technology the world in general and the developing countries, in particular find themselves in very deep trouble, and to the most of people this came as a sudden shock. It would not have come as a surprise to the Mahatma were he alive today. "This civilisation" he wrote in the beginning of the last century, "is such that one has only to be patient and it will be self-destroyed. . . . Now thousands of workmen meet together and, for the sake of maintenance, work in factories and mines. Their condition is worse than that of beasts. They are obliged to work, at the risk of their lives at most dangerous occupations, for the sake of millionaires."[15] Writing specifically about machinery he records, "Machinery is like a snake-hole which may contain from one to a hundred snakes. . . . I cannot recall a single good point in connection with machinery".[6] After the lapse of more than two decades, he maintained the same belief. "The future of industrialism is dark. . . . Industrialism is, I am afraid, going to be a curse for humanity. Exploitation of our nation by another can not go on for all time. Industrialism depends entirely on your capacity to exploit, on foreign markets being open to you, and on the absence of competitors."[17] And one can quote many other similar utterances. These were among the statements of our Father of Nation which lesser men like us found most ridicule. Is it not remarkable that they are now the common coinage of world-wide discussion.

Unlike the club of Rome or Professor E.F. Schumacher, Gandhi did not employ nor did he require, a computer to arrive at his conclusions. Common sense told him that Western-style industrialisation for the whole of mankind could never be implemented. God forbid that India should ever take to industrialism after the manner of West. If an entire nation of 300 millions (the figure is now 1210 millions) took to similar economic exploitation, it would strip the world bare like locusts. The 'main point of departure' of his thinking, however, was not resources, nor was it ecology (though he put great emphasis on both). This needs a closer examination of the context which has the following aspects.

Gandhi wrote his Manifesto *(The Hind Swaraj)* in 1908. Then, the mind of India was deeply stirred by two currents of thought—The ideological and cultural influence of the west-railways, hospitals, courts, machinery, universities and legislatures, etc. along with the Western World View and Values; and the Indian Renaissance led by Swami Dayanand (Arya Samaj), Swami Vivekanand (Ram Krishna Mission), Bladavasky (Theosophical Movement), etc.

By the close of the first decade of the last century, the public opinion inside and outside the Indian National Congress had began to take the desirability of modern civilization as granted. This cultural question was also linked with the future constitutional set-up in the independence movement. There were roughly two trends in the Congress—one represented by Gokhale who believed in the Parliamentary form of Government in which the village was expected to occupy the same position as those of the local bodies in England. The other trend was represented by Annie Besant, Bipin Chandra Pal and C.R. Das, according to whom the village was to be the primary and basic unit of political set-up.[18]

Picking up the latter trend, Gandhi tried to reverse the course of national movement towards the village. Therefore, he challenged the very basis of modern civilisation, which was responsible for impoverishing the Indian villages. The basis of modern civilization, according to Gandhi, lay in modern technology; hence his entire critique was focussed at it.

But the immediate cause and context of Gandhian philosophy of industrialisation came from his discussion with the patriotic Indians in London who wanted to 'adopt modern methods of violence and modern civilization to drive out the British.'[19] Since Gandhi had evolved a different approach in South Africa, he came to the conclusion that their approach is suicidal and opined that if they would revert to their own glorious civilization either the English would adopt the latter and become Indianized or find their occupation of India gone."[20]

However, the ultimate purpose of Gandhi was to present a critique and a manifesto of real civilization. According to him, "Civilization is that mode of conduct which points out to the man the path of duty. Performance of duty and observance of morality are convertible terms.[21] Examining the larger question of machinery, he comes to the conclusion that the real civilisation is fundamentally rural in character. Man is so made by nature as to require him to restrict his movements as far as his hands and feet will take him. God has set a limit to a man's locomotion in the construction of his body . . . ." am so constructed that I can only serve my immediate neighbours, but in my concept I pretend to have discovered that I must with my body serve every individual in the universe. Thus in attempting the impossible, man comes in contact with different natures, different religions, and is utterly confounded." So Gandhi says, "Machinery is the chief symbol of modern civilization; it represent a great sin[22]—large cities, slums, displacement of human labour, fast means of locomotion pollution, exploitation, concentration of power, etc., all are the bye products of this machine civilization. But the basis of the real civilization is the force of love which is also called soul force or truth force and not the brute force. "The Universe would disappear without that force."[23] Of course, there are wars and uses of force but hundred of nations live in peace. Wars are interruptions due to uneven working of the force of love or its neglect. Here, he tries to find solution of the ills of present day troubles in the spirit of Indian civilisation. "The tendency of the Indian civilisation is to elevate the moral being that of the Western civilization is to propogate immorality.[24]

Gandhi found a revalidation of these fundamental postulates in the Indian civilization and its philosophy of economics, which rests on mutual cooperation rather than cut throat competition, on simple living and high thinking instead of useless multiplication of wants. India has been predominantly a spiritually-oriented country, which implies a life of simplicity, self-control, self-reliance and peace of mind. The Western culture is by and large materialistic, hedonistic and economically speaking money and profit-oriented. Khadi is a symbol of a culture of simplicity and self-control; hence it is in keeping with the spirit of Indian culture.

There are three symbols of Indian culture—Grind *(Chakki),* Hearth *(Chulha)* and Wheel *(Charkha).* There are ample references to the wheel in Vedas. During Ramayana and Mahabharata period, silk and handmade super fine clothes were prevalent. There are numerous references about the rich heritage of super fine hand made clothes in ancient and medieval India by historians like Travineir, Hunter, Taylor, Rev. Ward Talcharkar, Monier Williams, Barneir, etc.[25] This is only to show that hand woven and hand spun textile cottage industry has been a proud heritage in India. It is ingrained in our culture and tradition. It was only during the British rule that it received a set back. The greedy British businessmen-*cum*-rulers destroyed the indigenous industry to boost up Lankashire (Manchester) markets. It is a pathetic story of intrigues, exploitation and loot. There was a time when Indian cloth captured the English market because of its beauty, variety and durability. However, heavy taxes were imposed by the British Parliament to stop the natural flow of Indian goods on account of which Indian cloth worth 7 shillings was sold in 20 shillings. Then, there were cruelities, perpetuated upon the weavers to the extent that their thumbs were often cut to render them incapable of weaving. Dadabhai Naoroji, the Grand Old Man of India, described all this in detail in his "Poverty and Un-British Rule in India.[26] It is not incorrect to say that to a great extent, the British affluence is the basis of exploitation and loot by the British rulers in India in particular and their other colonies in general. On one hand, Indian raw materials were purchased at cheaper prices, there was a virtual ban on Indian goods due to several prohibitive laws and custom taxes. To surpass all there were physical brutalities perpetuated by the British rulers on the Weavers and other artisans unheard in human history which is corroborated by a number of authoritative works. In a letter to the then Governor of Bengal, the Court of Directors wrote on 17.5.1866: "Every Englishman throughout the country ... exercising his power to the oppression of the helpless Natives. . . . We have the strongest sense of the deplorable state from the corruption and rapacity of our servants ... by a sense of the most tyrannic and oppressive conduct than was ever known in any age or country."[27]

Such unfortunate was the beginning of the connection between Britain and India based on greed and oppression. And to the misfortune of the Indians, the same has remained in subtle and ingenious forms and subterfuges up to the last day of the British rule in India with ever increasing impoverishment.

It is true that Gandhi's 'Hind Swaraj' is an indictment of industrial civilization. But this does not mean that his opposition was either indiscriminate or total. With the passage of time, his attitude became more realistic. During the course of years there was a gradual transition from the exalted heights of the ideas of 'Hind Swaraj' to the more cautious realism in his articles first in 'Young India' and then in the 'Harijan'.

"Ours has been described as the machine age," observed Gandhi, "because the machine dominates our economy. Now what is a machine? One may ask. In a sense, man is the most wonderful machine in creation. It can neither be duplicated, nor copied."[28] He had, however, used the word, not in its wider sense, but in the sense of an appliance that tended to displace human or animal labour instead of supplementing it or merely increasing its efficacy. That was the first differentiating characteristic of the machine. The second characteristic was that there was no limit to its growth or its evolution. That could not be said of the human labour. There was a limit beyond which its capacity or mechanical efficiency could not go. Out of this circumstance arose the third characteristic of the machine. It seemed to be possessed of a will or genius of its own. Machine is antagonistic to man's labour. Thus, it tended more to displace man, one machine doing the work of hundred men, if not a thousand, who went to swell the army of the unemployed and under-employed, not because it was desirable, but because that was its law. The onward improvement in machines did not impress him, but had repelled him. "It then dawned on me that to suppress and exploit the millions, the machine was a device par excellence; it had no place in man's economy if, as social units, all men were to be equal. It is my belief that machine has not added to man's stature and it will not serve the world, but disrupt it, unless it is put in its proper place. Then, I read Ruskin's Unto This Last; during a train journey to Durban, and it gripped me immediately. I saw clearly that if mankind was to progress and to realize the ideal of equality and brotherhood, it must adopt and act on the principle of Unto This Last; it must take along with it even the dumb, the halt and the lame. Did not Yudhishthira, the Prince of Righteousness refuse to enter heaven without his faithful dog?"[29]

In the machine age, these had no place. Under it the fittest alone survived to the exclusion and at the cost of the weak "That is not my picture of independence, in which there is no room for the weakest," observed Gandhi. "That requires that we must utilize all available human labour before we entain the idea of employing mechanical power."[30] He told the Industries Ministers from the Congress provinces, when they met him on July 31, 1946, "We stand today in danger of forgetting the use of our hands." To forget how to dig the earth and tend the soil is to forget ourselves. To think that your occupation of the ministerial chair will be vindicated if you serve the cities only, would be to forget that India really resides in her 700,000 villages units. And what would it profit a man, if he gained the whole world but lost his soul in the bargain."[31]

In October 1924, soon after he has broken one of his memorable fasts, in an interview to a student from Santiniketan, Ramachandran, he poured out his heart on this subject. In reply to a question as to whether he was against all machinery? "How can I be", said Gandhi smiling at the naive question "When I know that even this body is a most delicate peace of machinery? The spinning wheel itself is a machine; a little toothpick is a machine. What I object to is the craze for machinery, not machinery as such. The craze is far what they call labour saving machinery. Men go on saving labour till thousands are without work and thrown on the open streets to die of starvation. I want to save time and labour, not for a fraction of mankind, but for all. I want the concentration of wealth, not in the hands of a few but in the hands of all. Today machinery merely helps a few to ride on the back of millions. The impetus behind it all is not the philanthropy to save labour, but greed. It is against this constitution of things that I am fighting that all my might."

"Then", said Ramachandra, "you are fighting not against machinery as such, but against its abuses which are so much in evidence by today"

"I would unhesitatingly say 'yes', but I would add that the scientific truths and discoveries should first of all cease to be the mere instruments of greed. Then the labourers will not be overworked and the machinery instead of becoming a hindrance will be a help. I am aiming not at eradication of all machinery, but limitation." When logically argued out that would imply that all complicated power driven machinery should go. "It might have to go", admitted Gandhi, "but I must make one thing clear. The supreme consideration is man. The machine should not tend to make atrophied the limbs of man. For instance, I would make intelligent exceptions. Take the case of the few useful things ever invented, and their romance about the device itself. Singer saw his wife labouring over the tedious process of sewing and seaming with her own hands and simply out of his love for her he devised the sewing-machine in order to save her from unnecessary labour. He, however, saved not only her labour but also the labour of every one who could purchase a sewing machine."

"But in that case there would have to be a factory for making these singer machines, and it would have to contain power driven machinery of ordinary types."

'Yes' said Gandhi, "smiling at Ramachandran's opposition." "But I am socialist enough to say that such factories should be nationalised or state controlled. They ought only to be working under the most attractive and ideal conditions, not for profit, but for the benefit of humanity, love taking the place of greed as the motive. It is an alteration in the conditions of labour that I want. This mad rush for wealth must cease and the labourer must be assured not only of a living wage but a daily task that is not a mere drudgery. The machine will, under these conditions, be as much a help to the man working it as to the state, or the man who owns it. The present mad rush will cease and the labour and the labourer will work, as I have said under attractive and ideal conditions. This is but one of the exceptions I have in mind. The sewing machine had love at its back. The individual is the one supreme consideration. The saving of the labour of the individual should be the object, and honest humanitarian consideration and not greed, the motive. Thus, for instance, I would welcome any day a machine to straighten crooked spindles. Not that the blacksmiths will cease to make spindles—they will continue to provide the spindles—but when the spindle gets wrong every spinner will have a machine of his own to get it straight. Therefore, replace greed by love and every thing will come right."[32]

This long conversation between Ramachandran and the Mahatma is important from many points of view. The views expressed in 1924 seem to mark a significant departure from those of 1909. One can see above that Gandhi had already realized that there was a line between machinery and industrialism. In the passage quoted above, it seems that he had recognized that all forms of industrial organization were not necessarily wrong. In certain cases, the centralized use of machinery might be unavoidable if the object was the lightening of the burden of human labour. Gandhi pleaded for social control or nationalization in these cases.

Professor D.P. Mukerji referring to the passage quoted above observed: 'At this point Gandhiji presumably believed that the state was, and would be, an agency for transforming greed into a love for humanity, though elsewhere he was less hopeful. All this appears to be a move away from the uncompromising position taken up in the 'Hind Swaraj'. . . For Western readers the change is like that from Tolstoy to William Morris."[33]

During the mid-thirties the demand for the industrialisation of the country arose inside and outside the Congress; the modern liberals like Jawaharlal Nehru, the left Nationalists like Subhas Chandra Bose, the radicals like M.N. Roy and the emerging forces of Socialism inside and outside the anti-imperialist platform—all stood for industrialisation.

Gandhi could understand which way the wind was blowing. The assumption of the office by the Congress posed concrete issue in relation to industrialisation. A man of compromise in bare essentials, he was prepared to relent to a great extent but not at the cost of his basic faith.[34]

In 1937 to the question whether he was against the machine age, he replied "To say that is to caricature my views". I am not against machinery as such but I am totally opposed to it when it masters us:

'You would not industrialise India?'

"I would indeed, in my sense of the term. The village communities should be revived. Indian villages produced and supplied to the Indian towns and cities all their wants. India became impoverished when our cities became foreign markets and began to drain the villages dry dumping cheap and shoddy goods from foreign lands."

'You would then go back to the natural economy?'

"Yes, Otherwise I should go back to the city. I am quite capable of running a big enterprise, but 1 deliberately sacrificed the ambition, not as a sacrifice, but because my heart rebelled against it. For I should have no share in the spoliation of the nation which is going on from day-to-day. But I am industrializing the village in a different way"[35]

Till the last day of his life he stuck to his deep faith of industrialising the villages of India—The real India as he termed it—in his own way. On the eve of the independence the issue came to the force as quite as obvious. The socio-economic policy of the independent India had to be given a definite orientation. In this background, in reply to a correspondent he wrote:

> "I do not believe that industrialisation is necessary in any case for any country. It is much less so far India. Indeed I believe that independent India can only discharge her duty towards a groaning world by adopting a simple but ennobled life by developing her thousands of cottages and living at peace with the world. High thinking is

inconsistent with complicated material life based on high speed imposed on as by Mammon worship. All the graces of life are possible only when we learn the art of living nobly."

Whether such plain living is possible for an isolated nation, however, large geographically and numerically, in the face of a world armed to the teeth and in the midst of pomp and circumstances, is a question open to the doubt of a sceptic. The answer is straight and simple. If the plain living is worth living, then the attempt is worth making even though only an individual or a group makes the effort.

But "at the same time, I believe that some big industries are necessary I do not believe in arm-chair or armed socialism. I believe in action according to my belief, without waiting for whole sale conversion. Hence, without having to enumerate key industries, I would have state ownership, where a large number of people have to work together. The ownership of the products of their labour, whether skilled or unskilled, will vest in them through the state. But as I can conceive such a state only based on non-violence, I would not dispossess moneyed men by force but would invite their cooperation in the process of conversion to State ownership."[36]

The passages quoted above from Gandhi's writings are not exhaustive, but they are quite illustrative. It is evident from the foregoing that Gandhi went through a long period of transition and evolution from his extremist position of Hind Swaraj days to the later concept of state ownership of industries where a large number of people have to work together. The humanistic urge impelled him to move nearer and nearer to the socialist point of view regarding machinery in practice and conceded the necessity of key industries run on the basis of state ownership. But the concession he made should not be taken to mean that he deviated from his basic faith and eventually became an advocate for industrialization in the sense the term is usually employed. The contention is borne out by the last-quoted passage. The idealist Gandhi stood for the plain living while the realist element in him recognized and reacted, in its own way of course, to the given situation.[37]

Consistency to Gandhi was not merely repeating what one had said yesterday, last year or 10 years back; it was inconceivable to him that ideas should remain static, particularly when they did not concern the core of the matter. It was the basic approach that mattered, not the words or the manner in which they were couched. And this basic approach or philosophy was unalterable for him. No man remained more steadfast to his ideals and belief than the Mahatma. This was so in his views on machine and technology in spite of what seems to some as a complete reversal of attitude.

Now let us precisely see his basic approach in this context.

Firstly was his belief in the individual not as a matter of political doctrine leading to adult sufferage but as a human philosophy. 'In the midst of darkness, light persists; in the midst of death life persists', he had said; and it was this faith that in every man there is something of the 'Kingdom of God' that made him a humanist. His approach to machinery was so much tinged with this faith in the individual; when he gave the sewing machine as an example of a 'useful' machine devised by Singer to save his wife, the tedium of sewing, he was asked where he would draw the line between a good and bad machine to which Gandhi replied; 'The individual is the supreme consideration. Just when it ceases to help the individual it encroaches on his individualism'. To him an individual was the central piece in the picture; not a mere cog in a giant machine but one with feelings, emotions, one who reflected the glory of the creation. "The machine" he said, 'should not tend to make atrophied the limbs of man.'[38]

Talking to M. Frydman, a polish engineer, Gandhi said in 1938, "To use the language of the Bible, 'What shall it avail a man if he gain the whole world and lose his soul'."[39] Elaborating this, Professor J.K. Mehta, the famous economist observes, "World is on one side, the soul is on the other. Matter is on one side the spirit is on the other. Prakriti is on one side, Purush on the other. You can choose whichever you like; you cannot have both. Look either towards the matter or towards the soul and thus identify yourself either with the matter or with the soul." Gandhiji's objective of life is realisation of the self. If you have to attain this objective you have to choose that mode and pattern of life that would enable you to draw your attention away from matter and focus it on the indwelling soul. Does machinery enables you to focus your attention on the self within you.[40] Professor Mehta, himself answer this question by quoting what the Mahatma, said on the 8th September 1920 that "Europe is today only nominally Christian. In reality, it is worshipping mammon. It is easier for a camel to pass through the eye of a needle than for a rich man to enter into the kingdom. Thus, really spoke Jesus Christ. His so-called followers measure their moral progress by their material possession."[41]

Why is it difficult for a rich man to enter into the kingdom of heaven? Because a rich man's mind is focussed on all the material means of living. And machinery helps one to satisfy his craving for such material means and makes it difficult for him to realise his self.

The second cardinal point in his approach was the central place of the village in the national economy Till Gandhi enunciated his view, villages were looked upon as appendages to the towns, mere dung heaps, without sanitation, education or any amenities of a civilized society. To those in the villages, who have no work for the most part of the year, to those living in lakhs of villages who do not get clean drinking water or can get it only after trekking a long distance, and to those in the villages whose children always go to sleep half hungry, thetic fibre factories, big airports, modern hotels sky trappers, an endless range of domestic-gadgets and the like—make no sense at all. Here, the men begin with nothing at home. Nothing like a breakfast for them. They go to work hungry, toil from down to dusk get back after having put quite a good deal of their sweat in the process.

The Mahatma felt that a strengthened and economically sound rural economy would revitalize the country's economy because India lives in villages; where nearly 75% of the population are agriculturists. He preached hence 'the gospel of rural mindedness.'[42] A rural economy of self-contained villages also could be the basis of a non-violent economy. He felt that the small communities moulding their lives on the basis of voluntary cooperation would be the best environment for the extinction of exploitation. The regeneration of India he felt to be impossible without village reconstruction. Hence he gave a slogan 'Back to the village.'[43] He gave a call to every body to go and work in villages, develop rural economy, rural industry and rural skill. In small self-sufficient villages cottage and small scale industries can prosperous which in its turn can lead to equitable distribution of national wealth and will generate more employment. Big urban concentrations, on the other hand, result in the large scale and heavy industries leading to monopoly and accumulation of wealth in a few hands. Economic concentration is bound to lead to political centralisation. Centralisation, in its turn supports violence. He was of the definite view that non-violence could be realized not on the basis of factory civilization but only on that of self-contained village.[44]

He had sought to build India from the bottom, that is, from the poorest and the weakest and hence followed the centrality of the village. "Under my scheme nothing will be allowed to be produced by the cities which can be equally well produced by the villagers. The proper function of the cities is to serve as a clearing houses of village products."[45] He wanted the villages to grow as thriving independent production communities which can cater to their own 'vital wants' as well as to those of the towns in the neighbourhood and yet inter-dependent where such dependence is necessary.

It is mainly this belief which led Gandhi to the concept of decentralization of economy, which would avoid concentration of economic power and the monopoly that is attended upon it. He realised that centralisation of economy and concentration of economic power either in the state or in the hands of a handful of industrial or commercial magnets not only elevate the rank either of the political and economic bureaucracy or the propertied class; individuals are reduced to the rank of robots and machine-tenders and loose their significance as independent social, political and moral entities. Economic swaraj can pave the way of political swaraj and so also social and moral swaraj only when the economic system is decentralised and diffused, organised on small-scale and local basis and individuals are made an essential ingredient of the economic process, determining its nature and character, and tone and temper. As Wilfred Wellock has observed: "In order to liberate individual from the robotism and ensure the fullest development of human person, one of the means to this end is the establishment of small agro-industrial communities, in which every person has a status of a responsible worker and citizen and enjoys organic relationship with a community which control its economic and political life by mean of guilds, councils, and such other institutions as it deems advisable."[46] Under such a system industries and crafts can be organised on small scale or village scale and owned and operated either individually or co-operatively.

Decentralisation would also check urbanisation and the industrial slums that have become an ugly feature of modern cities with their increase in a number of social evils. Decentralisation enables one to live closer to Nature and the Mahatma instinctively sensed that the healthy physical and moral growth of man depended greatly on ecological communion with Nature. The more man moves away from Nature, the more helpless he becomes, till the ultimate is reached in the giant megalapolises as that have grown all round the world—Tokyo, Shanghai, New York, London, Bombay or Calcutta—where machines think like human beings and human beings live like machines.

Another characteristic feature of Gandhi's views on technology is his 'pragmatism'—not in the narrow conventional sense of being practical at the expense of idealism or being disinterested in fanciful theory or conjecture but only interested in what can be done immediately and now. When he read Ruskin's Unto the Last it was not something to which he would give intellectual allegiance but a philosophy of life that had to be practised, at once. It was for this reason that Cardinal Newman's favourite hymn (Lead Kindly Light) was one of his favourites particularly where Newman sighs "I do not wish to see the distant scene, one step enough for me."[47] It was the next step that mattered to him—whether it was politics, or education or constructive work. So it was in economics. If he pleaded for Khadi he was not being just a romantic idealist. In fact, he listed all its advantages and then asked his critics to suggest any other alternative occupation to the millions who are punished with forced idleness for a big part of the year. "Do not make the majority of your countrymen as compulsory thieves"—he pleaded for in his view anyone who eats without working is a thief. "My sole claim for Khadi", he argued, "is that it offers an immediate, practicable and permanent solution to the twin problems of enforced idleness and chronic starvation.[48]

It is for this reason that he wanted a dynamic balance between man and machine. He felt, and rightly, that there was an interaction between the two and only when both matched in harmony that the output would be most fruitful and productive. It was no use, he argued, providing the most sophisticated equipment to a man who could make little or nothing out of it. "The human body itself is a wonderful piece of machinery", he said, 'let us make use of 300 million machines lying idle in the villages before importing labour-saving machinery'. It is better to utilise the 'machines' available in the country than to throw them out of the employment and making them a burden on the community since the social cost of such an exercise would be frightfully heavy. He argued, "Dead machinery must not be pitted against the millions of living machines represented by the villages scattered in the seven hundred thousand villages of India. Machinery to be well used has to help and ease human efforts. The present use of machinery tends more and more to concentrate wealth in the hands of a few in total disregard of millions of men and women whose bread is snatched by it out of their mouths.[48]

When we look back on this basic approach of the Mahatma, can it be said honestly that it was either wrong or even irrelevant today The problems for which he tried to find pragmatic solutions have all become even more acute. Unemployment and underemployment has reached frightening proportions—nor can the conventional solutions offered by large scale urban industrialisation be said to touch the fringe of the problem, let alone solve it. Assuming the crude labour force participation rates in both rural and urban areas to rise reflecting largely the effect of age structure shift and some general rise in participation rates, especially of women, the size of the labour force can touch the 800 million figure in 2020. This implies an annual average addition of over 8.6 million over the entire period. Hence, in the next decade the Indian planners will have to cope with the larger pool of labour force. The pressure on capital and natural resources exerted by swelling labour force may be even more intense. That means a significant proportion of resources have to be used to create employment opportunities. In the mean time the country has to withstand the labour force explosion and plan to transform this serious threat to growth and stability into a powerful aid to progress.

After examining several studies of employment, unemployment and underemployment done in South Asia, the world famous economist and Nobel laureate Gunnar Myrdal remarked: "In general these studies have led to ask the kind of questions Western economists would wish to investigate in their own countries. At the same time, however, it is often acknowledged that the Western technologies cannot be transferred intact to a South Asian environment."[50] A committee of experts on Unemployment Estimates appointed by the Government of India, after a thorough review of Unemployment conditions in India with the use of western theoretical concepts, came to the conclusion that: "It is now realized that the concept as adopted in developed economics is unsuitable for an economy like ours with its preponderance of self-employment and production within house-hold enterprise."[51]

In view of the difficulties involved in applying the Western concepts to the Indian conditions, this committee proposed to give up the practice of estimating and presenting one dimensional estimates on employment and unemployment. In the words of the Committee, "In our complex economy, the character of labour force, employment and unemployment is too hetrogenous to justify aggregation into single dimensional magnitudes."[52]

From the economic efficiency point of view also, a developing economy with labour abundance and capital shortage, should choose technologies characterised by higher labour output and lower capital output ratios. In the words of W.A. Lewis, "Special care should be taken in those countries which have a large surplus unskilled labour for in such circumstances, money wages will not reflect the real cost of using labour. In these circumstances, capital is not productive if it is used to do what labour could do equally well, given the level of wages. Such investment may be highly profitable to capitalists but they are unprofitable to the community as a whole since they add to unemployment and not output."[53]

The steadily deepening economic crises quite visible even in the mid-fifties of the last century failed to open the eyes of planners. Rejection of indigenous models in the field of restructuring our economy after independence was accompanied by our persistance with wholly alien models of economic development. This helped only to compound our misery.

The etymology of the word development hints the same. The word develop is a 12th or 13th century word. The Italian form of this, according to Oxford English Dictionary, is 'Velupare', which means significantly 'to unwrap', 'to disentangle,' 'to rid free of'. The opposite of develop is 'envelope' which means 'to hide', 'to cover up', 'to put constraints upon'—which is what we do when we envelop something. When we develop we do the reverse. We remove constraints whatever they may be. The word develop maintains its original definition in photography. When we develop a film, we reveal what is already latent in that film. We can not put new things into the film and call it developed. Development is thus a process of revealing, as we continue with the dictionary definition, it says to unfold, as a tale or as a story develops to lay open by removal of that what enfolds. That is to say, something more comes out of that which already exists. Development should proceed on this basis rather than blindly following the models of development propounded by the Western theorists taking into account their own problem and circumstances. This is precisely what the Mahatma preached.[54]

Our set of problems are different. India is an over-populated country has already crossed 120 crore mark as far as the number of population is concerned. The vast population of the country which should be used as an asset have become a tremendous liability and a method must be devised to make this huge mass a productive asset. Though the manpower mobilisation programmes have been attempted in the various five year plans, yet the progress has been poor. Surely, here is a vast source of untapped wealth which if harnessed can make the country prosperous. What does it matter, if initially, these people can earn only a little through such small scale and village level industries? Surely it is better than nothing. Gandhi was not averse to improvement in techniques of production. He had himself offered a prize in 1927 for a better model of Charkha that could be easily worked by the villagers and easily repaired by the village carpenters. Time and again, he made it abundantly clear, "I would welcome every improvement in the cottage machine, but I know that it is criminal to displace hand labour by the introduction of power driven spindles unless one is, at the same time, ready to give millions of farmers some other occupation in their homes."[55] At another place, he made it emphatically clear, "I would prize every invention of science made for the benefit of all. There is a difference between invention and invention. I should not care for the asphyxiating gases capable of killing masses of men at a time. The heavy machinery for work of public utility, which can not be taken by human labour has its inevitable place, but all that would be owned by the state and used entirely for the benefit of the people."[56]

Another misconception about Gandhi was that he was against power driven machinery. True, he did not, like Lenin, make power the sheet anchor of his new society. Perhaps, he was painfully aware of the impossibility of doing so for even today the number of villages electrified is not very large and those which are electrified do not get sufficient electricity. But this does not mean that he was against using power so long as it did not throw men out of employment; he would certainly have welcomed its widespread adoption where it relieves the physical burden of the worker and helps him to earn higher wages.

Modern science and technology have reinforced the basic validity of Gandhi's approach. Science itself has become multi-disciplinary and it is no longer possible to regard human knowledge as compartments listed into narrow segments. Modern economists and sociologists favoured decentralised production as the only solution for the evil of uncontrolled urbanisation and the latest trend in the west is to set-up small manufacturing in rural communities where men live close to the land, and can walk to work. Electronic and electrical industries no longer require the vast conglomeration of men and machinery and can be decentralised without any change to the economic viability of the enterprise.

The dynamic balance between man and machine which the Mahatma had intuitively sensed as necessary is now accepted by most thinkers as the only possible approach for a really productive effort. Japan has demonstrated in the last few decades that the optimum 'man-machine' mix can significantly raise productivity which in turn has been responsible for its phenomenal growth, often turned a miracle. In India too it is being realized that what is needed in the rural sector for quick result is an 'appropriate technology', that would match the skills and resources available in the area. They should be tailored to meet the actual instead of indiscriminate import from the West. What is suitable for India may not be suitable elsewhere and in each case, one has to make sure that the level of technology is such as to match the skills and resources in the community. It is this approach with Bapu had taught when he pleaded for the spinning wheel in the village—and though with the passage of time some changes are necessary and even desirable, it is being realised that, essentially, his approach was a sound and valid one; and what applies to the spinning wheel, is equally applied to the village industries.

Notes and References

1. Dr. S. Radhakrishnan, "Speeches and Writings," Third Series, (New Delhi: The Publications Division, July 59 to May 61).
2. The club of Rome has among its membership such economists of eminence as Aurelio Peonm, an Italian economist who heads the management firm of Itloconrilt in Rome; Kongoro Vemura, President of the Japanese Federation of Economic Organizations; and Alexander, King of Britain, who is Director General for Scientific Affairs of the Office for Economic Cooperation and Development. Aurelio Peccei, The Human Development (Oxford: Pergamon Press, 1977).
3. *Ibid.*
4. Alvin Toffler, Future Shocks (New York: A National General Company, 1971), p. 430.
5. The Global 2000 Report to the President, Vol. I, p. 1, quoted in Romesh Diwan and Mark Lutz (eds.) Essays in Gandhian Economics (New Delhi: Gandhi Peace Foundation, 1965), p. 165.
6. E.F. Schumacher, Future is Manageable (New Delhi: Impex India, 1978), p. 16.
7. *The Tribune*, Chandigarh, 26.2.1987.
8. E.F. Schumacher, Roots of Economic Growth (Varanasi: Gandhian Institute of Studies, 1962), p. 50.
9. *Ibid.*, pp. 50-51.

10. J.D. Sethi, Gandhi Today (New Delhi: Vikas Publishing House, 1978), p. 112.
11. E.F. Schumacher, Roots of Economic Growth, *op. cit.*, p. 52.
12. *Ibid.*, p. 55.
13. E.F. Schumacher, Small is Beautiful: A Study of Economics as if People Mattered (London: Abacus, 1989), p. 126.
14. *Ibid.*, p. 133.
15. M.K. Gandhi, *Hind Swaraj* (Ahmedabad: Navajivan Publishing House), p. 97.
16. *Ibid.*, p. 97.
17. *Young India*, 12.12.1931, p. 355.
18. Jai Narain, Gandhi's View of Political Power (New Delhi: Deep & Deep Publications, 1987), pp. 44-46.
19. M.K. Gandhi, *Hind Swaraj, op. cit.*, p. 16.
20. *Ibid.*, p. 65.
21. *Ibid.*, p. 60.
22. *Ibid.*, p. 94.
23. *Ibid.*, p. 77.
24. *Ibid.*, p. 63.
25. Ramji Singh, "Gandhi Attitude Towards Industrial Civilization," Technological Advancement and Large Scale Production.
26. Dadabhai Naoroji, Poverty and Un-British Rule in India (New Delhi: Publications Division, Ministry of Information and Broadcasting, Government of India, 1961).
27. *Ibid.*, p. III.
28. *CWMG*, Vol. LXXXV, p. 95.
29. *Ibid.*, p. 96.
30. *Ibid.*
31. *Ibid.*, p. 97.
32. *Young India*, 13.11.1924, pp. 377-78.
33. D.P. Mukerji, Diversities (New Delhi: People Publishing House, 1958), p. 213.
34. Buddhadeva Bhattacharyya, The Evolution of Political Philosophy of Mahatma Gandhi (Calcutta: Calcutta Book House, 1969), p. 214.
35. *Harijan*, 27.2.1937, p. 18.
36. *Ibid.*, 1.9.1946, p. 285.
37. Buddhadeva Bhattacharyya, *op. cit.*, p. 216.
38. *Young India*, 13.11.1924, p. 378.
39. *CWMG*, Vol. LXVIII, p. 266.
40. J.K. Mehta, Gandhian Thought (New Delhi: Ashish Publishing House, 1985), p. 135.
41. *CWMG*, Vol. XVIII, p. 235.
42. *Harijan*, 16.5.1936, pp. 107-11.
43. *Ibid.*, 4.11.1939, p. 331.
44. Jai Narain, "Rural-Urban Dichotomy: The Need for a Fresh Look", in *Gandhi Jyoti: Journal of Gandhian Thought*, Bhagalpur University, July, 1989, Year 6, No. 4, p. 15.
45. *Harijan*, 23.1.1939, p. 438.
46. Wilfred Wellock, New Horizons (London: Houseman's Bookshop), p. 42.

47. Bertram Newman, Cardinal Newman: A Biographical and Literacy Study (London: G. Bell & Sons, 1925).
48. *Young India,* 13.10.1921.
49. *Harijan,* 14.9.1935, p. 244.
50. Gunnar Myrdal, Asian Drama: An Enquiry into the Poverty of Nations (New York: Pantheon, 1968), p. 22-21.
51. Government of India, Report of the Committee of Experts of Unemployment Estimates, Planning Commission, New Delhi, 1970, p. 30.
52. *Ibid.,* p. 31.
53. W.A. Lewis, The Theory of Economic Growth (London: George Allen & Unwin, 1955), p. 356.
54. Jai Narain, *op. cit.,* p. 14.
55. *Young India,* 5.1.1925, p. 377.
56. *Harijan,* 22.6.1935, p. 146. vcx

4

Theory of Trusteeship

Perhaps the most important and controversial issue of economic philosophy is the right to private property The controversy as it developed, mainly between *Laissez faire* economists and communist economists, led scholars to no definite conclusion. This (right to property) remained more a matter of dogmatic attachment to ideology than of rational convictions. The former believes in the absolute right to property. They maintain that there is automatic adjustment in the economy because whatever is produced is automatically consumed or the supply creates its own demand.[1] The forces of demand and supply independently make the equilibrium. Hence there is no need of any intervention by the state. They believe that each man is the best judge of his own interest. Given the complete freedom he would not only make efforts to better his own lot; but also promote general good. These celebrated words of Adam Smith, are the backbone of their philosophy. "It is not from the benevolence of the butcher, the brewer or the baker that we expect our dinner, but from their regard to their own interest. We address ourselves, not to their humanity but to their self-love, and never talk to them of our own necessities but of their advantages."[2]

The Marxists rejected the classical model on the ground that it inevitably led to the growth of monopolies and imperialism on one hand, and the perpetual immersion of the working class on the other, suggested the revolutionary overthrow of the entire politico-economic system, the socialisation of all means of production and the total elimination of 'bourgeoisie' through the dictatorship of the proletariat.

The Mahatma rejected both these solutions. He rejected the Marxist solution because he believed it to be based on violence and tyranny He also rejected the capitalistic solution because he considered it to be based on exploitation, competition and tyranny. The question of property relations assumed a great significance for him, since in his first order ideal society there would be no state or government, and these relations would have to be organised on a voluntary basis in such a manner that they are consistent with his basic philosophy. He was of the confirmed belief that instead of changing the property relations, if we change the uses to which property is put we can have the desired results. For this he advocated trusteeship as a relevant choice between the existing but unacceptable system of Capitalist organisation and its 'inevitable' throw by violence. He believed that as for as the present owners of wealth are concerned they have to make a choice between war and voluntary converting themselves into the trustees of their wealth. The choice is not between the two parties, that is wealth owners and their workers, but also for the society as a whole. Thus, he seeks to harmonize the economic relations and to conciliate the ultimate values into a state of equilibrium through Trusteeship.

Trusteeship was not just an economic expedient for Gandhi. It was no make-shift for him. It was a way of life. In his own words, "My theory of trusteeship is no make-shift, certainly no camouflage. I am confident that it will survive all other theories. It has the sanction of philosophy and religion behind it."[3] Indian philosophy, religion and morals are replete with this. The ancient Indian concept of rulers or kings was that of a real trustee. Ramachandra may be a legendary figure but the philosophy contained in the concept of Ramarajya bears testimony of the fact that under the Indian cultural heritage the rulers wielded power not for their own sake but for the sake of their subject. Bharat reigned over Ayodhya during Ramachandra's absence as the latter's trustee. Lord Krishna acted as the charioteer of Arjuna in the battle of Mahabharata, not with any ulterior motive or expectation of any gain from the battle, he acted as a trustee of Arjuna to give satisfaction to the latter.

The heads of Hindu joint families in those days used to live the life of true trustees. According to K.M. Munshi, "He held the family property and was expected to manage and administer it for the welfare of the family. He was expected to watch with care the advancement of its younger members belonging even to collateral branches and had to give asylum to the orphans, widows, destitutes in the family."[4] Writing specifically about the property, Dr. S. Radhakrishnan has pointed out, "Property according to the Hindu View, is a mandate held by its possessors for the common use and benefit of the commonwealth. The Bhagvata tells us that we have a claim only to so much as would satisfy our hunger. If any one desires more, he is thief deserving punishment."[5]

Thus the concept of trusteeship should be viewed in the context of the values it stood for. The doctrine is as old as the ages. But it was the Mahatma who tried to apply this philosophical teaching to the concrete realities of life for the solution of the existing economic problems.

Pyare Lal maintained, "Gandhi based his trusteeship doctrine on a celebrated verse in the ancient Hindu philosophical scripture 'Ishopanished', which says: "All that is in the universe is pervaded by God, Renounce first, therefore, in order to enjoy. Covet not any body's riches."[6]

The words like, aparigraha (non-possession) and 'samabhava' (equability) had gripped him.[7] He now came to realize that the principles of non-possession and renunciation of one's property or possession or assets as advocated in the Gita can be given effect to by way of trusteeship where by the propertied people while retaining their property can still divest themselves of such possessions by holding the property in form of trust for the real beneficiaries. His study of English Law also came to his help in deciding upon his divesting himself of all possessions. To quote from his autobiography, "My study of English Law came to my help. Snell's discussion of the maxims of Equity came to my memory. I understood more clearly in the light of Gita teaching the implication of the world trustee ... I understood Gita teaching of non-possession to mean that those who desired solution should act like trustees who, though having control over great possessions, regards not an iota of them as his own."[8]

In a letter to Polak on October 14, 1909, who was at that time in India, Gandhi employed the word 'trustee' for the first time. He wrote, "Then the British rulers will be servants and not masters. They will be trustees and not tyrants, and they will live in perfect peace with the whole of the inhabitants of India."[9] Laying his heart bare before the august audience assembled on the occasion of the opening of the Benaras Hindu University on February 4, 1916, he appealed to the 'richly bedecked noblemen' present on dias to strip themselves of the jewels and 'hold them in trust' for their countrymen in India.[10]

Let us see how he develops his theory?

Proudhan, the French philosopher said, 'all property is theft.'[11] Gandhi, on the other hand maintained that all property is trust. He was of the opinion that all forms of property and human accomplishments are either gift of nature or the product of social living. As such they belong not to the individual but to the society and therefore, should be used for the good of all. In his own words, "Everything belonged to God and was from God, and therefore, it was for his people and not for a particular individual. When an individual have more than his proportionate portion, he becomes trustee of that portion for Gods people."[12] He further argued, "Suppose I have come by a fair amount of wealth either by way of legacy or by means of trade and industry—I must know that all my wealth does not belong to me; and what belongs to me is the right of an honourable livelihood, no better than that enjoyed by millions of others. The rest of my wealth belong to the community and must be used for the welfare of the community".[13]

Gandhi divided property in two parts; gifts of nature and product of social living. The gifts of nature include land, mines, natural resources, etc. The second part deals with man-made property.

"All land belong to Gopal where then is the boundary line? He asked?[14] Land, mines and other natural resources, are the gift of nature. No individual has made them. God created these not for any particular individual or group of individuals. Man has only occupied a piece of land and demarcated it. He is only the maker of a boundary line. He can not be called the real owner of that property. Let us take an example. There is a landlord in a village having 100 acres of land. From where he got his land? 'From his forefathers', can be the safest answer. His forefathers got the land from their forefathers and so on. Actually what would have happened. Some one from that family might had occupied that portion of land and created a boundary line. That person was not the creator of land but the creator of that boundary line. The land which should have belonged to other persons also, belong to one particular landlord because of the boundary line.

Same is the case with man made property A capitalist has accumulated huge wealth and established several industries. He alone can not make that. There may be so many persons who helped that capitalist in accumulating that wealth. Thus, Gandhi emphasized that the ownership of the labourers and the peasants is something more than mere moral ownership. Because the rich can not accumulate wealth without the help of the poor in the society. Since they have helped the capitalist in accumulating the wealth they have their share in that also. Otherwise also the bounties of nature, felt Gandhi, are meant for the good of God's creation, for the benefit of the entire world. Each is entitled to acquire only that much of wealth or property that is essential for his immediate need or his existence. None has a right to acquire more than what is needed to satisfy his absolute and immediate needs particularly, when millions are unable to satisfy their most basic requirements. He wrote, "You and I have no right to anything that we really have until these . . . millions are clothed and fed better."

He allowed the people with talent to earn more but asked them to utilize their talent for the good of the suffering people. "I would allow a man of talent to earn more. I would not cramp his talent. But the bulk of his greater earning must be used for the good of the state just as the income of all earning sons of the father go to the common family fund. They would have their earnings only as trustees, i.e., owners in their own rights but owners in the right of those whom they have exploited. . . . I will not dictate to them what commission to take but ask them to take what is fair, e.g., I would ask a man who possesses Rs. 100 to take Rs. 50 and give the other Rs. 50 to the workers. But to whom who possesses Rs. 1,00,00,000—I would perhaps say take one percent for yourself, so you see that my commission would not be fixed figure because that would result in atrocious injustice."[15]

An industrious person with more than average intelligence, may acquire by legitimate means, more property than idle men and men of average or below average intelligence even without resorting to violence and exploitation. He admitted, "It is my conviction that it is possible to acquire riches without consciously doing wrong. For example, I may light on a gold mine in my one acre of land."[16] Some time earlier he wrote in form of a reply to Shankar Rao Deo who raised an issue whether crores can be earned by legitimate means. "Surely a man may conceivably make crores through strictly pure means assuming that a man may legitimately possess riches. . . . If I own a mining lease and I tumble upon a diamond of rare value I may suddenly find myself a millionaire without being held guilty of having used impure means.[17] But although such wealth or property may be legitimately acquired without violence and exploitation, he was not prepared to accept it as a source of one's real happiness and his balanced growth. Rather he felt that such possessions and affluence stand as stumbling blocks on the way of self-realisation and blossoming of an integrated personality and all round development of the individual since worship of the mammon and cultivation of manliness do not go hand in hand. As a remedy for such an untenable position arising out of the possession of wealth flowing into one's purse almost without any conscious effort on his part for the accumulation of the same, Gandhi suggested cultivation of a spirit of detachment for wealth and utilisation for oneself only a portion of it that is needed for meeting one's 'legitimate needs' and 'honourable livelihood'.

But the question naturally arises, what is to be done with the wealth that remains beyond what is required to provide an honourable livelihood? How this surplus wealth shall be utilised? Gandhi himself a liberated soul, would perhaps expect of all others the identical conduct. But a practical idealist that he was, he realised that it is highly painful to renounce one's wealth and strip oneself of all the possessions except one's absolute minimum. Possession itself gives a sense of satisfaction and security and people normally are hesitant to part with it. The solution according to Gandhi, therefore, lies in shedding possessiveness, if not possessions, and greed for wealth if not wealth itself. The owners of wealth may still hold their wealth but consider their superfluous wealth as the property of the community and themselves as trustees of such wealth to be utilized for the benefit of the community. As K.G. Mashruwala, has appropriately observed, "On this matter (matter of private property) Gandhi has perhaps more radical views than the most extreme communists. He would like to dispossess every person of all kinds of belongings. If he tolerates the institution of private property, it is not because he loves it, or holds it necessary for the progress of the humanity but because he has yet to discover a truthful and non-violent method of abolishing that institution. I think that all socialists believe that possessions are absolutely essential to make mankind happy. Gandhiji does not accept that position in theory. But as a practical proposition he feels that mankind is not going to give up possessions with in a time which can be estimated."[18] As the Mahatma has himself said, "I accept the proposition that it is better not to desire wealth, than to acquire it and becomes its trustee. But what I am to advice those who are already wealthy or who would not shed their desire for wealth? I can only say to them, that they should use their wealth for service."[19]

He accepted trusteeship as a practical proposition which shall liberate the wealthy and possessing class of their sin of acquisitiveness and greed and effect of change over in favour of egalitarian society. Hence elaborating the Upanishadic mantra Tena Twaktena Bhunjitha he said: Earn your crores by all means. But understand that your wealth is not yours, it belongs to the people. Take what you require for your legitimate needs and use the remainder for the society."[20]

He was conscious of the fact that both physical and intellectual ability differs from man to man. Some are capable of working with greater vigour and energy than others and their labour sincerely performed and honestly executed, may prove more productive of material wealth than that of others who are less energetic and enterprising. Besides people with better intellectual ability and vapour may devise ways and means for greater material prosperity and intellectual excellence of the nation. The material prosperity and progress of the nation depend upon enthusiastic performance of such capable, energetic, enterprising and imaginative individuals and not on the half-hearted work of the idler, sick, and the mentally deficient citizens. Hence, Gandhi's ideas do not imply that men of greater ability and vigour shall not work more than what is necessary to earn their absolute minimum. It also does not propagate the idea that men of more than average physical strength and vigour, resourcefulness and enterprise, intellectual ability and excellence, shall allow their additional ability and energy to be frittered away or wasted. Nor does it fix a premium on idleness, inactivity, inefficiency, mental incapacity and intellectual deficiencies. Gandhi a pragmatist realised that the society shall be poorer, unless such men of ability keep themselves active throughout. He clarified, "We do not want to produce a dead equality. Where every person becomes, or is rendered incapable of using his ability to the utmost possible extent. Such a society must ultimately perish."[21]

What Gandhi actually desires is that such individuals with more than average, or unusual ability shall work as per their capacity but shall get in return for themselves only what is required for fulfilling their legitimate needs.

He had ample faith in the selfless and self-sacrificing nature of man. If the privileged people or the capitalists, are exploiting the toilling millions, and are living at the latter's expense, it is not because they are fundamentally bad but because they have become victims of the evil system that goes by the name of capitalism. There is a finer, subtler, and a more vital chord, according to Gandhi, in every human heart, that is noble, self-sacrificing and full of compassion for others. Sometimes the dust of greed, selfishness and egoism may accumulate on this chord, but properly handled this subtle chord in human heart shall transmit the melodious music of sacrifice, self-sufferings and renunciation for the benefit of the others. "There are chords in every human heart. If we only know how to strike the right chord we bring out the music."[22]

Besides he said latter: "We must appeal to the good in human beings and expect response."

Apart from his faith in man, his faith in the reformability of every human being however deprived and degraded led him to accept the position that the capitalists and the privileged people in the society, even if they are normally egoistic, selfish and exploitative in nature when properly handled can be made to serve the interest of the society, by way of renouncing their possessions and privileges and acting as the trustees. As Gandhi said, "I have sought the friendship of the capitalists in order to induce them to regard themselves as trustees for the benefit of the labourers, and that they may take their own food feeding them."[23]

Through the device of trusteeship, the capitalists and the privileged classes were given an opportunity by Gandhi to reform themselves. As a pragmatist, he realized that inspite of all persuasions, there may be many hard nuts that may not be easily cracked. Many moneyed men, capitalists, industrialists, commercial interests and landlords may not easily respond to such a moral appeal. Hence, when he found that many propertied people were not voluntarily converting themselves into trustees by shedding their greed and acquisitiveness, although he was not accustomed to practise any physical or mental coercion and blackmail, did not desist from administering a dose of warning to the possessing class. On the eve of Salt Satyagraha he wrote, "All these (moneyed men, landlords, factory owners, etc.) do not always realize that they are living on the blood of the masses, and when they do, they become as callous as the British principals whose tools and agents they are. If like the Japanese Samurai they could but realize that they must give up their blood stained gains, the battle is won for non-violence. It must not be difficult for them to see that the holding of million is a crime when millions of their own kith and kin are starving and that, therefore, they must give up their agency."[24]

Accordingly, while advising the *Zamindars* and *Talukdars* to imbibe the spirit of Japanese nobles, read the sign of time, revise their notions, and hold their wealth as trustees for the good of the people and the ryots, he warned them: "There is no other choice than between voluntary surrender on the part of capitalists of the superfluities and consequent acquisition of the real happiness of all on the one hand, and on the other by impending chaos into which, if the capitalists do not wake up betimes, awakened but ignorant, famishing millions will plunge the country and which, not even the armed force, that a powerful government can bring into play can avert".[25]

Though Gandhi was firmly dedicated to the application of non-violent technique of persuasion and conversion and non-violent non-cooperation for the attainment of any objective. But in this case he specifically warned while writing in the Constructive Programme: "A violent and bloody revolution is a certainty one day unless there is a voluntary abdication of riches and the power that riches give and sharing them for the common good."[26] He repeatedly pointed out to the capitalists that their wealth was the cause of their worries and anxiety, unhappiness and insecurity. "They who employ mercenaries to guard their wealth may find those very guardians turning on them."[27] Writing in *Harijan* he further warned the wealthy sections of the society, "As for the present owners of wealth, they would have to make choice between class war and voluntarily converting themselves into trustees of their wealth."[28]

But Gandhi was not prepared to condone violent methods for the sake of realisation of his ideas of Trusteeship. Non-violence is too precious an ideal to be sacrificed by Gandhi. Besides the concept of Trusteeship was devised as an alternative to the violent overthrow of privileges so that violent method can not take precedence, yet if the privileged sections of the society, inspite of all manners of persuasion and moral pressure fail to live up to the ideal of trusteeship, the technique of social compulsion short of violence or coercion can be employed against them.

"All exploitation", observed Gandhi, "is based on co-operation willing or forced, of the exploited". Hence if the real producers—the labourers and the peasants resort to satyagraha, accumulation of wealth will fizzle out and the spring of the prosperity of the wealthy sections of the society will dry up. Speaking about the conversion of the recalcitrant landlords into trustees, Gandhi also suggested adoption of the same formula of non-violent non-cooperation. He said, "The moment the cultivators of the soil realise their power, the Zamindari evil will be sterilized. What can the poor Zamindar do when they say that they will simply not work the land, unless they are paid enough to feed, and clothe and educate, themselves, and their children, in a decent manner? In reality the toiler is the owner of what he produces. If the toilers intelligently combine, they will become an irresistible power."[30]

But the non-violent non-cooperation although a potent instrument can compel the wealthy section of the society to act as trustees, is dependent on the promise that the labour or the working class must become conscious of the strength and should be ready to assert its right. Besides the strength of the labour comes from its unity and collective behaviour. But as is often found in real life, labour is not united and when some labourers non-cooperate with the employers, others are ready to take their place. Under these circumstances requisite amount of pressure can not be exerted on the propertied classes to compel them to act as trustees.

Gandhi being a very practical idealist, having realised, the limitations of the concept of voluntary assumption of trusteeship by the rich and the need for the adoption of the strategy of pressure to be exercised by the labourers, came around to the significance of statutory measures or legislation for giving effect to his idea of trusteeship. But the statute that Gandhi had in his mind is not one which is imposed from above by the all pervading state that represents violence in its concentrated and organised form. It shall not be planned out and implemented by a coterie or clique of the ruling party or the bureaucracy under whose spell comes the entire nation and the entire economy.

His ideal picture of social and political organization, comprehended a system of self-sufficient and self-governing village republics, democratically organized, with Gram Panchayat as the basic unit of the government erected on the basis of consent of the people. The legislation regulating the wealth of the propertied class shall therefore emanate from such Gram Panchayats after a free and full discussion and proper appreciation of the principles by people in general. "Such a statute will not be imposed from above. It will have to come from below. When the people understand the implications of trusteeship and the atmosphere is ripe for it, the people themselves beginning with Gram Panchayats will begin to introduce such statutes. Such a thing coming from below, is easy to swallow. Coming from above it is liable to prove a dead weight."[31]

The statues or legislations had found favour with Gandhi as technique of last resort to give effect to the idea of Trusteeship. He did not overlook the potency of the technique of persuasion and conversion to aid, and effectualise the statutory enactments. Rather he felt that persuasion and conversion should precede statutory enactments so that it will make the propertied classes mentally prepared to accept the statutory enactments intended to give effect to trusteeship system. As he said, "Conversion must precede legislation. Legislation in absence of conversion is a dead letter."[32] But the technique of conversion that he suggests is not by way of prayer and petitions, but by exhibition of potency of democratic forces or public opinion. In his own words, "If the owning class does not accept the trusteeship basis voluntarily its conversion must come under the pressure of public opinion."[33]

Apart from this, Gandhi also felt that the state may be depended upon for the introduction of trusteeship. Educating the people in the principles of trusteeship so that it provides a basis to the statutory trusteeship system, or educating the workers and peasants to be conscious of their rights and dignity so that necessary social conditions conducive to trusteeship are created, is a time consuming process. But unless the state intervenes in time some national assets may be spoiled by unimaginative and useless owners of those property. Although Gandhi was afraid of the power of the state and the violence perpetuated by it, yet for the sake of the long-term interest of the nation he was prepared to allow state intervention to force trusteeship upon the possessing and the privileged class: "I would be happy indeed if the people concerned behaved as trustees, but if they fail, I believe we shall have to deprive them of their possessions through the state."[34]

SUCCESSOR OF THE TRUSTEES

The question of inheritance is vital for any scheme of socio-economic reconstruction. While advising the Congress ministries in 1937 to tax the rich persons heavily, he dealt the question of inheritance also. "For the inheritance should rightly belong to the nation."[35] The following extracts from Gandhi's later writings throw more light on the subject.

Question: How would the successor of a trustee be determined? Will he only have a right of proposing a name, the right of finalisation being vested in the state?

Answer: Choice should be given to the original owner who became the first trustee, but the choice must be finalised by the state. Such arrangement puts a check on the state as well as the individual.

Question: When the replacement of private by public property takes place through the operation of the theory of trusteeship, will the ownership vest in the state, which is an instrument of violence or in associations of a voluntary character like village communes and municipalities, which may of course derived their final authority from state made laws?

Answer: That question involved some confusion of thought. Legal ownership in the transformed condition vests in the trustee, not in the state. It is in order to avoid confiscation that the doctrine of trusteeship comes into play; retaining for the society the ability of the original owner in his own right.[36]

In the next issue of 'Harijan' he again answers to several questions on inheritance in trusteeship.

Question: "You have asked rich men to be the trustees. Is it implied that they should give up private ownership in their property and create out of it a trust valid in the eyes of law and managed democratically? How will the successor of the present incumbent be determined on his demise?"

Answer: "God who is All Powerful has no need to store. He creates from day-to-day; hence men should also, in theory, live from day-to-day and not stock things. If this truth is imbibed by the people generally, it would become legalized and trusteeship would become a legalized institution. I wish it becomes a gift from India to the world. Then, there would be no exploitation and no reserves, as in Australia and other countries for white men and their posterity. In these distinctions lies the seed of a war more virulent than the last two. As to the successor, the trustee in office would have the right to nominate his successor subject to legal sanction."[37]

When Gandhi wanted to fetter the original trustees' choice making it a subject to 'legal sanction', he acted as a pragmatist who felt that the trustees however, above the average men and however, self-sacrificing they themselves may be, may have some weakness for their own children. If the trustees are given unrestrained power to choose their successor they may choose their own people to succeed them as trustees. This may be particularly true in case of statutory trustees who have not voluntarily renounced their possessions or possessiveness, but have been forced to act as such under the pressure of the statute enacted either by the village Panchayat or the state. That is why he suggested that the nomination made by the original trustees need be confirmed by the state.

Gandhi has been quoted here at fair length to explain his theory of Trusteeship. This section is being concluded with a practical trusteeship formula which K.G. Mashruwala and N.D. Parikh drew up and was placed before Gandhi who made a few changes in it. The final draft reads as under.

I. Trusteeship provides a means of transforming the present capitalist order of the society into an egalitarian one. It gives no quarter to capitalism but gives the present owning class a chance of reforming itself. It is based on faith that human nature is never beyond redemption.
II. It does not recognize any right of ownership of private property except so far as it may be permitted by society for its own welfare.
III. It does not exclude legislative regulation of ownership and the use of wealth.
IV. Thus, under state regulated trusteeship an individual will not be free to hold or use his wealth for selfish satisfaction or in disregard of the interest of the society.
V. Just as it is proposed to fix a decent minimum living wage, even so a limit should be fixed for a maximum income that could be allowed to any person in a society. The difference between such minimum and maximum should be reasonable and equitable and

variable from time to time so that the tendency would be toward obliteration of the difference.

VI. Under the Gandhian economic order the character of production will be determined by social necessity and not by personal whim or greed.[38]

Professor M.L. Dantwala, felt that the "trusteeship formula as evolved by Kishore Bhai and others was somewhat vague and relied too much on the good sense of the trustee. Dantwala raised a pertinent question, whether trusteeship could be regulated by law or any sanction by society. Basing on these doubts, he revised the draft with two purposes—one, to make the trustee liable to social and if necessary, legislative control; and two to put in some of his socialist ideas in it. This revised draft when submitted to Gandhi, he wrote down his acceptance, rejection, amendments on it and reasons for it. The Photostat of this document is available with Professor Dantwala.

Gandhi's revised draft as prepared by Professor Dantwala reads as follows:

> In the point one, the words "into an egalitarian one" were Dantwala's addition and were accepted. Another small change was the word 'reforming' instead of transforming in the original draft.

In the point two, Dantwala suggested an important change which was accepted by Gandhi. The original draft had stated "except so far as may be necessary for the service of the society." Dantwala querried: Who would decide what is necessary and suggested "as may be permitted by the society".

Point three is worth-noting in view of Gandhi's distrust of the coercive authority of the state or legislative sanctions. It recognizes the limitations of self-regulations. This is confirmed by point four. Dantwala used the word 'legal'. Gandhi changed it to 'state regulated'.

In point five, a significant change was made by the Mahatma which reveals his ideal of the ultimate social order. The draft submitted by Dantwala read as follow: The difference between such minimum and maximum incomes should be reasonable and equitable. "Gandhi would consider the ratio of

1:12 suggested by Kishorilal Mashruwala as too high." The text as it stands is Gandhi's alteration. In the margin of my copy writes Professor Dantwala, 'I have in his hand writing a substitute draft which reads: The ideal aimed at being the obliteration of the difference, which I think reads better and is more categorical.'

Lastly, the learned Professor suggested that prevention was better than cure and that instead of permitting a person to accumulate wealth and then himself a trustee, why not *ab initio* ensure that the economic system does enable anyone to accumulate wealth? Gandhi's reaction was sharp. He wrote down: 'the issue is not of permitting accumulation of wealth, but that of regulating (disciplining) what is already accumulated'.[40]

The principle of trusteeship has been subject to much misconceived criticism. It has been described as a 'make-shift', as an 'eye wash' as a shelter for the rich and as 'merely appealing to the more fortunate ones to show a little more charity. It has been generally objected to, on the ground that as a means of affecting social transformation this theory, its ethical content notwithstanding, is ineffective. Professor M.L. Dantwala in his 'Gandhism Reconsidered' quotes a Marxist appraisal of the doctrine. "The division of the society into the property owning and the property-less classes, which is the characteristic of capitalism, is sought to be retained in Gandhism also. The only difference in Gandhism is that the erstwhile capitalist, property owning classes will consider itself trustee on behalf of the proletariat. The change is purely on the subjective sphere. The objective conditions of production will continue by remaining as they were in capitalism. Production will continue by unplanned private competition among the individual trustees. These conditions of production have a compelling logic of their own which will lead to the same contradictions as are witnessed under capitalism today. The class appropriation of surplus value, which trust production will continue in a pious guise, will mean larger and larger accumulations of the capital on the one hand and pauperization of the masses on the other. . . . These evils can not be banished by wishing a change in the hearts and minds of the owners of property."[41]

Similarly, Professor Hiren Mukerjee, makes out, "This apostle of pity wanted a sea change in human relationships, but he had a great deal more than the convinced conservative's caution in bringing it about; he was ready to be gentle even with fragrantly self-seeking and basically anti-social vested interests; and in his pre-occupation with the right kind of means for social change, he would make compromises and concessions to the 'status quo' which were often paradoxical and in their implications as in the idea of the rich being 'trustees' of the poor, positively pernicious."[42]

Professor Mukerjee further added, "Social transformation by moral suasion which changes the hardest of hearts and by making sure of individual self-reformation guarantees the quality of the transformation, is thus not an exclusively Gandhian contribution to social thought. No doubt, it is extremely important, but from history one gathers the knowledge that, as T.K.N. Unnithan puts it, when projected to a practical 'social perspective', it tends to become impractical. Not to recognize its limitations and to be blind to the objective factors without which said change can not really take place, and yet to harp on it as the sovereign remedy of the society's ill is to take deceptive moral unction to one's soul and to put on a mantle of myth as a safeguard against the chilling blasts of real life problems.[43] At another place, Professor Mukerjee lamented, 'It will be idle to speculate what India's contribution to Asian and world history might have been if Gandhi held no such concepts as that of 'Trusteeship' of the rich for the poor and based himself instead on the independent strength of the toiling masses whom he loved no doubt but never thought adult enough for purposes of social struggle."[44]

E.M.S. Namboodiripad has attacked not only his philosophy but his intentions also. In his own words, "Not only in relation to the rural poor, but also in relation to the working class and other sections of the working people, his was an approach which, in actual practice, helped the bourgeoisie. His theory of trusteeship, his insistence on certain moral values as the guiding line for any political activity, the skilful way in which he combined his own extra-parliamentary activities (constructive programme and satyagraha) with the parliamentary activities of his lieutenants, the characteristically

Gandhian way of combining negotiations with the enemy even while carrying on mass direct action against him—all these proved in actual practice to be of enormous help to the bourgeoisie in (a) rousing the masses in action against imperialism and in (b) preventing them from resorting to revolutionary mass action. This ability of his to rouse the masses and yet to check them, to launch anti-imperialist direct action and yet to go on negotiating with the imperialist rulers made him the undisputed leader of the bourgeoisie."[45]

The criticism of the theory has not been levelled only from the Marxist quarters. Even a sympathetic reviewer of Gandhian economics like Professor J.J. Anjaria doubts its validity as a long-term solution. "As a short-term measure, this is excellent; coercion is ethically bad; on any large scale, it is also not expedient. But the run away from the problem by merely appealing to the more fortunate ones to show a little more charity—awful word—is no solution".[46]

Nobel Laureate, Gunnar Myrdal, who calls Gandhi 'a radical liberal' maintains in his 'Asian Drama' that "the trusteeship idea is fundamentally a concept that fits into paternalistic, feudal, pre-democratic society. It is so flexible that it can serve as a justification for inequality. Possibly Gandhi realized this, for he demanded a moral revolution, a change of heart among the rich. But in the real world, such a revolution is unlikely and the trusteeship ideal is nought but a vision of society where the rich are charitable so that the poor can remain weak . . . by his stress on the principle of trusteeship, and his friendliness towards many in exalted economic positions, he established a pattern of radicalism in talk but conservatism in action that is still very much a part of the Indian scene.[47]

Jawaharlal Nehru, Gandhi's political heir and most trusted disciple, wrote in his autobiography, "Again I think of the paradox that is Gandhiji. With all his keen intellect and passion for bettering the down-trodden and oppressed, why does he support a system which is obviously decaying, which creates this misery and the wastes? He seeks a way out, it is true, but is not that way to the past barred and bolted? And meanwhile he blesses all the relics of the old order which stands as obstacles in the way of advance feudal states, the big zamindaris and taluqdaris, the present capitalist system. Is it reasonable to believe in the theory of trusteeship—to give unchecked power and wealth to an individual and to expect him to use it entirely for the public good? Are the best of us so perfect as to be trusted in this way? . . . And is it good for the others to have even these benevolent supermen over them".[48]

Whether it is the association of ideas around the world trusteeship or a delebrate refusal to understand the principle or pre-conceived determined attack on the doctrine, that is responsible for these misconceptions, it is difficult to say. "Whatever it may be", writes, Professor Dantwala, "I shall content myself with restating, at the cost of repitition the basic principles of doctrine."

1. The erstwhile capitalist is reduced to the status of a manager of the trust property. But the change is not confined to the name. The schedule of rights, privileges and obligations of the two is basically different. The capitalist instead of being sent to the concentration camp as under the socialist dispensation, is given an opportunity of conforming to the ethics of the new society. It is misnomer to call the class of trustees the property owning class. They are not different from the property managing class under the socialist economy.
2. The trustees will not be allowed to appropriate for his personal use more than twelve times the income of the poorest paid workers. The difference in income of the managerial class and the common run of the workers, permitted in erstwhile Soviet Russia was much wider than is allowed under Gandhism. Yet, the critics accuse Gandhism of allowing "larger and larger accumulations of capital on the one hand and pauperization of the masses on the other." It may also be pointed out that since the instruments of production under Gandhism will be comparatively simple and cheap, the danger of managerial class appropriating political and economic power will be much less than under socialism.
3. Production under Gandhian economy will not be unplanned. The character of production will be determined by social necessity and not by personal

whim or greed. What warrants the critics have for asserting that "production will continue by unplanned private competition", is difficult to ascertain.

4. In case the trustee does not confirm to the discipline imposed by doctrine, and, as critics fear, goes on appropriating the surplus value under a pious guise, the Gandhian techniques will not rest content with "wishing a change in the hearts and minds of the owners of the property".[49]

Prof. N.K. Bose, in his 'Studies in Gandhism' refutes the charge that the Gandhian theory of trusteeship is another name for class-collaboration. "Apart from its wider idealistic application, even with in the sphere of economic life, the Gandhian theory of trusteeship does not make for class collaboration but class liquidation, as a friend of mine once very happily put it. This liquidation will result in all men turning into labourers and placing their mental and material resources at the service of humanity taken as a whole, will be effected not by the forceful regimentation of the exploiters by the exploited, but by a change of heart brought about among the exploiters by the non-violent non-cooperation of those on whom the former depend for the making, the retention and the employment of their wealth. In course of that struggle the exploited will also become free from the weakness which have given rise to the present social inequalities. Under the new constitution of things, brought into being by the joint endeavours of today's hostile classes, all men will live as servants of the community, willingly and joyfully, through a complete reorientation of life's values in a new direction. Through economic equality, society will also in its turn secure for everyman full opportunity for the development of his physical, mental and moral powers without allowing him to restrict similar opportunities in others. And the product of those talents will be shared by all in common."[50]

It would be no exaggeration to say that the Mahatma was a more radical revolutionary than Mao-Tse-Tung. Gandhism seeks to combine Lincoln's Love of liberty with Lenin's urge for equality, without resorting to the barrel of a gun.[51] While framing the trusteeship formula, he proposed to fix a decent minimum living wage but at the same time he emphasized to fix the maximum income also that would be allowed to any person in the society At the same time, he maintained that the difference between such minimum and maximum income should be reasonable and variable from time to time. When K.G. Mashruwala suggested the ratio of 1:12 between minimum and maximum. Gandhi considered it too high and refused to fix any definite figure but emphasized that difference between minimum and maximum is to be bridged up ultimately, when every body will be getting equal share in the national income.

Such a perfect society was not stressed even in the communist economies. They had not been able to fix a maximum income for their citizens. The top Communist Party functionaires, bureaucrats and military officers earned money which was several times greater than a common man there. At present and even in the future there are no efforts to bridge this gap.

It is no doubt true that with the socialisation of the instruments of production, the *dejure* ownership will pass into the hands of the workers, but the very size of these giant machines will as a matter of fact, put the expert managers in complete control of them. There is no such thing in the trusteeship firms.

If the contention that socio-political make up of a society is reflex of its economic pattern is true, it is inevitable that a society with economic arrangements based on mechanised industry should produce a bureaucratic state. What had actually happened in Communist countries, inspite of the liquidation of capitalism, provides a good illustration of this. The communist revolution instead of resulting in a society with larger freedom for the common man created a state which hedged freedom more drastically than is done in a bourgeoisie society. Instead of 'withering away of the state' or even a tendency in this direction there was greater and greater intensification of state in such societies.

The main thrust of trusteeship is very broad and deep and is thus not easy to comprehend. There is no historical example of it to go by. Besides full trusteeship cases has not been experimented anywhere. The problem with this doctrine is that either it has been bitterly criticised or eulogized but not experimented. Gandhi had a way of prescribing sugar coated quinine for the maladies of the society. He would administer the bitterest of truth under a thick coating of ahimsa. But his followers have developed a way of lapping up the sugar and spitting out the quinine. The theory of trusteeship has been dealt in the same manner. That is why the country has not yet been able to enact a statue on trusteeship though several efforts have been done for this.

The late Dr. Ram Manohar Lohia had given notice of his intention to move an 'Indian Trusteeship Bill' in the Lok Sabha in March 1967. It was supposed to provide for the voluntary conversion into trust corporations of concerns owing a industries, plantations, banks, trade, transport, etc. worth Rs. 10,00,000. If the share-holders of any such concern offered to become trustees and accepted the workers as their partners, the Government would constitute a panchayat of trustees to manage the affairs of that concern. The share-holders and the workers would elect 5 trustees each and the Central and State Governments and the local municipal committee would together nominate 5 trustees to represent the interests of the consumers and the community. The existing managing agents of the concern would become the managing trustee of the new trust corporation. The bill made detailed provisions for efficient management of trust corporations in the light of Gandhi's views on trusteeship. The Bill also provided that the net profits of the trust corporations, after the provisions being made for depreciation and provident funds, should be credited to the Ministry of Finance for being allocated to the different states according to the recommendations of the Finance Commission.

The President of India withheld sanction to the introduction of this bill in Lok Sabha on the ground that aforesaid provision made it a Money Bill. Dr. Lohia had appealed to the President for reconsideration; but death snatched him away before he could pursue the matter.[52]

On November 21, 1969 George Fernandes introduced the same 'The Indian Trusteeship Bill' in the Lok Sabha but it lapsed without discussion. Picking up the thread Atal Behari Bajpayee introduced the same on 18th April, 1975 but it also lapsed with the dissolution of the Lok Sabha in 1977. The Janta Trusteeship Bill by Professor Ramjee Singh of April 20, 1978 also met the same fate.[53]

Gandhi had hoped that statutory trusteeship would be India's gift to the world. But uptil now we have not yet been able to fulfil this moral responsibility. Perhaps we are afraid of the bill. Ganesh D. Gadre has depicted our state of mind through a story from Panchtantra.

"There were four wise men. One of them was worldly wise and the other three were otherwise. They had set out to make some money and were passing through a forest. In that forest they found a few scattered bones of a tiger. The first wise man whispered a mantra and arranged the bones into a skelton. The second wise man with his mantric powers, put flesh and skin on the skelton. The third wise man then uttered another mantra and infused vital breath into the body. The animal, as soon as it regained life swallowed up the three wise men. The wordly wise man saved himself by climbing the top of a tree before beginning of these "Experiments with Truth."

'The mantra of trusteeship', writes Gadre, can influx life into the skelton of Gandhism which, if revived, will swallow us along with our comfortable armchairs.[54] Because of this fear we always try to find out some scapegaoat here or there in its implementation. It will snatch away from our rulers, leaders, industrialists, bureaucrats, intelligentsia and other elites their luxuries and comforts and will distribute them into the masses. Perhaps we belong to the race of that wise man who saved himself by climbing up a tree. The theory of trusteeship can transform the docile "Daridranarayana" into a vigorous Narasimha that will tear to shreds all subtle systems of exploitation of man by man. This fear haunts us. When we will have enough courage to experiment with it and will belong to the tradition of the three wisemen who would in the pursuit of Truth, prefer self-sacrifice to self-preservation, then and only then, we will be able to realize Gandhi's dream.

It is heartening to note that recently some eminent social scientists have shown some renewed interest in the theory of trusteeship. Professor S.L. Malhotra, Professor R.P. Mishra, Professor D. Gopal and Dr. J.D. Sethi have shown particular interest in this field. Dr. J.D. Sethi in his 'Gandhi Today' have termed 'Trusteeship—The Grand Alternative'.

Trusteeship aims at achieving larger social benefits rather than work for a narrow economic objective such as profit;

indeed its area of participation is quite wide. As it is more egalitarian than all other systems (corporations, state capitalist or socialist bureaucracies; systems of industrial democracy and mixed economy models), it makes participation not merely formal or of unequal economic, political or status weights, but bases it on the principle of alround equality. Trusteeship cuts across classes in such a way as to produce over a longer period a classless system. Trusteeship is also self-government not only of workers but of entire community. Above all, trusteeship being divorced from the profit motive, introduces the element of fraternity without which neither equality nor freedom can be adequately safeguarded."[55]

In the present day India, the theory has become more relevant. Here, we have a mixed economy model with a large public sector and a very large private sector. But the distribution of resources is highly skewed in both, much more sharply in industry than in agriculture. The one hundred largest industrial firms control the lion share of the economy. What is more frightening here is that the concentration of economic power in these houses keep on increasing. So long as even a single avenue remains open for big business, there is nothing to stop it from expanding. Even if all new avenues are closed, it can still accumulate assets on two accounts: (i) by accumulation from existing earnings from business, and in (ii) by buying up other small business firms. Short of straightforward nationalisation, there is nothing in the prevailing system which can suggest reduction in economic concentration. But consequences of nationalization are even more dangerous. It leads to the creation of a new bureaucratic class in whose hands all kind of power, political, economic and administrative, not compounded. Perhaps that is why we are again revertial to disinvestment in public sector.

Trusteeships provides an alternative mechanism for reducing the concentration of economic power. Professor J.D. Sethi has suggested three steps for this. At first, a certain percentage of assets of large houses will have to be transferred to a set of trustees. In the first phase, though they will cease to have any ownership, they will have jointly with others, control over their use. That control will be jointly exercised by labour, consumer interests and government representatives. The important point is that all the four interests will be trustees. Workers will be allowed to take a share from the profits earned by these companies. But a part of their extra earnings, such as bonus, will be transformed into shares so that the rate of capital accumulation can be accelerated. Secondly, in the next phase, except in small and medium industries, all other industries will have to follow the principle of trusteeship, for which a properly prepared scheme will be put on the statute book. Thirdly, some basic principles with respect to prices, distribution, wages profits, etc. will have to be laid down for trusteeship firms.[56]

It will be dangerous to view trusteeship as a complete system. In view of Professor Sethi, trusteeship as a complete system will have to pass through several stages. The first stage, therefore, has to be an attempt to persuade the hundred large firms or families to part with their resources according to some slab system. For example, the top twenty families may be asked to part with 20 per cent of their resources, the next twenty may be asked to part with 15 percent and so on and the last twenty houses may be asked to give up 5 per cent only. This would be the first step towards initiating the system of trusteeship and simultaneously achieving the reduction in the consensus of economic power. If the capitalists refuse to hand over their resources, mass action on Gandhian lines would be necessary.

The trustees of the newly acquired properties will not be the capitalists alone. They would also be taken from among workers' representatives and other public men who would represent the larger interest of society.

The real problems for this partial trusteeship would relate to the choice of products, pattern of production, technological choices, internal restructuring of the remuneration system, allocation of resources, marketing, etc. After all, the economic units under trusteeship will not be able to divorce themselves from the practices of other units run by the private or public sectors. For example, a certain amount of money will have to be spent on advertising if the trusteeship units wants to remain in business in competition with firms in the private sectors producing similar goods. They will have to follow certain principles of market production and so on. Here the Government can play a very positive role to sustain this trusteeship experience. Finally, the votaries of this new system should be ever prepared to launch satyagraha as a dynamic force to stop any possible reversal of the scheme, etc.

Once these steps are taken, writes Professor Sethi, the next set of steps can be formulated on the basis of this experience.

A slip and fall is common to earthly personality. Absolute best or perfection remains as a goal. So depending on the circumstances, every person is subject to change. That is why checks and balances are needed. For any work a starting point is must. With a doubt a beginning can never be made. Our goal is to walk hundred miles. There lies our perfection and success. But to doubt the putting of even one foot before hundred miles never brings perfection and success. As a result, we remain static where we stand. No doubt, the best and perfect men are there. Apart from all these people, even the worst and imperfect are trusted for carrying so many things. Then, why not we trust the best and the perfect? Every thing is relative to every thing. Only thing is, some where, some how, trust should be put for beginning trusteeship system. So far, nobody has given, a fair and sincere trail.

Even today there are people doubting about the efficacy of trusteeship. This is due to the lack of understanding about the nature and role of faith in the Indian tradition. The Indian life from the dawn of civilization has been moving peacefully, because it is dominated by faith rather than by intellect. The unique greatness of Indians lie in taking the torch of faith with the cells of intellect. There, they are highly convinced that faith alone unites the whole of mankind and the intellect always stands for division and division.

History proved that the functioning of faith is less powerful than the functioning of intellect. Therefore, the best and the perfect may faulter in acting as trustees. But the only thing is, it is time taking. So, a trial and error method should be applied to the theory of trusteeship today.

No man is without faith. From the dawn of rationality man has been relying upon his faith. Gaining faith is the mark of progress. Progress lies in fulfilling his goals, or promise. Every individual moves with a promise in his hands; and thus enjoy a firm faith in reaching that promise; no matter what happens to others. He may agree that his faith is right but its quality should pass through the consent of the society. No doubt truth needs no majority support. Yet, the concerned faith needs to be broader in its outlook, so as to accommodate some more apart from the faith holding individual. Actually clashes come because people do not share common faith.

When man looses faith, he had to surrender himself to other. That is surrendering totally is to fulfil the goals or promises of other individuals. This may benefit him, but it is almost dependence and thus, a slavery. So, a man of faith alone can enjoy individuality. Through individuality, he exercises his will, through his wills he exhibits his freedom, and through his freedom, he holds responsibility for all his acts.

'Wrong faith' is better than pretending faith. A man may hold wrong faith because of his ignorance or ambiguity. This can be set right once he get clarification from a right source. But pretending faith is always dangerous because it is willingly and continuously done knowing the true nature of faith. This leads to the distortion of every act willingly. Its goal is to achieve only mean ends. Further, it works with weak minded people, who lacks boldness to face the problems of life. At times, the pretending faith may yield good or the best results. This is possible only when a courageous person holds it knowing clearly the fulfilment of the promise for the betterment of all. The span of its continuance is very limited then. It never drowns anybody. Moreover, it promotes the progress by removing all the doubts or obstacles only danger comes through the people with half knowledge, lack of courage, confidence and conviction with false dignity.

Gandhi spotted out pretending faith in both capitalism and communism. That is why he warned the people to be more careful with pretending faith. Gandhi further clarified that people may have a wrong faith in the workability of trusteeship system. When man is bound to lead his life on 'faith' in himself, 'faith' in nature and 'faith' in neighbouring man, to develop a wrong faith is only to insult himself. But at the same time he was very cautious in warning man not to overpower his faith to fulfil mean ends. Means must be good for him. Otherwise even if the end is achieved, it loses its value and significance. His only faith is that human nature is subject to change. Hence, any brutish or cruel nature can be transformed by appealing to the heart of man, sincerely with love. This faith, if strengthened is sure to bring expected progress in society.

Men of ordinary calibre with narrow goals and with ulterior motives are bound to misunderstand Gandhi. They should accept that Gandhi never tried to amass wealth or fame for either himself or for his family. His total surrendering to the common cause of Sarvodaya itself is sufficient to repose faith in his thought. His supreme consideration is man. His final goal is to attain global peace for all living beings. What an evolved faith he cherished and worked for. Nowhere he gave room to pretending faith. May be at times as an ordinary man, he too exhibited wrong faith. But his greatness lies in openly confessing it and rectifying it for the benefit of all. His uniqueness can also be seen in the soliciting a pauper and a prince to lead a life of human being first. Thus, Gandhi, a giant of supreme faith has elevated trusteeship system as a boon to peaceful living. To break heads on the issue of its possibility, without giving even an iota trial denotes again our hypocrisy No leader of our land, after the departure of Gandhi has put his mind and soul in this theory. No trace in there from ruling and non-ruling; exhibiting its interest in bringing this system into practice. Then, why should the so-called big brains to talk about the failures or drawbacks of this system. It is here, Gandhi is being intellectually assassinated time and again. Again this is an evidence of cowardice act. It is supporting and feeding our wrong faith and pretending faith. We remained under foreign domination because of our wrong and pretending faiths. Why to extend the same again and again. This is high time for the Indians to put a full stop to their nasty pretending faith. To serve others by insulting and selling their own souls, is beyond any redemption. Now every thinking individual has to reconstitute his faith and frame it within indigenous love, sacrifice and service.

The required thing is a will to act. Tons of theories, prolonged speeches, glorified decorations, heavy garlands, colourful ribbon cuttings will never save man. Nor can they satisfy the starving stomach. All the disparities existing among men be peacefully resolved by applying the trusteeship in thought, word and deed. This is the urgent need of the hour.

Critics may view that trusteeship is utopian in their nature. It is true that every idea looks like an utopia in the beginning. But given a proper attention and careful practice, nothing is beyond the human capacities. Every solution is always to solve a problem. Behind these solutions a lot of great thought is put, Gandhi having studied the grave situation in human societies, where there is an increasing gulf between 'have' and 'have nots' aimed at establishing a classless society. As a great psychologist he thought that every solution which is based on faith alone can serve and save mankind. He realised that human faith tied with truth and non-violence alone is the most powerful one to bind the whole humanity into one, despite its dissensions and disparities. In this respect Gandhi is a great visionary in trying to establish one world family.

Every individual by becoming a trustee for himself and for others can cater to the needs of the society. This may dispel all the disparities both in the individual and social levels and contribute to the welfare of all. Except this solution, there is no other alternative to the modern maladies of the mankind. This has universal application. The only thing before us is to digest the philosophy of trusteeship without having any partisan attitudes. The subjective approach combined with the objective reality is bound to give a correct perspective of trusteeship. Since the dawn of nationality, at every age, man has been knowingly or unknowingly working as a trust. This is limited to himself and his family. As the population increases, globally the accumulation consciousness has yielded to the formation of allied groups. In due course, the ambition for domination and expansion of territory led man to wage relentless wars. The result is bloody revolutions. Man is not at peace. Under this complex system of life, man has to be saved and protected. This noble cause of saving the whole mankind made Gandhi to choose trusteeship. Here lies the greatness of Gandhi.

Notes and References

1. J.B. Say, Treatise on Political Economy, Translated by C.R. Prinsep (Boston: Wills and Lilly, 1867), pp. 78-79.
2. Adam Smith, An Inquiry into the Nature and Causes of the Wealth of Nations (New York: The Modern Library, 1937), p. 14.
3. *Harijan*, 16.12.1939, p. 376.

4. K.M. Munshi, Reconstruction of Society Through Trusteeship (Bombay: Bhartiya Vidya Bhawan), pp. 15-16.
5. S. Radhakrishan's, "The Individual and the Social Order in Hinduism" in E.R. Hughes (ed.) The Individual in East and West (London: Oxford University Press, 1937), p. 127.
6. Pyare Lai, Mahatma Gandhi: The Last Phase, Vol. 2 (Ahmedabad: Navajivan Publishing House, 1958), p. 624.
7. M.K. Gandhi, An Autobiography, *op. cit.*, p. 221.
8. *Ibid.*
9. *CWMG, op. cit.*, Vol. IX, p. 481.
10. *Ibid.*, Vol. XIII, pp. 210-16.
11. S.C. Biswas (ed.), Gandhi: Theory and Practice, Social Impact and Contemporary Relevance (Shimla: IIAS, 1969), pp. 124-25.
12. *Harijan*, 23.2.1947, p. 39.
13. *Ibid.*, 3.6.1939, p. 145.
14. *Ibid.*, 2.1.1937, p. 375.
15. *Young India*, 26.11.1931, p. 369.
16. *Harijan*, 8.3.1942, p. 67.
17. *Ibid.*, 22.2.1942, p. 49.
18. K.G. Mashruwala, Gandhi and Marx (Ahmedabad: Navajivan Publishing House, 1960), p. 101.
19. *Harijan*, 8.3.1942, p. 67.
20. *Ibid.*, 1.2.1942, p. 20.
21. M.K. Gandhi, My Socialism, compiled by R.K. Prabhu (Ahmedabad: Navajivan Publishing House, 1949), p. 24.
22. *Harijan*, 27.5.1937, p. 136.
23. M.K. Gandhi, My Picture of Free India (ed.) by A.T. Hingorani (Bombay: Bhartiya Vidhya Bhawan 1965), p. 40.
24. *Young India*, 6.2.1930, p. 44.
25. *Ibid.*, 15.12.1944, p. 396.
26. M.K. Gandhi, Constructive Programme : Its Meaning and Place, (Ahmedabad: Navajivan Publishing House, 1970), p. 26.
27. *Harijan*, 1.2.1942, p. 20.
28. *Ibid.*, 31.3.1946, p. 63.
29. *Amrit Bazar Patrika*, 3.8.1934.
30. Quoted in Benudhar Pradhan, The Socialist Thought of Mahatma Gandhi, Vol. II (Delhi: GDK Publications, 1980), p. 465.

30. *Harijan*, 5.12.1936, p. 339.`
31. *Ibid.*, 31.3.1946, pp. 63-64.
32. Pyare Lal, Towards New Horizons (Ahmedabad: Navajivan Publishing House, 1959), p. 91.
33. *Ibid.*
34. *Modern Review*, October 1935, p. 412.
35. *Harijan*, 31.7.1937, p. 197.
36. *Ibid.*, 16.2.1947, p. 25.
37. *Ibid.*, 23.2.1947, p. 39.
38. *Ibid.*, 25.10.1952, p. 301.
39. M.L. Dantwala, "Trusteeship and its Value Implications", *Gandhi Marg*, Vols. 8 and 9, Nov.-Dec. 1985, p. 505.
40. *Ibid.*, pp. 506-07.

41. M.L. Dantwala, *Gandhism Reconsidered* (Bombay: Padma Publications Ltd., 1945), pp. 54-55.
42. Hiren Mukerjee, *Gandhiji—A Study* (New Delhi: People Publishing House, 1960), p. 204.
43. *Ibid.*, p. 206
44. *Ibid.*, p. 202.
45. E.M.S. Namboodiripad, *The Mahatma and the Ism* (New Delhi: People Publishing House, 1959), p. 115.
46. J.J. Anjaria, *An Essay on Gandhian Economics* (Bombay: Vora and Co., 1944), p. 31.
47. Gunnar Myrdal, *Asian Drama: An Inquiry into the Poverty of Nations*, Vol. II, *op. cit.*, p. 755.
48. Jawaharlal Nehru, *An Autobiography* (London: Bodley Head, 1936), p. 528.
49. M.L. Dantwala, *op. cit.*, pp. 55-56.
50. Nirmal Kumar Bose, *op. cit.*, pp. 57-58.
51. Ganesh D. Gadre's in S.C. Biswas, *op. cit.*, p. 123.
52. *Ibid.*, pp. 128-29.
53. Jai Narain, Gandhi's Theory of Trusteeship, Paper III, Lesson No. 6, Post-graduate Diploma Course in Gandhian Studies Through Correspondence, Department of Gandhian Studies, Panjab University, Chandigarh.
54. Ganesh D. Gadre, *op. cit.*, pp. 122-23.
55. J.D. Sethi, Gandhi Today (New Delhi: Vikas Publishing House Pvt. Ltd., *1978)*, p. 168.
56. *Ibid.*, p. 170.

5

Labour-Capital Relations

Ours is an age of rapid change, unrest, and conflicting ideologies. Society is unsettled and individuals are apprehensive as groups of nations and organised groups within nations struggle for power and control over material resources and men's minds. It is in such a world setting of tension and cleavage that the present day industrial relations should be viewed. The term 'industrial relations' includes not only the dealings between labour organisations and the industrial management but also all aspects of labour in an economy including wages, productivity, employee security, management's employment practices, union policies and governmental actions on labour matters.

All of us during most of our life time, are affected by or directly concerned with industrial relations—as owners or managers of business firms, as employees, as labour leaders, as union members, as public officials, as consumers and as citizens. It is no exaggeration to say that the understanding and wisdom of management, labour, government, and the public in handling industrial relations will, to a considerable degree determine the future of any economy. Although, these problems in one form or another are present in every economy but they are becoming more intense and momentous with increasing urbanisation, industrialisation, and domination by large corporation and big unions. Now-a-days labour capital conflicts may not only cripple significant sections of the economy but also imperil the health and safety of the people and even halt temporarily the functioning of government.

As it has grown in strength organized labour has become one of the most potent factors for change in our economy and society. Unions have enhanced the job security of employees, greatly increased workers' participation in decisions affecting the forms and conditions of their employment, and have given labour a significant role in community affair. Improving the dignity and psychological well-being of the working man is important in a political democracy, which assumes a citizenry able to be persuaded by reason, and a free enterprise economy, which rests on the willing cooperation of the employees. Large scale unionism has, however, intensified the conflict between groups for political control and has aggravated the problem of centralization of authority.

In our kind of economy and political system the effects of industry upon man and society may be more significant than the physical output of our factories. In the words of Professor J.M. Clark, "The most important product of industry is what it does to the lives of the people who work in it and for its own safety it needs to contribute to making well-balanced individuals whose social faculties are neither atrophied nor perverted."[1] Wars and other national emergencies only serve to emphasize that a nation's existence depends on the strength of its human resources.

In a vital subject like labour-capital relations, any solution must tackle the tough problems that face the country in its field—the problem of paralysis strikes in a world of clashing economic systems; the influence of policies upon output and industrial progress; the question whether collective bargaining can be made to work without sacrificing the public interests and multiplying the evils of monopoly; whether unions may weaken the effectiveness of industrial management and force the country into syndicalism or the corporative state; splitting the population into management-minded and working class groups with significantly divergent views and social values, thus causing misunderstanding, distrust and social cleavage.

Many of these problems are exceedingly complex and do not yield to simple, unqualified answers. Often social and psychological as well as economic and political factors are involved. For example, the contention that union policies which increase workers' job security are reducing labour's incentive raises the question whether insecurity is a satisfactory stimulus to achievement and what harmful social and psychological results it may produce. In seeking answer to such issues one should not only analyse the available data from a broad humanistic approach but also recognise the limitations and qualifications to his conclusions. A live, human subject like labour can not be reduced to a set of mathematical equations from which an irrefutable solution can readily be derived.

Views on labour-capital relations are usually coloured by our own value judgments. Some may condemn unions, charging that they curtail freedom of the individual, are responsible for wasteful restrictions on efficiency, and impede the rate of industrial progress. Other may commend unions for introducing more democracy and justice in industrial relations, increasing employee security against arbitrary decisions by management and engaging in social welfare activities for the benefit of members.

In a business civilization, the activities of industrial management are not likely to conflict with dominant cultural values. Business is here respectable. Its successes are generally approved as meritorious achievement and progress, whereas success of a labour organisation may be rather difficult to assess by cultural standard of this civilization. Then too, business practices that conflict with the values in this society have been tolerated for a long period of time, for example, the regimentation and subordination of workers to management authority in industrial plant is considered to be normal and even not likely to receive much public condemnation as restriction upon individual liberty and freedom in near future.

The weight given to different social ideals or goals depends on one's economic and social philosophy. The economic individualist stresses freedom, efficiency, and personal achievement and development. Labour leaders are more likely to emphasize security, industrial democracy, justice and social welfare. And whereas the industrialists think of freedom as the absence of government regulation and oppressive taxation upon business, the union official is more likely to talk of the threat to the workers' freedom and independence arising from economic insecurity, poverty and social discrimination.

Clearly some values may conflict with others. Increased security is likely to be at the expense of freedom, industrial democracy and greater social welfare may limit managerial efficiency and inhibit industrial progress. Hence, none of these desires or objectives can be considered absolute. Society is continually working out, through practical compromises, the best balance among conflicting goals, all of which need to be included in a sound conception of the common welfare. In an economy any balance is only temporary, for concepts of welfare and social justice change. Pressure groups, including organized labour and business associations, strive to bring the balance closer to their particular value pattern.[2]

Karl Marx discusses these relations in his own characteristic way. To him, this is not a new phenomenon but the 'history of all hitherto existing society is the history of class struggle.'[3] He believes that class represented a very important entity. It has a collective unit of its own and its characteristic beliefs, nations and heritage. The individual has importance principally because of his membership of his class. He imbibes the notion and tradition of his class by environment and education. Economic relationship between men gets crystalized into economic classes which becomes thesis and anti-thesis in dialectic evolution of mankind. As soon as mankind emerges from the primitive state, it is seen that at every stage of society a particular class gets control and exploits the other. That it does so is no matter of chance, but is the result of the inexorable law of society. The class which exercises ownership of the means of production will dominate the rest when, for instance, the most important factor in the forces of production is agricultural, landowners will be the ruling class. The dominant class alone has freedom, and to preserve this must act the part of oppressors. They, therefore, create an executive and repressive instrument by use of which the hope to maintain their position and which is called the state. The subject classes had always strived to wrest this power. The subject classes had kept going the perennial struggle of slaves against masters (Greek history), plebeians against patricians (Roman history), serfs against feudal barons, journeymen against master craftsmen (medieval history), bourgeoisie against landed gentry, and finally proletariat against the bourgeoisie (modern history). The economically dominant classes have been keeping down and exploiting the other. Marx emphatically argued that these classes have conflicting economic interests and mainly because of this they are in constant struggle with each other.

There is a definite strain of determinism in the historical materialism of Marx. Social, political, ideological and institutional developments are the inescapable results of economic forces and development. In his own words, "The mode of production of material means of existence conditions the whole of social, political and intellectual life. It is not the consciousness of men that determine their existence, but on contrary it is their social existence that determine their consciousness".[4] At a certain stage of their development the material productive forces of society come into contradiction with the existing productive relationships or what is but a legal expression for these with the property relationship, within which they had moved before. From form of development of the productive forces these relationships are transformed into their fetters. Then, an epoch of social revolution opens. With the change in economic foundation the whole vast superstructure is more or less rapidly transformed. This finally leads to the inevitable victory of the proletariat and so on.

Even if one does not believe in Marxian philosophy yet the phenomenon of conflicting economic interests always keeps on wondering in one's mind consciously or unconsciously whenever he thinks about labour-capital relations. If it is felt that too much emphasis has been laid on the term 'economic' in these conflicting economic interest, this term can be dropped. Then we can come at a fairly balanced form that because of the 'conflicting interests' (which of course include the economic aspect in it as one of the important determinant) the labour-capital relations always remain strained. And with this background these relations are analysed.

A. ELIMINATION OF CLASS STRUGGLE (THE ULTIMATE OBJECTIVES)

Mahatma Gandhi has put the whole process in the reverse gears. He said that instead of assuming the conflicting interests among the workers and capitalists, can't we assume the harmony of interests? Though not as systematically as Marx, Gandhi has also made an effort to plan out a broad theoretical framework in which this whole hypothesis develops. Time and again he emphasized that class struggle was not the essential feature of the human nature. The elimination of the struggle is also possible. He has not only stressed the need for the elimination of the conflict between labour and capital but has also shown the ways and means through which this could be achieved. He felt that if the attempts are made to train the human mind in certain specific directions (as laid down on the basis of his principles of truth, non-violence and social justice), this struggle would come to an end. In an article in *Young India* he wrote, "I do not think there need be any clash between capital and labour. Each is dependent on the other."[5]

He, on the other hand, believed in class collaboration. "I have always said that my ideal is that capital and labour should supplement and help each other. They should be a great family living in unity and harmony, capital not only looking to the material welfare of the labourers but their moral welfare also—capitalists being trustees for the welfare of the labouring class under them."[6] He believed in the ultimate harmony of interests of not only labour and capital but of all the persons and for that matter society as a whole. In his view, the whole society has to progress through a collective effort. Coming specifically to labour and capital both should have one common objective, i.e., to produce more which will benefit both the classes. This is possible only when they live in peace and harmony with each other. But if there is tension between both production will suffer and it will have a negative impact on both the employers as well as employees. According to him, as far as possible, attempts should be made to create a family like atmosphere in an institution so that its members live in peace and harmony. Such an atmosphere would create an interdependent industrial community where the worker would try to increase the production and the employer would work for the welfare of his labourers.

Condemning the inevitability of class struggle and establishment of the dictatorship of the proletariat, he said, "Exploitations of the poor can be extinguished not by effecting the destruction of a few millionaires, but by removing the ignorance of the poor and teaching them to non-co-operate with their exploiters. That will convert the exploiters also. I have even suggested that ultimately it will lead to both being equal partners. Capital as such is not evil. Capital in some form or other will always be needed."[7] When both labour as well as capital are indispensable there is not fun to assume the inevitability of the conflicting interest between them. Leaving aside the Marxian doctrine, otherwise also it is clear that every capitalist is not an exploiter and every worker is not a work shirker. Both need each other and they can remain in best of the relations also.

Gandhi looked at the problem from another angle also. According to him, the main reason of the labour-capital trouble is the desire to accumulate wealth, both on the part of employers, as well as labourers. It is a common sense phenomenon that we need more and more wealth because we have a number of wants to satisfy. Human wants are unlimited. Means to satisfy them are limited. One can satisfy one want for one time. Or if he has more wealth he can satisfy one want for all the times or all the wants for one time. But one may not satisfy all the wants for all the times. Since the resources at our disposal are limited and then have alternative uses also. We need more and more money to satisfy our ever increasing wants.

Moreover, wants are the sources of pain. According to Professor J.K. Mehta, an eminent Indian economist "A want is a painful experience. This is evident from the fact that we wish to satisfy it and get rid of it as soon as possible."[8] Wants do not add to sum total of human happiness, it substracts from it a good deal. Professor Mehta further adds, "Removal of a want means removal of pains and procurement of pleasure. . . . If one wants to get maximum utility or pleasure of satisfaction, one should see to it that complete pain is removed and no fresh pain is felt in future."[9] Then the question arises what is to be done?

To free onself from this pain is to strike at the very root. Here Gandhi's stress on the reduction of wants becomes very relevant and useful also. He was of the opinion that instead of satisfying more and more wants we should try to eliminate them. When we satisfy a want we obey the voice of the wanting mind. One who yield to such a mind becomes virtually its slave. To remove the pain caused by the presence of wants by satisfying them is, therefore, an undignified way of getting pleasure. Instead of obeying the orders of a want, we can ourselves order the want to quit. When we satisfy a want we make it quiet for the time being. But when we order it to quit we do not merely make it quiet, we kill it.

Gandhi was of the firm belief that if the process of reduction of wants is followed then the human being will be free from a number of worries and tensions. They won't be needing much wealth to satisfy a number of wants (because they have already been limited). In the case of labour-capital relations also, if this becomes the attitude of both the parties, their conflict would automatically disappear.

The Mahatma approached this problem from another angle also. "We should not receive any single thing that we do not need," he wrote in 'From Yeravada Mandir.' We are not always aware of our real needs, and most of us improperly multiply our wants, and thus unconsciously make thieves of ourselves. If we devote some thought to the subject, we shall find that we can get rid of quite a number of our wants. One who follows the observance of non-stealing will bring about a progressive reduction of his own wants. Much of the distressing poverty in this world has arisen out of the breaches of the principle of non-stealing."[10]At another place he writes, "God never creates more than what is strictly needed for the moment with the result that if any one appropriates more than he really needs, he reduces his neighbour to destitution. The starvation of the people in several parts of the world is due to many of us seizing very much more than we need. We may utilise the gifts of nature just as we choose, but in her books the debits are always equal to the credits. There is no balance in either column."[11]

But he advised the moneyed to earn their crores (honestly of course) but asked them to dedicate themselves to the service of all. In this connection, he offered trusteeship as a relevant choice between existing but unacceptable capitalism and its violent overthrow by the proletariat. He was of the firm view that if the concept of trusteeship was accepted by the society, urge to own property would wither away. And if this urge withers away, personal as well as class conflicts would automatically disappear.

For the establishment of the harmony of relation between the labour and capital the Mahatma also suggested the principle of bread labour. By bread labour he meant mannual labour. He suggested that if the distinction between the mannual workers and the intellectuals, many of whom work on behalf of capitalists, was to be eliminated, there was a need for developing a sense of oneness between the one who carried on the mental work and the one who does only mannual work for producing a commodity. This sense of oneness can be generated if the capitalists or his representatives also do some mannual work. If they accept the concept of dignity of labour and work as mannual labourers for some time, it will generate an impression among the workers that the capitalists or their representatives are too, labourers like them doing the same work with their hands. Such impression is bound to soften greatly the bitterness that labourers have against the capitalists and can ultimately eliminate this bitterness. "There is a world-wide conflict between capital and labour, and the poor envy the rich. If all worked for their bread, distinction of rank would be obliterated; the rich would still be there, but they would deem themselves only trustees of their property, and would use it mainly in the public interest."[12]

Thus instead of class conflict, the Mahatma pleaded for the class collaboration, which according to him can be achieved if harmony of interest takes the place of conflict of interest. The harmony of interests can be achieved if both the employers as well as the employees understand the problems of each other. The doctrines of wantlessness, trusteeship and bread labour if practised can be of great help in achieving this harmony. Thus by following this way the class struggle can be eliminated to a great extent.

The above suggestion by Gandhi in fact, point to an ideal which the society must try to achieve. However, he was not ignorant of the prevailing situations and psychology of both labour and capital and believed in a pragmatic approach as well. He was a very practical man. He knew that this ideal of elimination of class struggle is a long-term objective which can not be attained for the time being. The next best possible solution for the present problem, could be the minimisation of the occurence of conflicts between labour and capital, if not its complete elimination.

B. MINIMISATION OF CLASS STRUGGLE (THE NEXT ALTERNATIVE)

Gandhi was opposed to all types of concentrations, since to him, centralisation was a menace and a danger to democratic norms. He argued, "Possession of power makes men blind and deaf, they can not see things which are under their very nose, and can not hear things which invade their ears."[13] Similarly, he emphasised "If India is to evolve along non-violent lines, it will have to decentralize many things. Centralisation can not be sustained and defended without adequate force."[14] Or 'centralisation as a system is inconsistent with non-violent society'.[15] Moreover, he was convinced that moral progress was possible only in a decentralised step-up as the end to be achieved is human happiness combined with full mental and moral development. And according to him, this end could be achieved only under decentralisation.

Accordingly, he affirms that without decentralisation it is impossible to ensure individual liberty and mental and moral growth of man. Similarly, it is equally essential for the realisation of this ideal which is not possible without adequate opportunities to individuals to participate in the management of their own affairs.

He pleads for the decentralisation of both economic and political power. The success of political decentralization in his view depends upon economic decentralisation. This follows from his conviction that a highly centralised management or political set-up is likely to bring dictatorship of one kind or another by self-interested and power-hungry minority imposing itself on a deluded and sub-servient majority.

Coming specifically to labour-capital relations in a decentralised productive unit there is a direct contact between the employer and the workers. There is also less use of capital which generally takes the form of machinery. Though in small scale units, the struggle between the labour and capital can not be altogether ruled out yet that will not be very intense in comparison with the large scale units. On the one hand, employers in small units are not in a strong position, since they are more dependent upon the labour for production because the extent of mechanisation is rather limited. On the other, the labour can not fight hard because not only has the individual labour developed personal relations with the employer but also because the number of labourers working in such a productive unit is rather small. Another redeeming feature of such industries is that the owner himself works in his unit as a labourer with other. He is in a better position to understand the difficulties of his labourers. They in turn understand the problems of their employer. Thus a perfect rapport is established between them leading to the solution of a number of problems. Thus, Gandhi recommended that, as far as possible, the production should be carried on in small scale labour-intensive units.

Gandhi does not advocate decentralisation only because of its economic and political advantages. To him decentralisation upholds the cultural or spiritual ideal of simple living and high thinking. The main aim of socioeconomic organisations, should not be the multiplicity of wants and accumulation of comforts and luxuries, although a minimum standard of living must be assured to all human beings. He was of the opinion that society should be organised in such a way that individual gets the maximum freedom and opportunity to develop his personality and character to the fullest extent. He was convinced that man could never attain peace and happiness with money only.

C. THE STRUGGLE AS A LAST RESORT

The Mahatma had mixed pragmatism with idealism. While he wished that there should be no class struggle at all, he knew that in the world of materialism, such an ideal may be difficult to achieve and there was every possibility that labour-capital struggle may take place. There might be strikes and lock outs. But these should be the last resorts and only if the struggle becomes inevitable. He was not completely against strikes provided these were actuated by just reasons and were conducted peacefully. In fact G.L. Nanda calls Gandhi as the 'first Indian labour leader.' It was he who led the labour strike of Ahmedabad mill workers in 1918. Before discussing this further let us first of all see how he led the workers in 1918.

Gandhi went to Bombay on 2nd February 1918, in connection with Kheda situation, he happened to meet Seth Ambalal Sarabhai there. Ambalal showed him some papers and informed him that it was feared that the workers would strike as a result of discontent over the question of bonus. He pleaded that undesirable consequences would result from such a strike and that Gandhi should intervene. Gandhi felt that Ambalal apprehensions were justified and so he decided to take measures to prevent developments.[16]

He went to Ahmedabad and began inquiring into the case of workers and the mill agents. He found that since August of 1917, the weavers were paid quite satisfactory 'plague bonuses'. He also discovered that many weavers who would have left Ahmedabad due to plague had been tempted by these plague bonuses to continue to work in the mills at the risk of their own lives. He found that in some cases the plague bonus was as high as 70 to 80 per cent of the workers' wages, and that the bonus had continued to be given even after the cessation of plague, since prices of foodgrains, cloth and other necessities of life had risen to more than twice, thrice, or four times the old prices.

The workers of the weaving department were agitated on learning that the mill owners contemplated stopping the bonus abruptly. Daily they used to go to Shrimati Anasuyabehn and explained to her their conditions. They demanded that they should be paid at least a 50 per cent increase as Dearness Allowance instead of the plague bonus. After coming to Ahmedabad, the Mahatma began to discuss the matter with prominent mill-agents. They too showed a keen desire to settle the matter. Gandhi had not decided hitherto to intervene directly in the dispute. On February 11, 1918, the Commissioner wrote the following letter to Gandhi:

> "There is likelihood of a serious situation arising between the mill-owners and the workers on the question of bonus.

> The mill-owners threaten to lock-out the mill, which will naturally cause great distress and hardship to the workers. I am, therefore very anxious to understand the real situation, I am informed that the mill-owners will, if at all, heed only to your advice, you are also sympathetic to them and you are the only person who can explain their case to me. I shall be thankful, therefore, if you can make it convenient to meet me for about an hour tomorrow."[17]

Gandhi saw the collector, the workers and the mill agents and held discussion with them. Ultimately both the parties decided to settle the matter by arbitration. In the arbitration board, Seth Ambalal, Seth Jagabhai Dalpatbhai and Seth Chandulal were appointed by the mill-owners and Gandhi, Vallabhbhai Patel and Shankerlal Banker were appointed on behalf of the workers, with the collector as the umpire.[18]

Gandhi went to Kheda soon after this. But he was informed by Anasuyabehn that the situation in Ahmedabad was critical and the mill-owners were on the point of declaring a simultaneous lock-out in all the mills. Gandhi reached Ahmedabad. He was informed that workers in a few mills had struck work. He expressed his regret to the mill-owners for what had happened, and informed them that the workers were ready to rectify their mistake. It must be stated here that it was not as if the mill-owners were free from all blame. But Gandhi concerned himself only with the mistake committed by his own side and showed his readiness to correct it. The mill-owners would not agree. They insisted that since the workers resorted to a strike after the appointment of arbitrators, the arbitration stood cancelled *ipso facto.*

Gandhi met the workers very frequently thereafter. He studied the scales of wages at Ahmedabad and Bombay, the demand of the workers, the financial position of the mills, the commission that the mill-owners charged before the war and after, and whether considering the increased cost of manufacture of cloth after the war, the industry could bear the burden of the increase demanded. On the basis of this study he came to the conclusion that the workers should not demand more than 35 per cent. He decided to inform the workers about this in order that they might keep their demands within restraint. But before doing so, he thought it well to tell the mill-owners about it and requested them to give him their detailed opinion and help. They evaded the issue. Then, Gandhi and his colleagues advised the workers to demand a 35 per cent increase. Those workers, who had demanded a 50 per cent increase till now after much persuasion finally accepted their advisers' recommendation to be content with 35 per cent.[19]

An element of doggedness already characterized both the sides. The mill-owners also established an association of their own to combat the unity of labour. Not only the city of Ahmedabad but the whole of Gujarat and to some extent the whole country watched this struggle, with great amusement which continued for about 25 days with great zest but without any bitterness. Let us see the *modus operandi* of the Mahatma during this struggle.

Even since the workers entrusted their problem to him, Gandhi put a restraint on their tendency for horseplay, diverted their bubbling enthusiasm along useful lines and tried to give the struggle a religious turn. He decided to enter into the life of workers, since superficial advice without intimate knowledge of the outer and inner life of the workers was likely to fail; even if it did not entirely fail, its success would be insignificant. The following means were, therefore, adopted for this purpose.

1. To visit the workers' houses, make detailed inquires regarding their mode of life, try and remove any defect noticed therein, advise and help the workers in their difficulties and share their happiness and misery to the extent possible.
2. To advise the workers regarding their conduct during the struggle, whenever they desire such advice.
3. To enlighten them on the issues and principles involved in the struggle daily at a public meeting for workers to be held at a fixed place.
4. To issue instructive leaflets everyday with a view to fixing firmly in their minds the principle and significance of the struggle, and to supply them with simple and elevating literature which would conduce to their mental and intellectual development and enable them to leave for posterity a heritage of the means for its progress.

Though the leaflets were published under the name of Anasuyabehn, they were as a matter of fact, written by Gandhi himself. Some of his speeches and leaflets are summarized as follows:

> In the initial days, Gandhi spoke on the importance of pledges taken by the workers. The pledge was as follows:
>
> I. Not to resume work until a 35 per cent increase on the wage is secured.
>
> II. During the period of lock-out—not to indulge in mischief, quarrelling, robbing, plundering or abusive language or cause damage to mill-owner's property, but to behave peacefully.[20]

Referring to some workers who complained that a 35 per cent increase was inadequate, he said:

> "Some workers say that we can demand more than 35 per cent. I say you can demand even a 100 per cent increase. But if you make such a demand, it would be unjust. Be content with what you have demanded in the present circumstances. If you ask for more, it will pain me. We can not make an unreasonable demand from anybody: I believe that the demand for 35 per cent is just."[21]

In the sixth day leaflet Gandhi explained that in order to be able to stand by the pledge it was necessary for one to culminate the virtues of truth, courage, justice, sincerity, tolerance and faith in God. The next day's leaflet contained some general but pointed expressions as to how the workers should use their idle hours. The struggle may continue for a long time, and some may have to face starvation. They may, therefore, have to do a type of labour they have never done before. Therefore, in order that they may regard all honest work as honourable, he said, "Any occupation that is essential for a man's life can not be considered as either high or low in comparison with other occupations. One need not be ashamed of working in an occupation other than the one he is used to. We believe that weaving cloth, breaking stones, sawing and splitting wood, or working in the field are the essential and honourable occupations. The heat and strength acquired by breaking stones, can not be acquired by handling a pen."[22]

The following expression in the eighth day leaflet need special attention:

> "We can never wish or do ill to the employer, and in every action of ours the idea of their good is also always present. We want to secure the good of the workers, while safeguarding the good of the employers."[23]

After this stage the tone of the leaflet was changed. Hitherto, it was felt that the mill-owners would test the workers for a few days and then take them back to work at the wage demanded by them. The workers were therefore, asked to have patience when they asked for alternative employment. It was explained to them that their desire for other work could be construed to mean that the workers did not want to return to their employers and that they harboured hatred towards them. The workers too, unemployed as they were had been patient and had literally carried out the instructions to remain peaceful. Now, however, it appeared that the non-acceptance of workers demand by the employers was not due to their inability to pay 35 per cent, but to sheer obstinacy.

Many attempts were made by the employers to persuade the workers to resume work and give up their pledge. It was also sought to scare them by the prospect of starvation; they complained about it to their advisors who kept them loyal to their pledge. Events however took a new turn on 12th March. The lock-out was ended on that day, and it was announced that mill would be open for all those workers who were prepared to accept the increase of 20 per cent. From that day onwards, the Mahatma decided to hold daily meetings in the morning for the simple reason that since the opening time of the mills was in the morning, some workers may resume work being misled by improper advice. The leaflet, issued on the day on which the lock-out was ended and strike by the workers commenced, contained advice not only to the workers but also to the employers. "In order that the workers may rise from their present conditions, there is no alternative for them but to remain firm to their pledge; and it is our conviction that the good of the mill-owners lies in the workers' keeping their pledge. Eventually the workers will gain nothing by taking labour from those who can not abide by their oath. A religious minded man will never rejoice in compelling any one to break his pledge nor be a party to causing such a breach."[24]

Twenty-two days passed in this manner. In one of the meetings, some one taunted Gandhi and Anasuyabehn. 'What is it to Anasuyabehan and Gandhiji, They come and go in their cars; they eat sumptuous food, but we are suffering death agonies; attending meetings does not prevent starvation.' These remarks reached Gandhiji's ears. These bitter words pierced his heart and he announced, "I shall not take any food or use a car till workers get 35 per cent increase or all of us die in the fight for it."[25] Hearing this hundreds of workers came to Gandhi with the persons, who had taunted him, to express their regret and to persuade him to give up his resolve to fast. Some were so excited that they told Gandhi that if Anasuyabehn who also had taken an oath to fast at the same meeting, would not withdraw it, they would take some extreme step. One worker came with a big knife tied to his waist and threatened to commit suicide. This sweet yet piteous dispute ended in Anasuyabehn having to agree to take food.

The situation created by fast was the subject of great curiosity, criticism and controversy. India had not yet witnessed its leaders making use of vows for the public good. Since Gandhi took this step even those who till now kept aloof became concerned. Leaders outside in different parts of the country also showed great interest, and all felt that this dispute should be settled soon.

Nor were the mill-owners quite unaffected. Undoubtedly many of them believed that it was just a device or desperate step to coerce them. Ambalal Sarabhai, who till now by his firm attitude sustained the other employers, was greatly pained by Gandhi's act. He came and sat by Gandhi for hours requesting him to give up his fast. Many other employers joined him in this request. All were anxious to persuade Gandhi to break the fast, but not so anxious to see the pledge of the workers fulfilled. Some mill-owners told Gandhi, "We will give 35 per cent increase to workers. This time for your sake." Gandhi flatly turned down the offer and said: "Do not give 35 per cent out of pity for me, but do so to respect the workers' pledge, and to give them justice."[26] Pleading the case of mill-owners, Ambalal further proposed, "It will be intolerable if workers defied us frequently counting on the support of outsiders. If this happens, there would be nothing like discipline among them. Besides, it is not proper that every time there is a dispute between us and the workers, we have to accept arbitration by a third party. In that case we shall have no prestige. We will immediately concede 35 per cent if you keep your self away from them for all the times in future, and leave matters between us and the workers entirely for us." Gandhi again refused flatly, Ambalal's proposal did not, therefore materialize.

The discussion then took another form. It was argued that the mill-owners' resolution should be accepted as a matter of principles. "Just as you have taken an oath, so have they" was the plea. Gandhi showed his incongruity by a counter-question. "It is open to a king to take an oath that he will tax his subjects heavily and harass them by not listening to any of their grievances." Gandhi wrote to Ambalal, "Respect your sense of justice more than your desire to break my fast. My fast gives me immense pleasure and therefore need not cause pain to any one."[27] Addressing the inmates of his ashram on the morning of the day of settlement, he said, "It is inevitable for people to feel that my fasts will weigh heavily on the minds of the employers, even inspite of my intentions that it should not. It is true that mill-owners have not been able to act freely owing to my weak conditions resulting from the fast. It is against the principle of justice to get any thing in writing, or lay down conditions, or take anything from a person, under duress. No satyagrahi should ever do so. I had therefore to compromise in regard to the settlement, and out of shame yielded partially to the employers.[28]

He, therefore, prepared himself to accept a compromise giving the workers a 35 per cent increase on the first day to enable them to up hold their pledge, a 20 per cent increase on the second day to honour the employers' resolve, and thereafter an increase to be decided by an arbitrator appointed both by the workers and the employers. It was realized that the arbitrator could not be expected to settle the dispute on the third day and could not order payment of a definite increase from that day, and therefore, it was agreed that a period of three months should be given for this purpose. What should the workers be paid pending the Award of the arbitrator? Both the parties settled this issue by a compromise. The workers reduced their demands by 7.5 per cent, the mill-owners increased their offer by 7.5 per cent, and it was decided—that the workers be given an increase of 27.5 per cent in the interim period. Professor Anandshanker who was acceptable to both the parties was appointed as the arbitrator.[29]

The workers and employers accepted the settlement with joy. Then, Gandhi broke his fast. There remains nothing to add to this history to say that the arbitrator finally decided that 35 per cent increase should be given to the workers.

In different parts of India, many times in the past struggles have taken place between mill-owners and workers, but not one of them was conducted as was this one, with clean weapons, on the strength of will power rather than wealth, and with complete sweetness.

The analysis clearly brings out the fact that Gandhi did realise that the present industrial structure had in it the germs of labour unrest. He also accepted that strikes and lock-outs at times become inevitable. But he was of the firm opinion that no strike or lock-out could go for ever. Sooner than later, both the parties will have to sit on the negotiating table. Settlement must ultimately be reached. Parties to a dispute in industrial relations must finally live and work together. They can not retire behind their respective frontiers to sulk in splendid isolation. Although they may sulk for a while after a period of open conflict, none-the-less they have at the same time to get on with the job and earn a living. The parties left to themselves sometimes fail to do what a third party ultimately can do for them and lay down the terms of a workable compromise.

The principal methods by which industrial disputes are settled, arranged in an ascending scale of participation by outsiders to the disputes, are negotiation, conciliation, mediation and arbitration. In negotiation only the parties to the dispute are involved. Conciliation involves a third party whose responsibility is limited to keeping the disputing parties together around the conference table. The mediator has the more positive role of assessing the views and interests of the parties in dispute and advancing suggestions for compromise for their consideration. The arbitrator goes further and has the responsibility for deciding the nature of the final settlement, acceptance of which may or may not be compulsorily required from the disputants.

But in this case, both the parties had agreed to accept the decision of the arbitrator. Gandhi had specifically told the workers, "If the arbitrator feels that a smaller increase is proper, we shall accept less, and our vow will not thereby be broken at all. We have accepted the principle of arbitration for all time. We believe we have not committed a mistake in deciding upon a 35 per cent increase, we, therefore, hope that we shall get that percentage. But if we find that we were mistaken we shall willingly accept less."[30]

Thus Gandhi approached this problem of labour-capital conflicts from another angle. First of all he pleads for the complete elimination of labour-capital conflicts and suggests the means and ways by which the harmony of interests can be established. But he knew that all this may not be possible in the present structure of society for the time being. As a second alternative, he suggests the minimisation of the struggle. For this, he recommends decentralisation of the economy through small scale and cottage industries.

And then, as a last resort, if strikes become inevitable, he gives several definite guidelines on the basis of which the struggles can be started. He accords the top priority to the first ideal (elimination of struggle), if first is not possible then the second best (minimisation of the struggle) and ultimately the struggle, if other avenues are not available. But he felt sure that through changes in the attitude of both labour and capital and through some institutional changes, not only could the frequency as well as intensity of the labour-capital struggle be reduced but the struggle itself could be eliminated altogether.

Labour-capital conflict is part of class conflict. Class conflict, as Karl Marx has advocated is the core of history, itself, and with war is 'one of the two plagues that has destroyed or mortally blighted past civilizations', according to Arnold Toynbee." The future of arbitration is a small and derivative part of the future course of history itself. Unless some one is willing to predict the course of history for us, it will be wiser to experiment on the Gandhian lines.[31]

Notes and References

1. J.M. Clark, Alternative to Serfdom (New York: Khopf, 1948), p. 50.
2. J.M. Clark, Guideposts in Time of Change (New York: Harper, 1949), Chapter 3.
3. Karl Marx and Frederick Engels, Manifesto of the Community Party (Moscow: Progress Publishers, 1975), p. 40.
4. Karl Marx, "Critique of Political Economy," *op. cit.*, p. 371.
5. *Young India*, 4.8.1927, p. 248.
6. *Ibid.*, 20.8.1925, p. 285.
7. *Harijan*, 28.7.1940, p. 219.
8. J.K. Mehta (ed.), Fundamentals of Economics (Allahabad: Pothishala Ltd., 1952), p. 11.
9. *Ibid.*
10. M.K. Gandhi, From Yeravada Mandir (Ahmedabad: Navajivan Publishing House, 1986), p. 14.
11. M.K. Gandhi, Ashram Observations in Action (Ahmedabad: Navajivan Publishing House, 1955), pp. 62-63.
12. M.K. Gandhi, From Yeravada Mandir, *op. cit.*, p. 22.
13. *CWMG*, Vol. XX, p. 505.
14. *Harijan*, 30.12.1939, p. 391.
15. *Ibid.*, 18.12.1942, p. 5.
16. *CWMG*, Vol. XIV, p. 185.
17. Mahadev Haribhai Desai, A Righteous Struggle (Ahmedabad: Navajivan Publishing House, 1968), p. 5.
18. *CWMG*, Vol. XIV, p. 215.
19. *Ibid.*, p. 212.
20. *Ibid.*, p. 214.
21. *Ibid.*, p. 217.
22. *Ibid.*, pp. 225-26.
23. *Ibid.*, p. 227.
24. *Ibid.*, p. 249.
25. *Ibid.*, p. 256.
26. *Ibid.*, p. 257.
27. *Ibid.*, p. 264.
28. *Ibid.*, pp. 265-66.
29. *Ibid.*, pp. 269-71.
30. *Ibid.*
31. Arnold J. Toynbee, A Study of History, Vol. IV (London: Thames and Hudson, 1977).

6

Rural Reconstruction

One of the most formidable and fundamental aspect of India's development effort has been to evolve a strategy to ameliorate the social and economic conditions of plus forty per cent who continue to live below the poverty line expecting something to turn up. Many half baked theories have been advanced, *ad-hoc* projects and schemes conceived and implemented, but the problem continues to evade solution. Rural politics and administration is a relatively complex interactional system, with many sub-operating units, their inter-se-linkages, and it is not easy to find out the nature of transaction with their external environment. We have not been quite serious in studying the rural social system as a separate and distinct entity with contours of its own interacting with the urban ecology and interests, shaping and influencing the politics and economy of the country as a whole. We had to pay a heavy price for it, but how long can we afford being complacent?

Rural development as a concept and as a reality has suffered intellectual importation heavily biased by philosophical and methodological assumptions quite unrelated to the actual configuration of problem situation. Statisticians, economists, sociologists, social workers and government agencies have, hitherto, overwhelmingly focused their attention on the study of the phenomena and problems of the urban society, though by far the greater portion of the Indian humanity lives in the rural area amidst condition of immense poverty.

The fundamental fact of Indian economy today is that there is a microscopic but powerful minority which systematically diverts huge rural resources from provision of basic minimum needs to the poor, to building up, maintaining and expanding modern facilities for the affluent. Even foreign aid has been consistently used to boost the living standard of this minority. Whatever is done, whatever is set-up, is quickly converted into just another establishment to create a mini New York in this poor land on the earth. Today the position is such that a man with his pocket full of money can get rooms and rooms in any five star hotel with all the luxuries of the world but a poor ailing person cannot get a single bed in any government hospital.

Most intelligent people, people who are in a position to deliver the good and those who have got the management expertise, are all meant only for the urban people. The elite is all city-based, metropolitan culture addicts. They are able to complete a mighty project in a capital city on schedule, on the dot, at the stroke of the hour. But when it comes to rural India, it does not happen so. Can we not bring about all around improvement in the villages within 5 or 10 years? Now more than 60 years are lapsing since we adopted planning. We are still not in a position to give a clear answer to that.

To those in the villages, who have no work for the most part of the year, to those living in more than two lakhs of villages who do not get clean drinking water or can get it only after trekking a long distance, and to those in the villages whose children always go to sleep half hungry; thetic fibre factories, big airports, modern hotels, skyscrapers, an endless range of domestic gadgets and the like, make no sense at all. Here man begins with nothing at home. Nothing like a breakfast for them. They go to work hungary, toil from dawn to dusk, get back after having put quite a good deal of their sweat in the process. The dignity of individual is something which is totally neglected. The payment of wages is of exploitation type.

India's present plight stems largely from a grievous choice made after independence to go immediately industrial. The

Father of the Nation had sought to give first priority to agriculture, accompanied by cottage industry or handicrafts followed by light or small scale industries and, then heavy industry. But Gandhi's ideas were rejected by his heirs who completely put the whole process in the reverse gears. The Indian National Congress turned socialist overnight at its annual session held at Avadi in January 1955. Thereafter big industrial units and the expansion of the public sector have been the craze with ruling leaders and regarded as a sign of progress in the country. They wanted to build India from top downward that is from the industrialists, managers and technicians, and hence followed the centrality of town. Instead of agriculture and labour-intensive and short-gestation period schemes, the Government had a strong preference for huge, expensive, capital-intensive schemes which were not merely time consuming, but also extravagant in the use of scare resources such as steel, cement, sophisticated technical expertise and foreign exchange.

The steadily deepening economic crises quite visible failed to open our eyes to the mistake we are committing. Rejection of Gandhian Model in the field of restructuring our economy after independence was accompanied by our persistence with wholly alien models of economic development. This helped only to compound our misery.

Gandhi had sought to build India from the bottom, that is, from the poorest and the weakest, and hence followed the centrality of the village. He stood for the integrity and foundations of the villages. In his own word, "Under my scheme nothing will be àllowed to be produced by the cities which can be equally well produced by the villagers. The proper function of cities is to serve as a clearing houses of village products."[1] He was pained to see the contrast between the two. "The poor villagers are exploited by their own countrymen—the city dwellers. They produce the food and go hungry. They produce milk and their children have to go without it. It is disgraceful."[2]

He was deeply anguished to see the disintegration and ruin of the villages. In his own words, "Our cities are not India. India lives in her seven and half lacs of villages. The city people are brokers and commission agents for the big houses of Europe, America and Japan."[3]

Gandhi started from analysing the causes of poverty owing to the British Rule. Like Dada Bhai Naoroji, Karl Marx, R.C. Dutt, Gandhi too, was of the firm opinion that poverty in India was a British Legacy and thus the principal cause of rural under-development. While pleading guilty during the great trial of 1922, he stated, "I came reluctantly to the conclusion that the British connection had made India more helpless than she ever was before, politically and economically". . . . Before the Biritish advent, India spun and wove in her millions of cottages, just the supplement she needed for adding to her meagre agricultural resources. These cottage industries, so vital for India's existence, have been ruined by incredibly heartless and inhuman processes as described by English witnesses. Little do the town-dwellers know how the semi-starved masses of India are slowly sinking to lifelessness. Little do they know that their miserable comfort represents the brokerage they get for the work they do for the foreign exploiter, that the profits and the brokerage are sucked from the masses. Little do they realise that the government established by law in British India is carried on for this exploitation of the masses. No sophistry, no jugglery in figures can explain away the evidence that the skeletons in many villages present to the naked eye. I have no doubt whatsoever that both England and the town-dwellers of India will have to answer, if there is a God above, for this crime against humanity is perhaps unequalled in history."[4]

His whole conception of rural development revolved around the development of villages and poor to attain a just social order. The postulates of swadeshi, khadi, trusteeship, bread labour (truth and non-violence being constant value parameters), non-exploitation, non-possession and equality were also rooted in the structure of our society, the religious and social faiths of people. In order to build up a just and equitable social order the development of villages is a necessity. Gandhi was not an advocate of the glorification of poverty but he was all for leveling the society. In the word of J.D. Sethi, "He called economic poverty a moral collapse of the affluent. Affluence co-existing with poverty is an absolute theft."[5]

The conception of Gandhi about village was neither narrow nor he intended to preach for keeping intact the old village devoid of sanitation, having old rotten houses, etc. Rather he visualized villages as productivity centres, applying adaptable technologies and having skilful workers and excellent environment. He wrote to Jawahar Lal Nehru on October 5, 1945, "While I appreciate modern thought, I find that an ancient thing considered in the light of this thought looks so sweet. You will not be able to understand me if you think that I am talking about the villages of today. My ideal village still exists only in my imagination. . . . In this village of my dreams the villager will not be dull. He will not live like an animal in filth and darkness. Men and women will live in freedom, prepared to face the whole world. There will be no plague, no cholera and no smallpox. Nobody will be allowed to be idle or to wallow in luxury. Every one will have to do body labour. Granting all this, I can still envisage a number of things that will have to be organized on a large scale. Perhaps there will even be railways and also post and telegraph offices. I do not know what things there will be or will not be. Nor am I bothered about it. If I can make sure of the essential things, other things will follow in due course. But if I give up the essential things, I give up everything."[6] His idea was not relief-oriented but he wished to build up the whole Indian economic and political structure on rural foundations.

The above statement of Gandhi points to the basic human needs which are fundamental to sustain life and living on this earth. This gives poorest of the poor to acquire productive capabilities. Unless these basic human needs are fulfilled, the process of development will tilt in favour of those few who have assets and better endowed than others. Not only it will deprive millions to be part of development process, it will also bring unrest in the world. Since the bulk of these millions live in rural areas, therefore, the structural reforms must start from there and once this platform is ready, the storeys of development can be erected. So, for him, conceptually, rural development is the basis of all development process. He does not believe in first creating inequality and then distribute development but he believed in equitable process of development from its very inception. He did not conceptualize rural development at one place but his ideas about village development and various aspects essential for taking up such developments such as villages sanitation, mechanization, rural industrialization, application and adoption of techniques, cooperation, decentralization, of power, etc. have village as the basic concern around which developmental parameters revolves around.

He visualized village as the basic unit of development of economic and political activity. To quote him, "A village unit as conceived by me is as strong as the strongest. My imaginary village consists of 1,000 souls. Such a unit can give a good account of itself if it is well organized on a basis of self-sufficiency."[7]

Elaborating his superstructure of rural development, he said, "Independence must begin at the bottom. Thus, every villages will be republic or panchayat having full powers. It follows, therefore, that every village has to be self-sustained and capable of managing its affairs even to the extent of defending itself against the whole world—It will be trained and prepared to perish in the attempt to defend itself against any on-slaught from without. Thus, ultimately, it is the individual who is the unit. This does not exclude dependence on and willing help from neighbours or from the world. . . . In this structure composed of innumerable villages, there will be ever widening, never ascending circles. Life will not be a pyramid with the apex sustained by the bottom. But it will be an oceanic circle whose centre will be the individual always ready to perish for the village, the latter ready to perish for the circle of villages, till at last the whole becomes one life composed of individuals, never aggressive in their arrogance but ever humble, sharing the majesty of oceanic circle of which they are integral units."[8] . . . At another place he elaborated, "When our villages are fully developed there will be no dearth in them of men with a high degree of skill and artistic talent. There will be village poets, village artists, village architects, linguists and research workers. In short, there will be nothing in life worth having which will not be had in the villages. Today the villages are barren and desolate and are like dung-heaps. Tomorrow they will be like tiny gardens of Eden where dwell highly intelligent folk whom no one can deceive or exploit. The reconstruction of the villages along these lines should begin right now. That might necessitate some modification of the scheme. The reconstruction of the villages should not be organised on a temporary but on a permanent basis."[9] While addressing the students at Vidyamandir training school at Wardha he asked them to drive away illiteracy from these villages. . . . Cast-off the cloak of foreign thoughts and ideals, and identify yourselves with the villagers."[10] He desired to exploit the inventive skills of the villages. Said he, "We will by concentrating on the villages see that the inventive skill that an intensive learning of the craft will stimulate will subserve the needs of the villager as a whole."[11] Thus he wanted to resuscitate the villages, to spearhead a "silent social revolution."[12] Removal of illiteracy and intensive learning of crafts were the keys to this revolution. These were the symbols to bring awareness, remove ignorance persisting since centuries as well to give productive work to idle hands to increase income of rural people.

Gandhi did not visualize static conditions in the villages. He was aware that wheel of development must move forward but the process of development must not create imbalances, "I have not pictured a poverty-stricken India containing ignorant millions. I have pictured to myself India continually progressing along the lines best suited to her genius. I do not however picture it as a third class or even a first class copy of the dying civilization of the West. If my dream is fulfilled and everyone of the seven lakhs of villages becomes a well-living republic in which there are no illiterates, in which no one is idle for want of work, in which everyone is usefully occupied and has nourishing food, well-ventilated dwellings and sufficient Khadi for covering the body, and in which all the villagers know and observe the laws of hygiene and sanitation such a state must have varied and increasing needs which it must supply unless it would stagnate.[13]

Gandhi's conception of village was not anchored on the modern (urban-industrial) notion of "development" but on the post-modern perspective of "quality of life", which today's men of ideas realized only after having the experience of the catastrophe wrought by modern urban industrialism. Generally, village may be: (i) a source of raw material, (ii) a market for goods produced in urban areas, (iii) an entity in itself. It cannot flourish under (i) and (ii) approach. The third system alone makes the village a worthy citizen.[14]

Gandhian concept of human equality is something basic and spiritual. Khadi gets pride place in the plan for village resurgence. The advantage of Khadi economy are: easy availability of operation, modest capital requirement, solution of unemployment, independence from monsoon conditions, promotion of equitable distribution of wealth, etc. The slogan of khadi, swadeshi and spinning wheel have appeared in Gandhian writings again and again. The mass poverty in rural area, the nearly negligible modern technical know-how, the dearth of capital and the availability of labour and local raw material are some of the key factors influencing Gandhian ideology to propagate the use of Khadi and production of Swadeshi goods and articles.[15] Gandhi wanted idle poor masses, who had no source, to supplement their agricultural income. He wrote, "The people of India are bound to remain idle atleast four months in a year. People who are thus forced to remain idle cannot but be revived. For crores of people the spinning wheel is the only occupation which can supplement their income for the fields, most emphatically, they have no other one."[16]

Those who consider Gandhian solutions in relation to village problems and Gandhian solution piecemeal can never honestly believe that a revolutionary transformation can take place by adjuring any kind of conflict in the name of non-violence. It would be dangerous to take Gandhi as a piecemeal. On the other hand, we have to accept it in totality or exercise option not to adhere to it at all. It is in this context that Gandhi had expressed: "If the villages perish, India will perish too. It will be no more India. Her own mission in the world will get lost."[17] On the other hand, if all Indian villages would come up to the Gandhian ideal, the country would be free from most of its worries.

In Gandhi's scheme, the foundation of rural development is based on the solid work of workers. A worker should not be power hungry and he should remain apolitical, i.e. away from power politics. He should be above village's factions and should not expect any rewards or gratitude for his work. He should work courageously and 'intelligently' with local help as far as possible. He should work as a village scavenger, train others in rules of sanitation and health care and import health education with an emphasis on nature cure and such simple medicines as castor oil, quinine, etc. He should be a master spinner, habitual user of Khadi, should take interest in encouraging and reviving village industries. He should be engaged in a craft so that he may earn his own livelihood. He should be a model of industry, fully utilizing all working hours. He should maintain a diary in which he should write a complete account of the daily work done by him. He prescribed 'Eleven Vows', viz., "non-violence, truth, non-stealing, celibacy (brahmcharya), non-possession, manual or bodv labour, control of the palate, fearlessness, equal respect for all religions, Swadeshi (restricting oneself to the use and service of one's nearest surroundings in preference to those more remote) and spirit of exclusive brotherhood."[18]

Besides, the village sewaks—village level workers are the main pillars for a success and it is they who should act as the custodians of village development. To find such dedicated workers is perhaps the most difficult problem even faced during that period when craze to serve the nation was at its zenith. According to Gandhi, 'an ideal village' is required to have (i) Orderliness in the structure, (ii) Orderly roads, lanes and drainage, (iii) Temple/Mosque kept beautifully clean, (iv) Dharamshala/small dispensary, (v) Own water works, (vi) Theatre and recreational facilities, (vii) School and education compulsory upto final basic course, (viii) Self-sufficiency in food and cloth, (ix) Money crops except opium and tobacco, (x) Defence against wild animals/robbers and compulsory service of village guards, (xi) People practicing non-violence and satyagraha technique, and (xii) Village panchayat exercising executive, legislative and judical powers in combination.

The unit of decentralized authority, as envisaged by Gandhi, i.e., 'Viable Village' is essential to be determined on the basis of population, from the point of view of viability of schemes, effective programme adoption and execution for rapid social development. Such a size will provide in-built market mechanism near to the centre of production for local goods and quick returns to poor not only in economic terms but he, emphatically advocated and dreamed this kind of model of political autonomy as a tool of effective decentralization of authority for social transformation. He was an 'individualist' thinker and visioned absolute economic and political independent individual living in social harmony within the overall circumference of national identity. Decentralization of authority is a pre-requisite of independence, and individual sufficiency will culminate into collective sufficiency. Such a political and administrative decentralization shall form the basis to sustain an integrated rural development structure of Indian Nation.

Similarly, there will be nothing in life worth having which will not be had in the villages. Today the villages are barren and desolate. The reconstruction of the villages alone these lines should begin right now. That might necessitate some modification of the scheme. The reconstruction of the villages should not be organized on a temporary but on a permanent basis. He wanted to resuscitate the villages, to spearhead a silent social revolution.

It must be noted here that Gandhian concept of rural development is certainly multi-dimensional encompassing the total development of man with stress on quality of development. With this conception of rural society, reconstruction was envisaged by Gandhi. He initiated some earlier works of rural reconstruction at Champaran in 1917 and he took his Constructive Programme at Sevagram in 1920 and at Wardha in 1938 which was an elaborate programme of rural development in an entirely different fashion and termed it as an instrument of permanent value.

His action plan involved the rebuilding of every aspect of human life (economic, educational, social and political), and envisaged a society based on self-supporting and self-governing villages. Gandhi first wrote Constructive Programme in 1941 and revised it in 1945. He regarded Constructive Programme as the truthful and non-violent way of winning complete independence (Poorna Swaraj). The concept of Poorna Swaraj was woven around the concept of Gram Swaraj, i.e., establishment of ideal village society.

He clarified to Nehru, "man is not born to live in jungle, he is born to live in society. If we are to make sure that one person does not ride on another's back, the unit should be an ideal village or a social order group which will be self-sufficient, but the members of which will be interdependent. This conception will bring about a change in human relationship all over the world."[19]

Gandhi while drafting his constructive programme took care of social, economic, political and moral aspects of development. His approach to Constructive Programme can be classified into five segments, viz., economic, educational, social, environmental and political. The Constructive Programme as revised has eighteen items with one more addition, i.e., improvement of livestock. These include: (i) communal unity, (ii) removal of untouchability, (iii) prohibition, (iv) khadi, (v) other village industries, (vi) village sanitation, (vii) new or basic education, (viii) adult education, (ix) women, (x) education in health and hygiene, (xi) provincial language, (xii) national language, (xiii) economic equality, (xiv) kisans, (xv) labour, (xvi) adivasis, (xvii) lepers, (xviii) students and one more to be included, and (xix) improvement of livestock.[20]

The main pillars of this Programme are:

	No. of items	
1. Economic:	4	The production and use of khadi.
	19	Improvement of livestock.
	13	Socio-economic equality.
	5	Development of village industries.
2. Educational:	7	Adoption of basic education.
	8	Adult education.
	12	National language.
	11	Provincial language.
3. Social :	1	Communal unity.
(i) National Interaction	2	Removal of untouchability
	3	Prohibition.
(ii) Target Groups for Social Development	9	Women.
	10	Adivasis.
	17	Lepers

4. Environmental:	6	Improving village sanitation.
	10	Education in health and hygiene.
5. Political:	15	Organisation of peasants and labour with a view to securing their just rights to them.
	18	Organisatin of students and youth for social work.
	14	Kisans.
6. Moral:		Truth and Non-violence.
7. End:		Panchayat Raj (Gram Swaraj) that is self-governing society at the village level.

The above classification exhibited, as the foundation of total development of India as envisaged by Gandhi. The constructive programme is basically a constant programme which should be updated with social and technological changes and needs. It is not a static concept but a dynamic concept of rural development. The economic parameters contemplates an 'economy of permanence' rather an 'economy of predation.' Non-violence is a central point to such a village economy of permanence.[21]

His concept of rural development is so integrated that it will be disastrous to disintegrated the same into separate components. The Gandhian idea of rural development is so comprehensive that it is synonymous with national development.

Gandhi, also advocated the theory of protectionism so that the wheel of development must move with equal speed. He was against importing development. For him development must start from the smallest to reach the zenith but with self-help, own skills, own resources and with an attitude to promote and propagate own production. No country of the world developed on other's shoulders (except colonial powers).

Gandhi felt the hunger of masses who are to be provided with work for winning bread. He wrote, "To those who are hungry and unemployed, God can dare reveal himself only as work and wages as the assurance of food."[22] But he was against giving "free food to those poor people" who are capable of earning their livelihood provided they are given work. One must do 'honest labour'[23] to earn his livelihood. He was all for giving such work which can lead to productive self-employment on a regular basis to these people. Wrote Gandhi, 'If I had my say I would close down all charitable institutions and alms-houses.[24]

Therefore, he was advocating opening of self-employment avenues based on local skills, technical knowhow and raw materials. Wrote he, "I feel convinced that the revival of hand-spinning and hand weaving will make the largest contribution to the economic and the moral regeneration of India. The millions must have a simple industry to supplement agriculture. Spinning was the cottage industry years ago and if the millions are to be saved from starvation, they must be enabled to reintroduce spinning in their homes, and every village must repossess its own weaver."[25]

Thus, Gandhi viewed village as the basic political and economic unit, inhabited by not poor, dirty, exploited and hopeless. Villages are clean places, having numerous opportunities of development, maximum autonomy, participation of people in political, social and economic development. Such a village is giving gainful, adequate and satisfying employment to all and each is involved in productive pursuits. If the basic framework and parameters are intact Gandhi seems not against using machines, technologies or even use of computer, radio, television but the same should be need-based fulfilling all basic necessities of life and employment to all.

Gandhi himself wrote, "The revival of the village is possible only when it is no more exploited. Industrialization on a mass scale will necessarily lead to passive or active exploitation of the villagers as the problems of competition, and marketing come in. Therefore, we have to concentrate on the village being self-contained manufacturing mainly for use. Provided this character of the village industry is maintained, there would be no objection to villagers using even the modern machines and tools that they can make and can afford to use. Only they should not be used as a means of exploitation of others."[26]

His elaborate concept of rural development, apart from villagers, in general draws our attention to specified sections of rural masses such as adivasis, lepers, and of course untouchables. These targeted sections, i.e. adivasis (not generally scheduled tribes) and untouchables (scheduled castes) who are capable of producing productive assets must be drawn into mainstream of life. This, in fact, constitutes the major section of our utterly poor classes living in extreme poverty. They even do not possess the only and basic rural endowment, i.e. land. Under the integrated rural development programme these classes alongwith other rural poor form largely the targeted groups. Gandhi went a step ahead by drawing attention to lepers by which inference can easily be drawn that he refers to people who can't do work, such as infirm old, diseased, disabled persons. But so far, any body is capable of doing work must be given work or he must work to sustain his livings. Obligation to work is essential under Gandhian principles. This has very far-reaching implication on our economic and social system. Every nation has its peculiar characteristics and without understanding these special parameters no social or economic theories can bear desired fruits. Gandhi understood the basic Indian social pattern, class structure, economic deficiencies and inherited mentalities. Apart from a handful of population and area, India was and is rural and without developing rural sector no development worth the name is possible in India. The key to India's development lies in its vast rural sector and if India could bring prosperity to its 75 per cent ruralities, India automatically reaches a stage of quality development as well as take-off stage which can breed development, further and further.

Gandhi sincerely felt that a strengthened and economically sound rural economy would revitalize Indian economy because India lives in villages. Where 75% of the population are agriculturalists. He preached, hence "The Gospel of Rural Mindedness."[27] A rural economy of self-contained villages alone could be the basis of a non-violent economy. He stated—"you have therefore to be rural minded before you can be non-violent, and to be rural minded you have to have faith in the spinning wheel."[28] He felt that the small communities moulding their lives on the basis of voluntary co-operation would be the best environment for the extinction of exploitation. The regeneration of India he felt to be impossible without village reconstruction. Hence he gave us a slogan 'Back to villages.' He gave a call to every body to go and work in villages develop rural economy, rural industry and rural skill. In small self-sufficient villages producing mostly for their consumptions a peaceful life devoted to the persuit of democratic values was possible. Big urban concentrations, on the other hand, result in the monopolization and accumulation of wealth by a minority. Economic concentration is bound to lead to political centralization. Centralization, in its turn, supports violence. He was of the definite view that non-violence could be realized not on the basis of a factory civilization but only on that of self-contained villages. Hence in order to faster the democratic notion of decentralization, which is integrally linked up with non-violence, it was essential to promote the self-sufficient small scale ecor .omy of the villages.

Pt. Jawahar Lal Nehru, expressed his doubt over this model and wrote, "The whole question is how to achieve this society and what its contents should be. I do not understand why a village should necessarily embody truth and non-violence. A village normally speaking, is backward intellectually and culturally and no progress can be made from a backward environment. Narrow-minded people are much more likely to be untruthful and violent."[29] Gandhi himself acknowledged the abnoxious essential realities of Indian villages. "Instead of having graceful hamlets dotting the land, we have dung heaps. The approach to many villages is not a refreshing experience. Often one would like to shut one's eyes and stuff one's nose; such is the surrounding dirt and offending smell." He further argued, "If the majority of the Congressmen were derived from our villages as they should be, they should be able to make our villages models in every sense of the word." But lamented "they have never considered it their duty to identify themselves with the villagers in their daily lives."[30] However, he was not willing to accept this state of affairs as a *fait accompli*, as an irredeemable situation. He was confident that the prevailing situation would be transformed by the villagers themselves provided proper help and guidance are extended to them.

Referring to the economic conditions of India, in a paper on 'The Human Dimensions of Economic Growth; Challenge of Stagnation in Under-Developed Countries' presented by him at the one Asia Assembly held in New Delhi in 1973, the world famous economist, Professor Gunnar Myrdal said:

> "Gandhi was certainly a planner, and a rationalistic planner but his planning was all embracing and laid main stress on sanitation and health, the raising of nutritional levels by more intensive agriculture; a redirection and not only an expression of education so that it becomes basic and not merely literacy and academic; and a redistribution of land and wealth to create greater equality."

"It is only in the latest years that we have more generally come back to Gandhi's ideas, when even some economists have been moved to press for an 'integrated planning' which is the modern term for what Gandhi was all the time teaching. My Indian friends will not be offended when I say that if Indian planning has not been more successful than it has actually been, the main explanation is that they have not kept as close as they should, to the fundamentals of the teachings of the Father of the Nation."[31]

It is heartening to note that, as the national crises has deepened, the alternative of a Gandhian solutions has been advanced as a panacea for her illnesses by Western Scholars like Professor E.F. Schumocher and Professor Gunnar Myrdal. Our planners and policy-makers should realize that urbanisation problems can not be solved through providing more of the infrastruture to the urban areas and ignoring the rural sector. The major problems of urban sector viz. problems of slums, housing, sanitation, pollution and the like are due to the ever increasing of already high pressure of population on cities. If we want to check the migration of population from rural areas to the cities, we will to provide them those jobs and other facilities in their existing homes in rural areas which they get in cities. This can be done only by moving towards Gandhi.

History has often been a relentless persecutor. Sentiments have seldom influenced its verdict. One of the basic functions of history is to teach succeeding generations the lessons it holds forth. If sentiments blind our eyes to the correct lessons from history, we will only be untrue not only to ourselves but also to the forebears and their memory and the contributions which we held as imperishable and clear. The verdict of history in this case will be but one, viz. a near total rejection of what Gandhi envisaged in the field of restructuring our economy, has resulted in a collapse of India's rural economy

Notes And References

1. Pt. Jawahar Lal Nehru moved the resolution on the socialistic pattern of the Society. Kamraj Nadar seconded it. A.M. Zaidi, and others (eds.): The Encyclopaedia of the Indian National Congress, 1955-57, Vol. 15 (New Delhi : S. Chard & Co. 1981), p. 24.
2. *Harijan*, 23.1.1939, p. 438.
3. *Ibid.*, 31.3.1946, p. 63.
4. *CWMG*, Vol. 23, p. 117.
5. J.D. Sethi, "Gandhi on Poverty and Employment," *Gandhi Marg*, August 1986, p. 263.
6. *CWMG*, Vol. 81, p. 320.
7. *Ibid.*, Vol. 85, p. 19.
8. *Ibid.*, p. 79.
9. *Harijan*, 10.11.1946, p. 394.
10. *CWMG*, Vol. 67, pp. 35-36.
11. *Ibid.*, p. 139.
12. *Ibid.*, p. 169.
13. *Harijan*, 30.7.1938, p. 200.
14. *Ibid.*, 4.8.1946, pp. 251-52.
15. Jawaharlal Nehru, Bunch of Old Letters (Bombay: Asia Publishing House), 1960, p. 506.
16. *CWMG*, Vol. 23, p. 12.
17. *Harijan*, 29.8.1936, p. 226.
18. *Ibid.*, 31.8.1934, p. 229.
19. *CWMG*, Vol. 82, p. 72.
20. M.K. Gandhi, Constructive Programme: Its Meaning and Place (Ahmedabad: Navajivan Publishing House, 1986).
21. Ashu Pasricha, Gandhian Approach to Integrated Rural Development (New Delhi: Shipra 2000), p. 77.
22. *CWMG*, Vol. 68, p. 447.
23. *Ibid.*
24. *Ibid.*, p. 447.
25. *Young India*, 21.7.1920, p. 4.
26. *Harijan*, 25.8.46, p. 281.
27. *Ibid.*, 16.5.1936, pp. 107-11.
28. *Ibid.*, 4.11.1939, p. 331.
29. Pyare Lal, The Last Phase, Vol. II (Ahmedabad: Navajivan Publishing House, 1965), p. 545.
30. M.K. Gandhi, Constructive Programme: Its Meaning and Place, *op. cit.*, p. 15.
31. *The Nagpur Times*, February 16, 1973.

7

Gandhi and the Capitalists

Economic historians find it too cumbersome a task in formulating a specific reply to the origin of the term 'Capitalism'. The popularity which it got in recent times was hardly acknowledged as such in economic theory by the classical writers. Adam Smith, the founder of modern economics was not acquainted with this term though his 'magnum opus', 'An Inquiry into the Nature and Causes of Wealth of Nations," has been considered as a foundation stone of the philosophical interpretation of capitalism. In his endeavour, he has attempted to explain burning questions such as the problems represented by the colonial regimes, the trading companies, the mercantile systems, the monetary questions and taxation, etc. In his own words, "A nation is first a workshop, where the labour of each is however diverse in character, adds to the wealth of all".[1] The father of modern economics supporting the *laissez faire,* system, with his dictum "invisible hand", seems entirely to be in favour of the private enterprise. Thus, he, either directly or indirectly, should be regarded, as a prophet of industrialism and hence capitalism.

This term is also not found in Gide, Cauwes, Marshall, Seligman or Cassel, to mention only the best known texts. In other treatises such as those of Schmoller, Adolf Wagner, Richard Ehrenburg and Philip Povich, there is some discussion on the term, but the concept is subsequently rejected.[2]

The term was first used by Karl Marx approximately during 1870's in his correspondence with his Russian followers. His references of 'bourgeoisie economy', 'Capitalist mode of production', and 'capitalist accumulation' were indicative of this system.[3] The Oxford English Dictionary, too, mentions the use of first reference to capitalism during 1854.

But it does not mean that capitalism as a system was not operative prior to this. There was capitalism even before a word was written about it. Capital accumulation has been a human tendency since time immemorial: obviously, every historic period, since man got his first tool has been capitalistic. In recorded history, there has always been merchants and traders. Vasco-de-Gama, Christopher Columbus, Sir Francis Drake are well known for their discoveries of new trade routes and civilizations. Much before this, there had been a large class of merchants and traders, which traded as far as China, India, Greece and Roman empire, to name only a few. Trade has been the source of capital accumulation in the hands of merchant class which helped to create prior conditions fruitful for the development of capitalism. The concept from its very inception has been known to be associated with system of private acquisition.

To Werner Sombart, who spent most of his time in writing on modern capitalism, the evolution of capitalism is a result of 'bourgeoisie spirit' of calculation and nationality. At different times, different economic attitudes have always reigned, and it is this spirit which has created the suitable forms for itself and thereby on economic organisations. To him pre-capitalist man was a natural man whose economic activity was based on simplicity catering for his moral wants. Capitalist system developed by the process of uprooting and dethroning of the natural system primitive and original outlook and values of life.[4]

Karl Marx analyses capitalism, not as a 'capitalistic spirit' or as a "system of production" but a 'particular mode of production in which way the means of production are owned and the resultant social relations are formed from the production process. To the owners of means of production he called bourgeoisie and those who are propertyless workers and labourers are proletariat. The propertyless wage earning class depends upon the mercy of bourgeoisie who by their continuous exploitation pile up their riches in substantial degree and finally give rise to capitalism.

Sometimes the term capitalism is made synonym with the doctrine of 'Laissez faire', 'Individualism' (the term used by Diecy) or 'Free Enterprise', where no state intervention is assumed. This view of capitalism leads us to suspicion whether such 'pure capitalism' could have ever existed. After the general depression in the 2nd quarter of the last century state regulated capitalism has become a dominant feature. Lord J.M. Keynes was propounder of the theory of state intervention to keep unemployment and over production balanced. The classical school assumed that there is a tendency for the economic system based on private property and profit motive to be self-adjusting at full employment level. Keynes challenged this assumption and attempts to show that the normal situation under *laissez faire* capitalism in its present stage of development is a fluctuating state of economic activity which may range all the way from full employment to widespread unemployment and hence state intervention is needed.[5] Thus, pure individualism is replaced by the corporate enterprise, monopoly and quasi monopoly, etc.

The beginning of capitalism in India is linked with the advent of colonial rulers and exhibited a feature almost common to all colonies. Initially, British colonial policy was to prevent any industrial development in India so as to keep away the risk of competition with the British industries. Hence, these colonies were treated by them for 'plunder and loot'. With the dawn of colonialism, the way of economic drain got enlarged. Indian basic raw materials were plundered to meet the demand of British industries and import of machine-made finished goods came to ruin the cottage industries of village economy. The policy of rulers was to make India permanent market for their industrial finished goods and a source of cheap raw material.

There appeared a change in industrial policy early in twentieth century encouraging industrial development of India.

But most of the industries were controlled by the British industrialists. Now they have started using colonies for investment of surplus capital. It gave momentum to the Indian capitalist structure. "While the Indian economy was forcibly included in the system of world capitalist economy that was taking shape, the colonial capitalist system development in close association with British capitalism and was powerfully supported by it."[6] The history of Indian capitalism thus begins with the modern cotton mills belonging to the Indian capitalists. The first cotton mill was founded by Davar in 1851 in Bombay.

If we look at the historical background, it is clear that from the very beginning, Mahatma Gandhi was in close touch with the business and trading class. He went to South Africa as a legal representative of Dada Abdulla, a proprietor of Dada Abdulla and Company which was a leading Indian firm in Durban in South Africa. Along with Dada Abdulla Seth, Tyeb Haji Kilan Muhammad was another big businessman who held the same position in Pretoria as was enjoyed by Dada Abdulla in Natal, came in contact with Gandhi. Those other Indian merchants, who came in his close contact were Parsi Rustomji and Adamji Miyakhan. Parsi Rustomji became his great supporter and supplied him the necessary funds for the hospital that was set-up and for the Pheonix Settlement. Commenting upon the merchants' support in South Africa, Gandhi said, "In South Africa, our merchants rendered valuable help in the struggle and yet because some of them weakened, the struggle was prolonged."[7]

For Satyagraha movement in South Africa, Gandhi was able to receive the financial help from the rich people of India also. Among the major donors were:

I.	Rustamji Samshedji Tata	Rs. 25,000
II.	Aga Khan collected at the All India Muslim League session	Rs. 3000
III.	J.B. Petit	Rs. 400
IV.	Nizam of Hyderabad	Rs. 2,500[8]

It is evident from the political strategy in South Africa as well as in India since 1916, Gandhi had been continuously in good relations with the merchants and business class. He succeeded in rallying a number of them around him. Addressing the businessmen of Ahmedabad on August 24, 1917, he said: "It is my view that until the business community takes change of all public movements in India, no good can be done to the country. Ahmedabad is the capital of Gujarat and wields much influence, if businessmen elsewhere starts taking livelier interest in political agitations, as you of Ahmedabad are doing, India is sure to achieve her aim."[9]

Gandhi's personal life was so simple that of an ordinary Indian peasant but his ashram being the headquarters of al social and political activities needed considerable finance. This ashram at Sabarmati was financially supported by rich merchants of Ahmedabad (though the poor had also their contributions according to their capacity but the major source of income was the donation by the rich). Admitting this in his autobiography, Gandhi records that the main purpose of opening the ashram in Gujarat was "the hope that monetary help from its citizens would be more available here than elsewhere."[10]

Most of the money for Gandhi himself and his programmes came from the rich capitalists such as Jamana Lal Bajaj, Ghanshyam Dass Birla and Ambalal Sarabhai. Once declaring about his friendship with the rich capitalists, Gandhi said, "I do count moneyed men as my best friend. I know that the critics are not wanting who consider my association with moneyed men a sign of weakness unworthy of a votary of truth and non-violence. My many friends know well the motive of my association with them. I receive money from them for my many constructive activities. My mission is to convert capitalists not into mere friends and patron of the millions of the unemployed but of willing sharer of their goods with them."[11]

A few richest capitalist developed their personal relationships with for the running of his ashram and for the implementation of constructive activities but he was consulted even on the smallest details of their personal and family life. To many he was their personal guide. G.D. Birla has written, "I was doing my best to support him with money . . . the commodity which he most lacked . . . in his struggle to help the depressed classes". Even he wrote to Gandhi by giving blank cheque. "Whenever you find any particular kind of work impeded for lack of funds, you have only to write to me."[12] On Gandhi's part "I always hesitate to approach you and your brothers for funds because whatever I ask you I get."[13]

Gandhi was mostly looked after by Birla. Even when Gandhi stayed in slum areas of Harijan quarters, Birla saw to it that he was properly housed and cared for. The Mahatma openly admitted that he had enjoyed Birla's hospitality for years. Whether he stayed at Birla's house or in the Harijan quarters, he was always Birla's guest. Perhaps that is why Sarojini Naidu once commented jocularly, "It costs a great deal of money to keep Gandhiji living in poverty".[14] Sevagram Ashram, which was taken up by G.D. Birla in 1935, he contributed at the rate of Rs. 50,000 a year for its maintenance. Besides the regular payment to Sevagram, Birla's contribution to social reforms and rural uplift work ran into millions."[15]

Birla's generosity for master's call was immediate with ready response. During the communal riots of Hindu-Muslims, Gandhi asked Birla to donate to the Aligarh Muslim University which was facing great financial hardships. Though it was impossible for Ghanshyamdas to refuse as he was in horns of a dilemma since his brothers were unwilling to help the Muslim University cause, because in their opinion it was anti-Hindu. In such a situation any donations would have created unpleasantness or family disputes. But to the devotee of Mahatma, there was no question to decline. Eventually, Birla decided to contribute Rs. 25,000 conditionally that his name should not be disclosed. Gandhi accepted it, though unusual for him to conceal any fact from the public. Four months latter, Gandhi wanted the amount of Rs. 1,00,000 for All India Deshbandhu Chitranjan Das Memorial Fund which Birla gave promptly. Once Rabindra Nath Tagore became involved in debts in maintaining the institutions of Shantiniketan and Ganshyamdas paid the amount of Rs. 60,000 at Mahatma's gesture.[16]

Jamnalal Bajaj was another prince merchant who identified himself with the Mahatma and his programmes. Soon after Gandhi came from South Africa, Jamnalal Bajaj came in direct contact with him. During the Nagpur session of Congress in 1920, Bajaj was the Chairman of Reception Committee, for the session. He went to Gandhi and said with some hesitation, "I want to ask some thing of you." Gandhi replied with some surprise, "Ask, and it shall be given, if it is at all within my power to give." "Regard me as your son Devdas," Jamnalal asked. Gandhi had positive reply, "Agreed, only I am giving nothing, you are the giver." This mutually and willingly agreed relationship between the father and the son went on increasing. Jamnalal purchased a car and kept it entirely at Gandhi's disposal.

Seth Jamnalal Bajaj spent nearly 25 lakhs of rupees for the national cause but there is no account of his unrecorded charities. Some of his important donations are given below:

I.	Gandhi Seva Sangh	Rs. 2,50,000
II.	Tilak Swaraj Fund	Rs. 2,00,000
III.	Satyagraha Ashram, Wardha	Rs. 1,00,000
IV.	All India Village Industries Association	Rs. 1,30,000
V.	Sabarmati Ashram	Rs. 35,000
VI.	Marwadi Shiksha Mandal, Wardha	Rs. 80,000
VII.	Scholarship to Muslim Students	Rs. 21,000
VIII.	Gujarat Vidyapeeth, Ahmedabad	Rs. 21,000
IX.	Marwadi Aggarwal Mahasabha	Rs. 61,000
X.	Sir Jagdish Chandra Bose Science Institute	Rs. 35,000
XI.	Benaras Hindu University	Rs. 51,000
XII.	Nagpur Flag Satyagraha	Rs. 10,000
XIII.	Gurukul Kangri	Rs. 18,000
XIV.	Nagpur Congress Session	Rs. 10,000
XV.	Rajasthan Kesari	Rs. 10,000
XVI.	Nasik Kumbha Mela Sewa Samiti	Rs. 10,000[17]

But it is difficult to assess the unrecorded amount he spent for the national movement which may certainly go in crores of rupees.

Under Gandhi's leadership, the national movement went side by side with many other activities such as constructive programmes and social reforms. And he freely used the capitalists' money for the implementation of these programmes. In his own words, "My own relations with the capitalist friends typify the attitude of the Congress towards the capitalist class. I freely accept the hospitality of the capitalist class like Birlas and make use of their money to serve the cause of the poor, but the latter do not expect anything from me. On contrary they are glad to be exploited by me in the interest of the poor. My relationship with them is ethical. I can never give up my association with the Capitalists because of fear of any body. To do so in my opinion amount to be a betrayal of the cause of the poor."[18]

The designs of the capitalists class were their own. G.D. Birla, father figure of the Indian capitalists and a great disciple of Gandhi, whose prime concern in taking part in the national freedom movement was the development of capitalism in India, clarified this stand in the third annual general meeting of the Federation of Indian Chamber of Commerce and Industry on 16th February 1930, "I am very sorry that we have not been able to influence the government or to convert them to our views, but we never anticipated that. It is impossible in the present circumstances and in the present political conditions of our country to convert the Government to our views; but I think the only solution of our present difficulties has in every businessman strengthening the hands of those who are fighting for the Swaraj of our country. . . . Swaraj is not a question of sentiments. It is a question of bread. The prosperity of the country depends entirely on the amount of political freedom which we get and I think that not only in the interest of the country but in the interest of the capitalists, the employers and the industrialists, we should try to fight and strengthen the hands of those who are fighting for Swaraj.[19]

Gandhi's friendship with the capitalists, their financial support to him and his programmes and their active participation in the freedom movement is viewed very seriously by the leftist from the very beginning. It was natural for the critics to say that such relationship with the rich capitalists and financial dependence upon them would surely be exploited by the bourgeoisie in their class interest. The Indian National Congress remained under the bourgeoisie hegemony. In the words of Bhagwan Josh, "Leading capitalists G.D. Birla and Parshotamdas Thakurdas delibrately failed the attempts of a few capitalists to form their separate party. According to them this was the surest way of getting alienated from the national movement. The strategy suggested by them was to stay with in the Congress and fight for hegemony.[20]

Communist international in its first world Congress held in September 1920 in Moscow observed that in India increasing hold of Gandhism is inimical to communism. "Tendencies like Gandhism in India thoroughly involved with religious conceptions idealize the most backward and economically most reactionary forms of social life, see the solution of the social problems not in proletarian socialism, but in reversion to these backward forms, preach passivity and repudiate the class struggle and in the process of the development of the revolution became transformed into an openly reactionary force. Gandhism is more becoming an ideology diverted against mass revolution, it must be combated by communism."[21]

Moscow took direct interest to fulfil this objective and appointed M.N. Roy to organise in India the communist movement. He found in Gandhi and his teachings an "unerring instinct for safeguarding class interests" and averted "that this strong instinct of preserving property rights above all betrays the class affiliation of Gandhi inspite of his pious outbursts against the sordid materialism of modern civilisation. His hostality to capitalist society is manifestly not revolutionary but reactionary. He believes in sanctity of private property but seeks to prevent its inevitable evolution to capitalism."[22] In July 1924, the Comintern decided to adopt M.N. Roy's advice that the Communist Party of India should be established as a branch of the Communist International. For fulfilment of these aspirations, the Bolshevik needed both, a revolutionary plan and revolutionary agents. Moscow trained Indian communists were taught that Gandhi was an agent of the British imperialists and his national Congress was a reactionary, counter-revolutionary organisation of the Indian bourgeoisie.[23] The Communist International developed in the mean time doubts about M.N. Roy's efficacy who was really finding it difficult to handle the India's nascent Communist Party from abroad. Rajani Palme Dutt, a member of Communist Party of Britain was then entrusted with the task of having organisational links between Comintern and the Communist organisation and groups in British India, who identified the leadership of Gandhi with the petty bourgeoisie elements which "wished on one hand to stand forward as a leader of the masses, but also feared to break with the propertied interests of the bourgeoisie.[25]

On Ist September 1928, at the Sixth World Congress of Comintern a resolution was passed. The Communists must unmask the national reformism of the Indian National Congress and oppose all the task of Swarajists, Gandhists, etc. 'It observed Gandhism' as the ideology which originally belong to the radical petty bourgeoisie movement which later on converted itself to the service of the big bourgeoisie.

The thesis entitled 'Platform of Action' of CPI which appeared in Pravada in 1930 said, "The policy of Gandhism on which the programme of the Congress is founded, uses a cloak of vague talk about love, meekness, modest and working existence, lightening the burden on the peasantry, national unity, the special historic mission of Hindustan, etc. But under this cloak it preaches and defends the interest of the Indian capitalists, the inevitability and the wisdom of the division of society into rich and poor eternal social inequality and exploitation".[26]

Actually the Indian communists could not observe the national reality, their opposition to national struggle under Gandhi's leadership was based on Comintern call for 'ruthless exposure of reformist leadership.' This direction from outside without understanding the national reality alienated the Communists to great extent from the masses of India. This led Chinese Communist leader Wang Ming who prepared a report on colonial countries to report in seventh World Congress of the Comintern in Moscow. "Our comrades in India have suffered a long time from "left sectarian" errors; they did not participate in all the mass demonstrations organised by the National Congress or organisations affiliated to it."[27] Then arrived Dutt-Bradley thesis following Dimitrou's dictum, in India in 1936 which called upon the CPI to rally the Congress left wing for an attack on the right wing leadership.[28] Many prominent Communist leaders joined the Congress and got top ranking status in the National Executive in 1937-38.[29] After his release from prison in 1936 M.N. Roy also said, "My message to the people is to rally in the millions under the flag of the National Congress and fight for freedom. Socialism or Communism is not the issue of the day and Communists and Socialists should realize that the immediate objective is national independence. We should realize that the National Congress is our Common platform."[30]

Thus in the last phase of the freedom struggle the attitude of Indian communists towards Indian National Congress and Mahatma Gandhi was diluted to a great extent, still here and there they went on criticising the Mahatma terming him pro-bourgeoisie and 'protector of capitalism in India'.

But Gandhi's attitude towards capitalism is as visible as sunlight. While maintaining good relations with the capitalists and heavily depending upon them for financial support he continued his attack on them. He had scarcely any soft corner for the Western capitalists system of production. For it can neither suit the Indian conditions nor the value system since it promotes acquisitiveness. It is true that capitalism has its history of success and its magical power offering panacea for the ills of under-developed poverty. He was also seriously confronted with this concerning problem of under-developed India and the increasing contrast between the affluent nations embracing industrialism and stated world of industrialized nations in which remainder mankind was struggling for hunger. Both the opposing models Capitalism (Western Free Enterprise) and Communism (State regulated system) had their own achievements and records to influence him. But he was not impressed by these models. He offered trusteeship as a relevant choice between capitalism and its inevitable throw by the proletariats.

The inherent imperfections of capitalism, its historical growth based on profit motive and exploitation which eventually led it to the highest form of exploitation known as Colonialism and Imperialism was plainly apparent to every body, Gandhi, thus comparing capitalism with his dream of perfections found its inherent contradictions as uncongenial to human progress. More apparently in Gandhi's terminology as opposed to his philosophic view of Truth and Non-violence, the system of capitalism could no longer deliver the good. Perhaps that is why he came to the conclusion, "I don't fight shy of capital. I fight capitalism."[31] He rejected it as a system and did not hesitate to call it 'satanic'.[32] His rejection is based on following grounds.

He found that advancement and success of capitalism gave new directions and channels of exploitation and dominance over under-developed nations. The Great Britain was the champion of colonial policy while other European countries such as the Dutch, the Portuguese and the French too had their colonies. India had been a victim of colonialism for more than three centuries. The Mahatma who fought tooth and nails against colonial exploitation held capitalism responsible for it. His indictment of Western civilisation simply shows his political attitude as a leader who was fighting against the so-called white man's 'civilising mission' in colonies. On sensing that the emerging elite was dazed and dazzled by the splendour of Western civilisation he openly raised his voice against it. He rather claimed the superiority of ancient Indian culture and appealed to the Indians to cling to it like a child clinging his mother. His patriotism was hurt when he found that the educated Indians, whether doctors, lawyers, teachers had become aliens to Indian culture under the influence of the West.

Capitalism as a system of production makes rich richer and poor poorer and thereby widening the gulf between sections of a society. Thus, it puts a total strain on national infrastructure. Further continuous depletion of natural resources on which the lust for capitalism stands, creates ecological and environmental imbalances. Gandhi had observed the behaviour and actions of the rich nations in their colonial ambitions and hence managed deliberately to reduce human suffering by conserving natural resources.

Gandhi also realized that capitalism in the form of imperialism is a promoter of war. Being humanist he presented an approach for the well-being all and to avoid the humanity from war and destruction. He found that under capitalism, tendency for profit maximization has been the major characteristic of the capitalists. The history of world wars testifies this fact. When Britain had monopoly as a leading industrialist in the world, the challenge put forth by Germany to its capitalist dominance aggravated antagonism between the two and eventually became the decisive factor which led to the first world war. He wanted to create such conditions which result in building of such an atmosphere or world order that is free of tension and war. In this direction he was fully acquainted with the fact that it is needed to transform man from ignorance and untruth.

But trusteeship is viewed in certain quarters as a cover to the capitalists. They quote the clause one of the trusteeship formula in defence of their view point. According to this clause, "Trusteeship provides a mean of transforming the present capitalist order of society into an egalitarian one. It gives no quarter to capitalism, but gives the present owning class a chance of reforming itself. It is based on the faith that human nature is never beyond redemption."[33] Though Gandhi has made it specifically clear here that trusteeship gives no quarter to capitalism, yet he is giving one more chance to capitalists to reform themselves. It is crystal clear that they are not going to reform themselves. No capitalist will surrender his property willingly Jamnalal Bajaj and G.D. Birla these two devoted disciples of the Mahatma could not transfer their property to a trust. Whenever trusteeship has been used by any capitalist, it has been used to maintain control over the property. Thus why to give a chance to man about whom our past experience is not good. There is every likelihood that he will utilise this 'chance' to maintain *status quo*. Thus to some of the leftists, Gandhi is protecting the capitalist through his trusteeship.

But their fear is groundless. A mere look at the other sentence of the same clause and other clauses of the trusteeship formula is sufficient to prove them wrong. He has made it emphatically clear in the first point that trusteeship is a method of transforming the present capitalist order of society into an egalitarian one. There is no room for capitalism in it. He just wants to give the capitalist one more 'chance' to reform themselves believing that human nature is never beyond redemption.

In the second point of the formula, Gandhi "does not recognise any right of ownership of private property except so far as it may be permitted by society for its own welfare "and further he is not excluding 'state' legislative regulations of ownership and the use of wealth. Again, 'an individual will not be free to hold or use his wealth for selfish satisfaction or in disregard of the interest of society'. Gandhi has gone to the extent of fixing a decent maximum income which a person can get. In his own words, "Just as it is proposed to fix a decent minimum living wage even so a limit should be fixed for a maximum income that could be allowed to any person in the society. The difference between such minimum and maximum income should be reasonable and equitable and variable from time to time so much that the tendency would be towards obliteration of the difference."[34] Even the Communist countries in the world could not fix a maximum income for their citizens, though the minimum income has been fixed. Party bosses, military officials and bureaucrats appropriate more than their share in national income in such countries. It would be "no exaggeration to say that Mahatma Gandhi was more radical revolutionary than Lenin and Mao-Tse-Tung of China. Gandhism seeks to combine Lincoln's love for liberty and Lenin's urge for equality without resorting to the barel of a gun."[35]

Another minor point raised by the leftists is that the Mahatma was against Communism. Giving more than due emphasis to some of Gandhi's utterances here and there they conclude that since he was against communism, it means that he was in favour of capitalism. There is no denying of the fact that whenever Gandhi get an opportunity he criticised communism. He was hostile to the techniques of Communism. He was thoroughly dissatisfied by its association with atheism and violence. As early as March 30, 1919, he had said in a speech in Madras, 'Bolshevism' is the necessary result of modern materialistic civilization. Its insensate worship of matter has given rise to a school which has been brought up to look upon materialistic advancement as the goal and which has lost all touch with the final things in life."[36] In this speech he pointed out that while self-restraint was the Satyagraha creed, Communism stood for self-indulgence. He warned that if the quest of spirit and love yielded to matter and brute force "we shall have Bolshevism rampant in this land which was once so holy". In an article entitled 'My Path' in the *Young India* he wrote: "I am yet ignorant of what exactly Bolshevism is. I have not been able to study it. I do not know whether it is for the good of Russia in the long-run. But I do know that in so far as it is based on violence and denial of God, it repels me. I do not believe in short violent cuts to success. Those Bolshevik friends who are bestowing their attention on me should realize that, however much I may sympathize with and admire worthy motives, I am an uncompromising opponent of violent methods even to serve the noblest of causes. There is, therefore, really no meeting ground between the school of violence and me."[37]

Though he was against Communism, it does not mean that he was in favour of capitalism. The principle of 'enemy's enemy my friend does not work here'. He criticized both communism as well as capitalism in the strongest terms. He had no admiration for the capitalistic economic system, and he passionately desired to change it. Poverty and Unemployment of the vast masses of India were the constant themes of his speeches and writings. He had constantly appealed to the rich to renounce the privileges of property and ownership. He had even asked the Indian princes to wash-off the sin of their 'gigantic autocracy' and to divest themselves of powers "which no human acting conscious of his dignity should possess". He always claimed to be the champion of the Daridranarayan. At the Round Table Conference, he said, "The Congress represent in its essence the dumb and the semi-starved millions scattered over the length and breadth of the land in its seven lakh villages. Every interest which is worthy of protection has to subserve to this interest and if there is genuine and real clash, I have no hesitation in saying that the will sacrifice every interest for the sake of the interest of the dumb millions".[38]

Economic equality is one of the items of his constructive programme. R.H. Tawney's description of the capitalist society as the 'religion of inequality',[39] has any meaning, Gandhi can not be regarded as its upholder. Writing about his constructive programme he made it clear that 'The whole of this programme will however be a structure on sand if it is not built on the solid foundation of economic equality.' The All India Spinners' Association (AISA) and All India Village Industries' Association (AIVIA) these voluntary associations started by him run their respective industries on a non-profit basis. That unlike a capitalist he is guided on price policies not by consideration of larger consumption and higher profits but soley by the principle of decent living condition for the producers becomes evident from his insistence on the minimum wages for spinners in the AISA, in total disregard of its effect on the sale of Khaddar. In his propagation of Khaddar he has courageously resisted the acme of capitalist wisdom of 'buying the cheapest and selling the dearest'. Anyone with respect for the capitalist norms of economic property and wisdom would not have dared to recommend to India so doggedly the adoption of the Charkha—perhaps the fittest emblem of uneconomic technique.

The capitalists who surrounded Gandhi may be having their own axe to grind. They might have taken advantage of their proximity to Gandhi but to conclude that Gandhi allowed them to take advantage of his position is a sin and entirely baseless. Rather his impact on the capitalists brought some of them in the national mainstream for active participation in the freedom movement.

Under Gandhi's influence Jamnalal Bajaj played a significant role in freedom struggle. Like true trustee of Gandhi's conception, he adopted honesty and fair practices in business dealings. He lived a very simple life and did not enjoy the luxuries like other capitalists. On Gandhi's little call he invested for the nation's cause as he could. Also he took his advice on economic matters and tried to run his industries on Gandhian pattern. Another top capitalist G.D. Birla saw in Gandhi the best political leader and religious man whose ideals and conduct impressed him and brought him closer to Gandhi. But like Bajaj one can not find in Birla complete integration of Gandhian values.

Under the first phase of his political strategy, he gave dignified place to the capitalists because of the fact that his main aim was to fight the Britishers. His ashram being the centre of all political and social activities needed considerable finance which was met by the capitalists. Thus along with using their money, he also gave them the chance to reform themselves and utilize their experience and talent for the nation's cause.

Truly one can not fight too many enemies at a time. Strategy needs to be chalked out on the basis of preferences. Gandhi was lucid in his preferential approach. At such a stage when he needed rich people in his fight against Britishers, he never risked to loose the landlords and capitalists. While the interest of the moneyed men was with the stability of the British rule, yet it was the subtile leadership of the Mahatma, who brought them under his umbrella.

Under the second phase of his strategy, capitalism as such (exploitators) would not have any place. Acceptance of Gandhian ideology would have made them 'trustees'. The transformation of capitalists, as visualised by Gandhi was itself a unique formula in the restoration of socio-economic order. Though this approach is dynamic and revolutionary but its beauty consists in its non-violent creed. Truth being preserved at each stage in its evolutionary as well as revolutionary process would have given a great solace to Gandhian credentials. If not by methods of appeal conversion and education, Gandhi would have come open against the bourgeoisie but after attaining the freedom. In a letter to Jawaharlal Nehru, he admitted "I am quite of your opinion that some day we shall have to start an intensive movement without the rich people and without the vocal educated class. But that time is not yet."[40]

Gandhi was however, no mere a thinker or a visionary who made castles in the air, but being a practical idealist he knew the fact that no man is at all perfect. Everyone is a mixture of good and bad. For the creation of better society, it needed to transform man from ignorance and untruth. His scheme tolerated capitalists on the ground that gradual transformation may bring about desired results but he vehemently opposed the system of capitalism. In his own words, "I have no absolute design on capitalists. I can have none as I do not believe in violence. But I do want cleanliness in capitalism as well as in labour. And I shall certainly resist capitalism being used to exploit the resources of the country for the use of "few by the foreigners or home born."[41]

In context of the nature of Indian capitalists and their role in freedom movement, the Mahatma presented a pragmatic approach. He also felt that exploitation of the poor can be curbed not by killing a few millionaires but he taught the poor working class the art of non-cooperation with their exploiters.

In the end a few words about the allegation, that he allowed some of the capitalists to take advantage of his position. It is an admitted fact that 'financial dependence is the worst type of dependence'. But to conclude on this basis that in lieu of this financial dependence Gandhi allowed the capitalists to exploit the situation is totally baseless. He did not allow any one to take undue advantage of the situation. We all know the fate of his own sons and other members of his own family. A man who has not allowed any of his family member any advantage of his position would allow other capitalists to take advantage of his position is an allegation which does not need any proof to be rejected straight forwardly. He himself did not take any advantage of his own position. Had he wished to become the Prime Minister or the President of the country after her independence in 1947, it would have been a cake walk for him. His was the most legitimate claim. There was nothing unusual in making such a claim. For architects of all great nations accepted the prized offices soon after they were victorious. This is very true of those leaders who led a successful revolution and established powerful regimes in their countries. But Gandhi is unique amongst all builders of nation. He never thought of accepting any office anywhere.[42]

Notes and References

1. Adam Smith, An Inquiry into the Nature and Causes of Wealth of Nations (New York: The Modern Library, 1937), pp. 13-14.
2. R.A. Edwin Seligman (ed.), Encyclopaedia of the Social Sciences, Vol. III (New York: The Macmillan Company, 1951), p. 195.
3. Karl Marx, Capital, Vol. I (Moscow: Progress Publishers, 1977).
4. Encyclopaedia of Social Sciences, *op. cit.*, pp. 189-208.
5. John Maynard Keynes, The General Theory of Employment, Interest and Money (New York: Harcourt Brace & Company, 1964), pp. 4-22.
6. V.I. Paulov, The Indian Capitalist Class (Delhi: People Publishing House, 1964), p. 179.
7. *CWMG*, Vol. XIII, p. 254.
8. E.M.S. Namboodripad, The Mahatma and the Ism (New Delhi: People Publishing House, 1958), p. 8.
9. *CWMG*, Vol. X111, p. 510.
10. M.K. Gandhi, An Autobiography or The Story of My Experiments with Truth, *op. cit.*, p. 46.
11. M.K. Gandhi, Capital and Labour (Bombay: Bhartiya Vidya Bhawan, 1970), p. 77.
12. G.D. Birla, In the Shadow of the Mahatma (Bombay: Vakils, Fetter of Simons Pvt. Ltd.), pp. 23, 32.
13. *Ibid.*, p. 34.
14. Quoted in Ved Mehta, Gandhi and His Apostles (New York: Andre Dutsch Ltd., 1977), p. 56.
15. Atulandanda, Chakrabarti, The Mahatma and His Men, G.D. Birla (New Delhi, Rupa and Co., 1968), p. 23.
16. P.C. Ghosh, Mahatma Gandhi: As I saw Him (Delhi: Chand, 1968).
17. T.V. Pavate, Jamnalal Bajaj: A Brief Study on his Life and Character (Ahmedabad: Navajivan Publishing House, 1962), p. 135.
18. M.K. Gandhi, Capital and Labour, *op. cit.*, p. 80.
19. Report of the proceedings of the Annual General Meeting of the FICCI, Vol. III, Third Annual Meeting, 1930, pp. 264-65.

20. Bhagwan Josh, Congress and Politics of the Capitalist Class: Party, Class and Nations, (Unpublished).
National bourgeoisie, specifically the capitalist class was one of the classes involved in all class anti-imperialist movement. They (industrialists, traders and merchants supported the national movement at a large scale. Aditya Mukherjee, Indian Capitalist Class and Congress on National Planning and Public Sector), 1930-47.
21. M.R. Masani, The Communist Party of India: A Short Story (Bombay: Bhartiya Vidya Bhawan, 1967), p. 16.
22. M.N. Roy, India in Transition (Bombay: Nachiketa, 1971), p. 236.
23. V.B. Sinha, The Red Rebel in India (New Delhi: Associated Publishing House, 1968), p. 15.
24. R.P. Dutt, Modern India (London, 1927).
25. Degras Jane, The Communist International Documents, 1919-43, Vol. II, London, 1971, p. 541.
26. *The Communist International,* Vol. VIII, No. 20.
27. Wang Ming, The Revolutionary, Movement in Colonial Countries (New York: Workers' Library Publishers, 1935), p. 64.
28. Rajni Rekme Dutt and Ben Bradley, "The Anti-Imperialist People's Front", INPRECORR (Vol. XVI, February 29, 1936), pp. 297-300.
29. Rajani Palme Dutt, *India Today* (Bombay: People's Publishing House, 1949), p. 397.
30. *The Tribune,* Lahore, November 23, 1936.
31. *Young India,* 7-10-1926, p. 348.
32. M.K. Gandhi, *Hind Swaraj, op. cit.,* p. 37.
33. *Harijan,* 25-10-1952.
34. *Ibid.*
35. Ganesh D. Gadre, "Trusteeship" in S.C. Biswas (ed.) Gandhi, Theory and Practice: Social Impact and Contemporary Relevance (Shimla: IIAS, 1969), p. 123.
36. *CWMG,* Vol. XV, p. 168.
37. *Young India,* 11.12.1024, p. 406.
38. *CWMG,* Vol. XLVIII, pp. 355-69.
39. R.H. Tawney, Equality (London: George Allen & Unwin Ltd., 1952), p. 19.
40. G.D. Tendulkar, Mahatma, Vol. VIII (New Delhi: Publication Division, Ministry of Information and Broadcasting, Government of India, 1969), p. 291.
41. *Young India,* 23.2.1922.
42. Jai Narain, Gandhi's View of Political Power (New Delhi: Deep & Deep, 1987), p. 150.

8

Gandhism, Communism and Socialism

Society is a moving phenomenon. It holds a changing scene, and presents a human drama enacted continuously. Master minds are busy in understanding the logic of this social drama. Often an endeavour is made to create a science of society. Natural science has indeed succeeded in establishing the lawfulness of natural phenomenon. The stage is set for a similar exercise in the study of society. And we now have the social dynamics. Society is a dynamic phenomenon, with growth and change as its basic characteristics. This change is often non-smooth. Differences and disputes, clashes and conflicts punctuate the process. Sometimes battles are fought, wars are waged.

At any point of time inequalities do exist in any society. They may refer to property, power, status, race, educational attainment or mere physical strength. With the passage of time development of science and technology tend to perpetuate, even accentuate, these inequalities. This is so for, the simple reason that fruits of development and accruing benefits remain confine to those who already hold the position and enjoy the privileges.

With inequalities going deeper and getting harder, the social structure groans under strain and tension. Solution is sought either through peaceful reforms and/or violent revolutions. Society moves on evolving a new structure relevant to the new needs. Master minds are busy in examining this process, are busy in exploring the laws of social change and are busy in providing models that ensure order and progress, stability and change. Marx and Gandhi were such master minds.

"Gandhi has often claimed in the course of his discussion with communist and socialist friends that he is a better communist or socialist than they. Their goal is identical."[1] Writing the introduction of K.G. Mashruwala's famous work 'Gandhi and Marx', Vinoba Bhave has used the words, 'Two Mothers' for Gandhism and Marxism as both of them regard the well-being of the poor and the oppressed with the intensely loving regard of the mother."[2]

The Mahatma himself admitted at one place "What does Communism mean in the last analysis? It means a classless society—an ideal that is worth striving for. Only I part with it when force is called to aid for achieving it."[3] Perhaps that is why it is often said that 'Gandhism is Communism minus violence.' Before commenting on this let us first of all see what are the similarities and dissimilarities between Gandhism and Communism.

The common point between Gandhi and Marx is the extreme concern of both for the suppressed and the oppressed, the resourceless and the ignorant, the dumb and starving sections of the society. They form the major part of the world. And their condition is wretched in this world which is abundantly full and capable of providing a larger measure of happiness to each and every one. Both want to establish an order, which would make these masses co-sharers in the gift of nature and fruits of human labour and genius.

Both Gandhi and Marx believed in and understood the power of awakened masses. Marx's belief that, theory becomes a material force as soon as it has gripped the masses, led him to place the highest emphasis on organizing the masses and energising them with correct theory. He never wavered in his belief that the emancipation of the masses was the work of the masses themselves. In his own words: "Human emancipation will only be complete when the real, individual man has absorbed into himself in the abstract citizen; when as an individual man in his every day life, in his relationships, he has become a specific being; and when he has recognized and organised his powers as social power so that he no longer separates this social power from himself as a political power."[4]

Gandhi was able to accomplish his great task of leading the people of India to freedom from foreign rule because he understood the masses and was extremely adroit in organising them, and rousing their enthusiasm and energy for the task of national liberation. The real seat of power is the people. If the individuals recognise the power in their hands and use it constructively to secure the social good (Sarvodaya) or to engage in Satyagraha against the unjust laws and the repressive measures of the state, the monopolisitc effectiveness of the state power would be reduced. The mightiest government can be rendered absolutely impotent if the people realizing their power use it in a disciplined manner for the common good.

The glaring economic inequalities of the society leading to the concentration of capital in the hands of a few evoked condemnation of both Marx and Gandhi. According to Marx, the existence of equality is naturally bound up with the true application of the rule: 'He who shall work, shall eat.' In the words of Frank Thakurdas, "Marx's sovereign concept, as we all knew, was of economic equality; his life and writings are a glorious epitaph on that; for after all it is economic injustice and economic exploitations that have characterised the whole course of human history".[5]

The state of inequality was morally degrading and economically untenable for Gandhi also. In an article, 'Gandhiji's Communism', Pyare Lal beautifully depicts, Gandhi's state of mind, "Economic equality of his conception did not mean that everyone would literally have the same amount. It simply meant that everybody should have enough for his or her needs. For instance, he required two shawls in winter whereas his grandnephew Kanu Gandhi who stayed with him did not require any warm cloth whatsoever. He required goat's milk, oranges and other fruits. Kanu could do with ordinary food. He envied Kanu but there was no point in it. Kanu was a young man whereas he was an old man of 76.

The monthly expenditure of his food was far more than that of Kanu but that did not mean that there was economic inequality between them. The elephant needs a thousand times more food than the ant, but that is not an indication of inequality. So the real meaning of economic equality was: "To each according to his need." That was the definition of Marx. If a single man demanded as much as a man with wife and four children that would be a violation of economic equality.

"Let no one try to justify the glaring difference between the classes and the masses, the prince and the pauper, by saying that the former needs more. That will be idle sophistry and a travesty of my argument," he continued. "The contrast between the rich and the poor is a painful sight."[6]

And equality according to Marx, comes to prevail when classless society is established after the successful results of the revolution. All kinds of equality—social, economic, legal and political—merge so as to prove that what we know by the name of equality is possible only after the liquidation of class antagonisms. All persons engaged in work, whether mental or physical, belong to the class of the toilers and intelligentsia that shows the existence of a new kind of collective life. "The organic unification in one classless collective of all workers will be a society of peaceful creative labour, equality and the happiness of all the people. This will be a society where, the first time in history, the personality of each worker will attain a full, general and perfect development."[7]

Marxist notion of equality assumes a humanistic form in the final stage of social development. That is, the existence of equality will emerge with the prevalence of 'glorious human values'. When the state withers away people lead a life of perfect co-operation. It is in such an ideal state that Rousseau's concept of moral equality shall prevail. Here proletariat will ultimately abolish its own supremacy as a class, and society would represent not as a group of mutually antagonistic classes but an association in which the free development of each should be the condition for the free development of all. When in the course of development class distinctions have disappeared and all production has been concentrated in the hands of a vast associations of the whole nation, the state will loose its political character and will wither away as there are no capitalists now whose interest it had been serving all through. In the words of Engels, "It will be sent to the museum of antiquities and will be placed side by side with the spinning-jenny and Bronze axe. A classless society based upon the doctrine from each according to his ability and to every one according to his needs will come into existence."[8]

Similarly, Gandhi's ultimate ideal was also stateless society whom he termed "Ramrajya or the kingdom of God on Earth." He further stressed, "I do not know what it will be like in heaven. I have no desire to know the distant scene. If the present is attractive enough, the future can not be very unlike."

"In concrete terms, then the independence should be political, economic and moral 'Political' necessarily means the removal of the control of the British army in every shape and form. 'Economic' means entire freedom from the British capitalists and capital, as also their Indian counterpart. In other words, the humblest must feel equal to the tallest. This can take place only by capital or the capitalists sharing their skill and capital with the lowliest and the least. 'Moral' means freedom from armed defence forces. My conception of Ramrajya excludes replacement of the British army by a national army of occupation. A country that is governed by even its national army can never be morally free and therefore, its so-called weakest member can never rise to his full moral heights.[9] At another place, he made it emphatically clear, "By Ramrajya I do not mean Hindu Raj. I mean by Ramrajya, Divine Raj, the kingdom of God. For me Ram and Rahim are one and the same deity. I acknowledge no other God but one God of truth and righteousness. Whether Rama of my imagination ever lived or not on this earth, the ancient ideal of Ramrajya is undoubtedly one of true democracy in which the meanest citizens would be sure of swift justice without an elaborate and costly procedure. Even the dog is described by the poet to have received justice under Ramrajya."[10]

Gandhi's ideal of stateless society brings him close to Marxian philosophy where ultimate ideal is also the establishment of stateless and classless society. Another similarity between Gandhi and Marx is that both were scientists. The scientific temper of Gandhi is brought out clearly in his autobiography, which he appropriately called 'My Experiments with Truth'. Throughout his life, he was conducting experiments of various kinds—experiments in food, in medicine, in living, in political action, in education and so on. His contribution in economies such as his demonstrations of the impossibility of solving any of man's problems through industrialization and his concept of trusteeship are all significant scientific contributions.

Marx, too was a great scientist. Engels called him the greatest living thinker. His scientific contributions have discovered the law of development of human history and the special law of motion governing the present day capitalist mode of production and the bourgeoisie society that this mode of production has created.[11] Paul Lafargue, Marx's son-in-law, has recorded, "Marx held the view that science must be pursued for itself, irrespective of the eventual results of research, but at the same time a scientist could only debase himself by giving up active participation in public life ... and holding aloof from the life and political struggles of his contemporaries." Marx used to say, "Those who have the good fortune to be able to devote themselves to scientific pursuits must be the first to place their knowledge at the service of humanity."[12]

Both Gandhi and Marx had no use for theory unrelated to practice. They both were interested in theory only if it served a practical purpose. In his 'Theses on Feuerbach' Karl Marx had argued, "Philosophers have interpreted the word in a various ways, the point, however is to change it."[13] Marx was a voracious reader. He was always plunged in a sea of books. Gandhi had not read very much as he inform us in his autobiography".[14] He heard of Freud only towards the ends of his life and read 'Das Capital' only in his 75th year. It is unlikely that Gandhi constantly immersed in the thick of political activities had the time necessary to devote to a proper study of this book. He certainly does not discuss at any length Marx's Theories in his writings. His trusteeship concept and his attitude towards capitalists would have been substantially modified if he had recognised the role of man's objective environment in moulding his character, views and attitudes. On the other hand, the insight that only a changed individual can change society is an insight that Gandhi shared with Marx, but an insight that the followers of both have often neglected.

Both Gandhi and Marx took the attitude that their own writings were subservient to their political practice, and were stimulated to fresh theoretical practices by the onrush of events and problems. They were not inclined to rest on their scholarly laurels. When some one suggested to Gandhi that he should mouth his ideas in a systematic and formal treatise, Gandhi answered, "For one thing, I have no time, for another, I am still experimenting. Hence, let the treatise develop slowly by itself if it does at all."[15] In a like situation Marx's response was strikingly similar. Three years before his death when he received inquiries regarding the eventual publication of his completed works, Marx replied dryly, 'They first would have to be written.'[16]

Gandhi and Marx distrusted the capitalist system. Gandhi took a somewhat unhistorical view and condemned 'modern civilisation'. Marx, on the other hand, felt confident that the capitalist society will be over thrown and replaced by a socialist state, committed to the harmonious development of human being, after an interim dictatorship of the proletariat. Both of them took a dim view of the impact of machinery on man. But the Mahatma attributed it to mechanisation as such, Marx blamed capitalist society for this adverse impact it had on human beings.

In 'Das Capital', Marx makes several references to the unfavourable impact that machinery has on labour in a capitalist society. "The character of independence and estrangement which the capitalist mode of production as a whole gives to the instruments of labour and to the product as against the workmen is developed by means of machinery into a thorough antagonism. Therefore, it is with the advent of machinery that the workman for the first time brutally revolts against the instruments of labour."[17] Marx's major complaint against capitalism is that it cripples the labour. In his early writings, he argued. "It is true that labour produces wonderful things for the rich, but for the weaker it produces privation. It produces palaces, but for the workers hovels. It produces beauty, but for the worker deformity. It replaces labour by machines, but some of the workers it throws back to a barbarous type of labour, and the other workers it turns into machines. It produces intelligence, but for the workers' idiosyncrasies."[18]

In the socialist society which Marx believed would be established by the forceful overthrow of capitalism, the labourer would come into his own and socialism would ensure the equality of all. Marx felt strongly on the subject of exploited labour and passionately desired their emancipation, and coming into being of a socialist society. Gandhi too, desired socialism and was opposed to private property, but hoped that rich could be persuaded to voluntarily place their wealth at the disposal of society. Gandhi feared that too much concentration of political power in the hands of the state would be detrimental to human freedom. But he was very serious about the establishment of socialism in India. On the eve of the independence he said, "I shall work for an India in which the poorest shall feel that it is their country in whose making they have an effective voice, an India in which there shall be no high class and low class people, an India in which all communities shall live in perfect harmony."[19]

Thus, it is true that there are certain common points between Gandhi's and Marxism. But their differences are nevertheless fundamental. The fact of the matter is that these too ideologies are irreconcilable.

VIOLENCE *vs.* NON-VIOLENCE

When it is said that Gandhism is communism minus violence, the impression created is that the 'minus violence' factor in communism is some small impurity, the removal of which will make it the same as Gandhism. In the words of K.G. Mashruwala, "As a matter of fact, even if it were possible to so equate Gandhism in terms of Communism, the minus violence factor is a major factor of considerable value. The implications of minor violence are so great as to make the equation as illusory as to say that red is green minus yellow and blue, or a worm is a snake minus poison."[20]

When Vinoba was once told that Gandhism differed from communism only in its strict emphasis on non-violence, he reacted, "Two persons were so physically alike that one could have well served as the double of the other in a political fraud. But there was a slight difference. One breathed, the other did not. The result was that a dinner was being prepared for one and a coffin for the other. The likeness between these two ideologies bereft to the above pair of doubles."[21]

Gandhi's greatness as a leader and thinker lay in his transformation of the individualistic message of non-violence into a successful technique for direct mass action. He always insisted upon adherence to truth and non-violence for achieving the end Marx does not care, about the quality of the means, provided they appear efficient enough for achieving the end as quickly as possible. The Mahatma always pleaded for the purity of means and did not accept the statement that 'end justifies the means', rather he advocated 'means justify the end.'[22] Ends and Means are convertible terms. The two are inseparable. The purity of one affects the purity of the other. Criticising those who do not give due importance to means, he said, "They say 'means are after all means'. I would say means are after all every thing. As the means are so the end. Violent means will give violent Swaraj. That would be a menace to the world and to India herself.....There is no wall of separation between means and end. Indeed, the creator has given us control (and that too, very limited), over means, none over the end. Realisation of the goal is in exact proportion to that of means. This is a proposition that admits of no exception. Holding such a belief, I have been endeavouring to keep the country to means that are purely peaceful and legitimate."[23]

The problem of means and end according to Marx, is a scientific problem. He regards ethics and politics, as applied sciences.[24] Of course in his early writings, he appears to hold that ethico-social discipline is a philosophical speculation "about the material condition of life rather than a science of society."[25] But later on he changed his views. From the year 1848 he stopped talking in terms of human nature, man in general, etc. These concepts are empty concepts according to him. They exist only in the misery realm of philosophical fantasy.[26]

Marx has no love for non-violence as a means. He accepts the maxim that 'end Justifies the end'. Violence is justified according to him, if, it helps in realizing the ideal. He held the history of all hitherto existing society as the history of struggles. Freeman and slave, patrician and plebeian, lord and serf, guild master and journey man, in a word, oppressor and oppressed, stood opposition to one another, carried on an uninterrupted, now hidden now open fight, a fight that each time ended, either in a revolutionary reconstitution of society at large, or in the common ruin of the contending classes.[27] Throughout the ages, the working class people, whether slaves, peasants or industrial workers, have been brutally exploited by the ruling classes. So it is natural that they struggle against oppression and strive for a fire and happy life. If for such an end they adopt violent means they can not be condemned.

Marx is of the opinion that without class struggle, there will be no social progress. The developmental progress of society is usually faster, if the struggle of the exploited against the exploiters is mere stubborn and organized. Therefore, the exploited has got the moral right to decide what type of means, he will use for realizing his objective quickly. Thus, Marx accords moral sanction to the adoption of any kind of means. If it is only through a violent means that the objective is achieved and achieved quickly, the adoption of such a means is morally justified. Further clarifying the Marxian stand on this issue V I. Lenin emphasizes, "If it is necessary to use any rude, cunning, unlawful method, evasions, concealment of truth, one should."[28]

Marxism does not advocate violence for its own sake. Claim some of its followers. In a letter to Gorky, Lenin has also written, "Opposition to all violence is our ultimate ideal—it is hellishly hard task."[29] They believe that violence is thrust upon the oppressed by the ruling class, and the majority of the population as a measure of self-defence and of vindicating the ethical ideal of non-exploitation represented by communism takes resort to just and necessary violence. The extent of violence which must be employed is a matter that depends on the intensity of the resistance which is countenanced. Gandhi, on the other hand, urges that all types of violence is an evil and therefore to be eschewed. Thus, Gandhi and Marx are diametrically opposed to each other with regard to the selection of means for the realization of the end.

SPIRIT *vs.* MATTER

The cornerstone of Gandhian philosophy is the supremacy of spirit over matter. Gandhi starts with the premise of an omnipotent and all pervading spiritual power which can be called by many names, Brahm or God or Truth. The existence of God or the supreme reality cannot be proved through the evidence of the senses. It is self-evident and can be realised only through inner experience of man. Man can have a revelation of the spiritual power intimately by a process of ethical discipline and thereby purifying one's heart through a life of truth and non-violence. It is only through renunciation of the luxuries of life and ridding oneself of the life of indulgence and sensate values that man can reach nearer God or the supreme reality.

Gandhi is over-confident about the presence of spirit in man. This consciousness of the presence of the spiritual power in man has induced Gandhi to believe in the basic goodness of man and to believe in the unity of all souls. For him, 'Whatever happens to one body must affect the whole of matter and the whole of spirit'.[30] For the spirit manifests in all life. "If one gains spiritually, the whole world gain with him, and if one falls, the whole world falls to that extent." Naturally for him, dealing of man with man is judged with spiritual considerations. "To me God is truth and love, God is ethics and morality; God is fearlessness. God is the source of light and life and yet he is above and beyond all these. God is conscience. He is even the atheism of the atheist. For in His boundless love God permits the atheist to live. He is the searcher of hearts. He transcends speech and reason. He knows us and our hearts better than we do ourselves. He does not take us at our word, for He knows that we often do not mean it, some knowingly and other unknowingly."[31] For, Gandhi's spiritualism has an inherent potency to combine the spirit of the Sermon on the Mount, Gautama Buddha's compassion, the Hindu concept of love and the Islam obedience to the will of God.

Viewed from the Marxian point of view, Gandhi's conception of spirit can not be appreciated at all. He on the other hand considers matter to be the ultimate reality and spirit only a reflex of matter. To him, "The more careful a man becomes about values, the more valueless, the more unworthy he becomes."[32] He maintains that one should not sink himself in the imagination of spirit. Rather one should be aware of one's flesh. "Although we should possess spirit, spirit should not possess us . . . only by being aware of his flesh is man fully aware of himself and only by being aware of himself, is he aware or rational."[33]

Marx is essentially a philosopher of matter and he has fused the materialistic traditions of Democritus, Hobbes, Descartes and Spinoza, with the dialetics of Hegelian idealistic philosophy. In Marx, the concept of matter is an all embracing concept, which includes not merely separate objects or processes or phenomena, but all objective reality. Lenin defining the concept of matter wrote: "Matter is a philosophical concept denoting the objective reality which is given to man by his sensation and which is copied, photographed, and reflected by our sensations."[34]

Marxian view of matter is not static, but dynamic. To them matter exists only in motion through which it manifests or reveals itself. All bodies starting with the atoms in the molecules to the whole man of cosmic and territorial bodies are in continuous motion. Likewise living organism and social life are in a state of flux. It is impossible to find a single particle in the world of matter which is in a state of eternal rest. It is for this reason that Marx regards life, consciousness and even social life as "higher form of motion of matter." Marx appears to be confident of the view that the forms of motion of matter are 'interconnected' and inseparable. Their unity and interconnection is based on the material unity of the world. If appropriate conditions are provided one form of motion can be converted into other.

Marx's concept of matter and motion apparently, is found to be strong metaphysical, basis for all his ideologies in the field of economics, politics and ethics. Gandhi takes the help of spirit in explaining and defending his ideologies. Thus on this aspect also they have taken the opposite stands.

The Concept of Human Nature

Every thinker who theorises upon the problem of social reconstruction and government is guided by certain preconceived assumptions regarding human nature. If he assumes human nature to be utterly selfish, wicked then he glorifies the role of state. But if the human being is considered to be wholly good and peaceful, in that case the state becomes unnecessary and the ultimate goal of a stateless society is envisaged. Marxists do not fall into either of the two categories, since they believe that human nature is a social construct and man the product of his environment. Consequently, he acts and thinks in accordance with its laws. Any change in human nature can only be possible by effecting a corresponding change in man's environment. Gandhi on the other hand repudiates both the assumptions pertaining to human nature, regarding him wicked on one hand and the product of social construct on the other. To Gandhi man is basically good, since he is a part of divinity. The ideal man, according to Gandhi, is the non-attached man, who is full of qualities of truth and non-violence, renunciation and self-sacrifice and that these virtues can be cultivated and men initiated into moral excellence till a stage comes when life becomes regulated and the need for Government is felt no more.

Thrust of Human History

To the Mahatma, history meant gradual unfolding of the spirit of love and non-violence resulting in an increasing awareness of universal brotherhood. He discarded the mercantalistic interpretation of history as given by Marx. Marx had believed that man was dominated by considerations of economic self-interests. According to him the ultimate causes of social changes and political revolutions are to be sought not in the minds of men, in their increasing insight into eternal truth, but in the changes in the modes of production and exchange, they are to be sought not in the philosophy but in the economics of the period concerned. "Social relations are closely bound with productive forces. In acquiring new productive forces, men changes their modes of production, they change all their social relations. The hand mill gives you society with a feudal lord, the steam mill society with the industrial capitalist."[35]

The whole universe and all the things in the history are explicable in purely materialistic terms and are rooted in the economic process. According to Marx the course of history is determined by the actions of groups not by individuals, and the only meaningful groups are those based on the modes of production which are termed as 'classes' in the Marxian language. In every society there have been two main classes having diametrically opposed interests. The history of hitherto existing society is the history of class struggle. The final phase according to him, is the impending struggle between the bourgeoisie and the proletariat. Marx distinguishes five economic systems or modes of production—primitive, communal, slave feudal, capitalist and socialist. Under the first means of production are owned by the society, under the second slave owner own them, under the third they are owned partially by the feudal lord, under the fourth the capitalist owns the means of production and the workers are compelled to work for him, under the fifth the workers themselves will own the means of production and with the abolition of the inherent contradictions of capitalism, production will reach its fullest development. Both from the point of view of production and of freedom each of these stages marks an advance over the one preceding it. This being in accordance with the law of dialectics harmonises in the synthesis of value in the thesis and anti-thesis. To understand social revolution man must distinguish between changes in the productive forces and the various ideological forms with which men become aware and fight under the banner of one or the other ideology. Marxists contend that most history has been written under this illusion and the true cause of the revolutions have remained cancealed till the advent of Marx. Engels claimed, Marx discovered the simple fact, hitherto concealed by an overgrowth of ideology that mankind must first of all eat and drink, have shelter and clothing, before it can pursue politics, religion, science, art, etc. and that therefore, the production of the immediate material means of subsistence and consequently the degree of economic development attained by a given people or during a given epoch form the foundation upon which state institutions, the legal conceptions, the art and even the religious ideas of the people concerned have been evolved and in the light of which these things must be explained instead of *vice-versa* as had hitherto been the case."[36] Thus the economic system of society which Marx calls the sub-structure always provides the real basis and the religious laws, ethics, etc. are the super-structure built upon and determined by it. As such in Marx's view, ideas are not supreme, it is not they which determine the form of society but society which determine their form. The dialectics of Marx when applied to the interpretation of history ends in a deterministic philosophy which militates against the fundamental concept of man's essential freedom and creativity.

Gandhi discards this economic interpretation of history and did not think in terms of a single factor determining the social process. Experience also shows that there is no single determinant of social phenomena. Whatever might be their origins, every sphere of life and society, political, social, economic, cultural, etc. acquire lives of their own and though all these aspects interlock and changes in one sphere affect the others, the effects are not always such as one would like to see. It was a widely held belief in radical circles when Gandhi was fighting against untouchability that he was wasting his energy in vain. The evil was a feudal relic and would disappear when the country was industrialized. India is now proud to be counted as the tenth largest industrial nation in the world but that has had little impact on the problems of untouchability and casteisms. There are even sociological studies to show that casteism has become stronger in the industrial areas. Political freedom has not automatically lifted the educational system of India out of rut in which imperial rule had left it. Socialist industrialization in the erstwhile USSR had not helped to rid that country of anti-semitism and has not changed everything that needed to be changed. A new ruling class had emerged intent on keeping the common people in their place. Women in highly industrialised Japan still lack basic equality with men. Such instances can be multiplied endlessly.

Gandhi selected the approach of a multi-pronged attack on all fronts and while engaged in the struggle for political freedom, set in motion programmes and processes for changes in other spheres of the country's life: for radical changes in the economic system based on a new productive technology, for a new educational system for changes in values in social life that would rid it of the evils of casteism, untouchability, the liberation of women and so on. These programmes were all conceived as parts of one integral whole which he named as the Constructive Programme.

Gandhi also rejects the gross materialism of Marx. Gandhi's interpretation of history is the extension of his metaphysics—the concepts of truth and non-violence and his belief in God. He has a firm faith that God the maker of us all is the director of this human drama being enacted in the theatre of this world. His unshakable faith in God leads him to believe in the Divine dispensation and the Will and the capacity of God to right the wrong and undo the injustice prevailing in the world.

Unlike Marx, Gandhi believes in the dynamic forces of the spirit, or God acting behind all social and historical movements. Not a leaf stirs without His order. The spirit is moving with a purpose progressively towards the realization of truth and perfection at all levels both in life of individual and society. As a corollary of this arises his belief in the force of religion in the history of man. Man's spiritual and moral progress stems from religion. It leads Gandhi to believe in the power of the spirit of man to shape the environment according to the law of spiritual evolution. Believing in the spiritual unity of all men, Gandhi argues that "If one man gains spiritually the whole world gains, if he falls the whole world falls to that extent." Viewed in this light, history becomes a gradual unfolding of the cosmic souls. To Gandhi, it is the progressive realization of non-violence. "If we turn our eyes to the time of which history has any record down to our own time we shall find that man has been steadily progressing towards ahimsa. Our remote ancestors were connibals. Then, came a time when they were fed up with cannibalism and they began to live on chase. Next, came a stage when man was ashamed to live the life of a wandering hunter. He, therefore, took to the agriculture and depended mainly on mother earth for his food. Thus from being a nomad he settled down to a civilised, stable life, founded villages and towns and from a member of family he become member of a community and a nation. All these are signs of progressive ahimsa and diminishing himsa."[37]

CAPITAL *vs.* LABOUR

There is also a basic difference between Gandhism and Marxism about capital and labour. On one hand we have Gandhi's concept of trusteeship which is heavily loaded with spiritualism and idealism, and on the other we have the hard materialism purported to be scientific which finds manifestation in his concept of surplus value. (Trusteeship has already been discussed in the present volume).

Marx on the other hand had given a completely different picture. He says that capital creates nothing but in itself created by labour. The wood as a tree created by nature has a value, but this is not exchange value and does not become such until human labour power has been extended upon it to transform it into objects, which can be bought and sold in the market. In short, the value of all marketable commodities is determined by the quantity of labour power which goes to produce them, but the worker however under the capitalist system does not receive a just share of value of his skill. Instead he gets less than that. Let us take an hypothetical example. Suppose the actual price of the product produced by the labourer is Rs. 100. And he is paid Rs. 75 as wages. This difference of Rs. 25 is appropriated by the capitalist and this is called the surplus value. Surplus value is thus difference between actual price and actual payment.

Actual price – Actual payment = Surplus value
100 – 75 = 25

This surplus is pocketed by the capitalist and this constitutes his profit—'a toll wrung from the grinding toil of the masses'. Competition impels the capitalist to beat down the worker's wage to the lowest possible point. This can be more readily and fully accomplished in large scale units of industrial organisations. Hence because of the larger profits, there is a progressive tendency towards consolidation which results in the concentration of capital in the hands of a very small class—the bourgeois. The poor grow poorer and the rich richer until finally the workers are impelled to organise.

Marx concludes that by its very nature capitalism is full of inner contradictions and is doubly doomed by the general law of capital accumulation and centralization which begins to operate automatically as soon as capitalist appropriates surplus value.

Marx does not believe that the capitalist will act as a trustee of the poor. There is a never ending greed of the capitalist which makes him more and more exploiter, till at certain stage, the only thing that the labourer has to 'lose his chains' and this is when a violent revolution takes place. There is hardly any need to elaborate how far apart Gandhi and Marx are in their stand here.

Religion and Politics

Similarly, their views about religion and politics are poles apart. Gandhi regards religion as very important for human life. He claimed, however, to be a practical religious idealist and was not much interested in the transcendental and eschatological aspects of religion. Religion signified, to him, belief in the ordered moral governance of the world and the spirit of faith in and dependence upon the absolute truth. Hence, it demanded a complete conservation of a man's being and personality to Truth which is God and implied an emphasis on the moral values of man as spirit. "For me morals, ethics, and religiòn are convertible terms. A moral life without reference to religion is like a house built upon sand. And religion divorced from morality is like "sounding brass good only for making a noise and breaking heads."[38]

Gandhi categorically said that he wanted to bring religion into politics. "For me the road to salvation lies through incessant toil in the service of my country and of humanity. I want to identify myself with everything that lives. In the language of Gita, I want to live at peace with both friends and foes. So my patriotism is for me a stage on my journey to the land of eternal freedom and peace. Thus it will be seen that for me there are no politics devoid of religion. Politics bereft of religion are a death trap because they kill the soul."[39]

Religion is based on the recognition of the superiority of moral vows. A religious life signifies the dedicated pursuit of these vows. Hence, the incorporation of religion in politics means a progressive movement towards the continued and faithful practice of moral vows of truth and love. The central point of Gandhian political philosophy is that the fundamental religious ethic common to all the great religions has to be made concrete in individual, social and political life. It is, hence, opposed to regarding political action as the sphere of the non-moral. Summarizing his reflections upon life in the last chapter of his autobiography, he wrote, "To see the universal and all-pervading spirit of Truth face to face one must be able to love the meanest of creation as oneself. And a man who aspires after that cannot afford to keep out of any field of life. That is why my devotion to truth has drawn me into the field of politics; and I can say without the slightest hesitation and yet in all humility, that those who say that religion has nothing to do with politics do not know what religion means."[40]

The Marxists are the sworn enemies of religion which in the words of Marx, is "the sob of the oppressed creature," "the heart of a heartless world", and "the opium of the poor." "The first word of religion is a lie," said Engels and Lenin was of the view, "Religion is one of the aspects of spiritual oppression. Thus religion from the Communist point of view is a gigantic deception.

The attitude of Marx towards religion is quite in keeping with his belief that consciousness is a derivative of matter. As is well known, Marx does not believe in the existence of any other thing than the matter. Religious interests, therefore, must be discarded because, 'nothing should' be allowed to compete with the individual's 'loyalty to the state'. Unlike Gandhi, Marx does not introduce religion in the field of politics. Rather, he makes definite to keep politics free from any spiritual or mystical outlook.

He also ridicules the idea of another world in the form of heaven. It is the most disgraceful manifestation of religious consciousness according to him. He is of the view that this longing for the heavenly world by man is due to the oppressive social and economic conditions of his life in his world. Thus, the religious estrangement is a protest against social tyranny. A time will come when 'in the social whole of men-labouring-in nature, religion would wither away and the question of theism *versus* atheism would simply become irrelevant.'[41]

Last but not least communism is based on certain set principles while Gandhian ideology is ever evolving. Vinoba Bhave has given a very interesting comparison between Valmiki Ramayana and Communism. It is said that Valmiki wrote the Ramayana long before the birth of Rama and Rama conformed to every word of it during his earthly career and so had also no occasion to worry himself about using his own judgement in order to take a decision. He had just to consult the book and act accordingly. Since the consequences had also been predicted, he was not worried about the results also. So, too, is the case with the communists. Lenin acted as Marx had prescribed. Common man also according to them are to merely follow Marx and they can straightaway reach their goals. "If at times there appear a discrepancy between the words of Marx and the actions of Lenin, the Pandits of Communism have of course to labour a little to prove that there is no real discrepancy. This is not very difficult, for, it is well known maxim of interpretation that a smriti-text (rule) must conform to a shruti-text (law). And, hence, if the rule is clear, then one need only so interpret the law that the former is justified! Do that and you get the line clear."[42]

It is quite otherwise with the Gandhian ideology. "If communism is a solid and imposing stricture of granite, Gandhism is an ever changing amoeba."[43] Gandhian ideas are ever growing. There is no finality in his approach. This is largely so because his concepts are not absolute but relative. He himself kept on modifying, elaborating and enriching his own concepts on the basis of his experience. If his later pronouncements contradict his earlier ones, he had asked not to worry about reconciling the two, but to accept the later and reject the earlier and proceed further.[44] Even in his major fights, he had no premeditated plans, no technique, no ordered arrangement, etc. Since he used to say, 'one step is enough for me'. Why should the Lord show him two? And what was the amount of authority to be attached even to his latest utterances? His answer was, "Do not be authority bound. Use your own talent. You might ask me while I am available. Thereafter every one is free to think and decide for himself."[43] That is why there is no unanimity of ideas even among his closest followers. Otherwise also it is better to allow thought to work freely than to beat and drive and shut it up into the rigidity of a system as has been done by the Communists.

Thus, there are fundamental differences between Gandhism and Marxism and the differences can not be stated by such simple equations as 'Gandhism is Communism minus violence' or 'Gandhism is communism plus God'. The differences between both are deeper than what can be expressed by a single equation with plus and minus signs.

Whenever Gandhi got an opportunity, he expressed his views against communism. As early as in 1919, he had said in a speech in Madras, "Bolshevism is a necessary result of modern materialistic civilization. Its insensate worship of matter has given rise to a school which has been brought up to look upon materialistic advancement as the goal and which has lost all the touch with the final things in life."[46] In this speech he pointed out that while the self-respect was the satyagraha creed, communism stood for self-indulgence. He warned that if the quest of spirit and love yielded to matter and brute force 'we shall have Bolshevism rampant in this land which was once so holy'. In an article entitled 'My Path' in the *Young India,* he wrote, "I am yet ignorant of what exactly Bolshevism is. I have not been able to study it. I do not know whether it was for the good of Russia in the long-run. But I do know that in so far as it is based on violence and denial of God, it repeals me. I do not believe in short violent-cuts to success. Those Bolshevik friends who are bestowing their attention on me should realize, that however, much I may sympathize with and admire worthy motives, I am an uncompromising opponent of violent methods even to serve the noblest of causes. There is, therefore, no meeting ground between the school of violence and me."[47]

Four years later writing in *Young India* he maintained the same belief. "But from what I know of Bolshevism, it not only does preclude the use of force, but freely sanctions it for the expropriation of private property and maintaining the collective state ownership of the same. And if that is so, I have no hesitation in saying that the Bolshevik regime in its present form can not last for long. For it is my firm conviction that nothing enduring can be built on violence."[48]

In reply to a question which several Zamindars put to him he said on July 25, 1934, "Socialism and Communism of the West are based on certain conceptions which are fundamentally different from ours. One such conception is their belief in the essential selfishness of human nature. I do not subscribe to it, for I know that the essential difference between man and the brute is that the former can respond to the call of the spirit in him, can rise superior to the passions that he owns in common with the brute and, therefore, superior to selfishness and violence which belong to the brute nature and not to the immoral spirit of man. That is the fundamental conceptions of Hinduism, which has years of penance and austerity at the back of the discovery of this truth. That is why, whilst we have had saints who have worn out their bodies and laid down their lives in order to explore the secrets of the soul we have had none, as in the West, who laid down their lives in exploring the remotest or the highest regions of the earth. Our socialism or communism should, therefore, be based on non-violence and on harmonious co-operation of labour and capital, landlord and tenant."[49]

When his attention was drawn to a question that, "when the rich became callous and selfish and the evil continues unchecked, a revolution of the masses with all the attendant horrors inevitably results. Since life, as you have put to it, is often a choice between evils, Won't you, in view of the lesson which the history of the revolution inculcates, welcome the rise of a benevolent dictatorship which would with the minimum use of force 'soak the rich', give 'justice to the poor' and thereby serve both?"

He reacted, "I can not accept benevolent or any other dictatorship. Neither will the rich vanish nor will the poor be protected. Some rich men will certainly be killed out and some poor men will be spoon fed. As a class the rich will remain, and the poor also, in spite of dictatorship labeled benevolent. The real remedy is non-violent democracy, otherwise spelt true education of all. The rich should be taught the doctrine of the stewardship and the poor that of self-help.[50]

The *Harijan* of August 4, 1946 carried a very interesting dialogue between Louis Fischer and the Mahatma. When Fischer called himself a communist. Gandhi said, "O, don't. It is terrible for you to call your self a communist. I want what you want, what Jaiprakash and socialists want, a free world. But the communists don't. They want a system which enslaves the body and the mind.

"Would you say that of Marx?"

"The Communists have corrupted the Marxists teachings to suit their purpose."

"What about Lenin?"

"Lenin started it. Stalin has since completed it. When the Communists come to you, they want to get into the Congress and control the Congress and use it for their own ends."

"So do the socialists. My communism is not very different from socialism. It is harmonious blendings of the two.

Communism, as I have understood it, is a natural corollary of socialism."

"Yes you are right, there was a time when the two could not be distinguished. But today socialists are very different from communists."

"You mean to say, you do not want communism of Stalin's type?"

"But the Indian communists want communism of the Stalin type in India and want to use your name for that purpose." "They would not succeed", replied the Mahatma.[51] There are so many other alike utterances and he maintained the same belief till his death in 1948.

Gandhi the lover of humanity and liberty found that Russian experiment of Bolshevism could scarcely prepare the necessary atmosphere for the fuller development of human personality. He strongly denounced the Stalinistic brand of communism which was prevailing in Russia at that time. He was specially allergic to the very idea of violence for the establishment of the new world order. Despite its passion for social justice and love for the poor, communistic rejection of God and religion and neglect of spiritual evolutions in man with his nobler instincts made Gandhi to oppose it vehemently.

Socialism

But his opposition to Socialism is not as strong as against Communists. Before 1934, he did not approve of the word 'socialism'. He was very much against it. In 1916, he had declared, "I am no socialist and I do not want to dispossess those who have got possessions, but I do say that personally those of us who want to see light out of darkness, have to follow this rule. I do not want to dispossess anybody. I should then be departing from the rule of ahimsa."[52]

But a change is evident from this earlier stand in 1924 when he admitted the necessity of nationalization or state control over certain key industries which was deemed as guarded approval of socialism. Again in a speech before the 49th meeting of the Federal Structure Committee of the Round Table Conference held on November 19, 1931, he gave a picture of how things were to shape themselves if a national Government was to come into being in India. As observed in the previous chapter, his association with the indigenous capitalists did not prevent him from taking the side of the poor and press the views of the common men. He supported the Indian capitalists' opposition to the financial safeguards and the Government's currency policy, and spoke against the British representatives on commercial discrimination. He argued that there must be no racial discrimination but the national government would have to discriminate in favour of the poor against the rich. Not only the government obligations, he proceeded but "existing interests should subject to judicial scrutiny when necessary". His formula was meant to be applied to the Indians equally. "If they have obtained concessions ... because they did some service to the officials of the days and got some miles of land, well, if I had the possession of the government I would quickly dispossess them." Referring to the representatives of moneyed men, he declared, "They are not representatives of those who lack even a place to sleep and have not even a crust of bread to eat. If the National Government comes to the conclusion that place (i.e., the patatial buildings of this white elephant which is called New Delhi) is unnecessary, no matter what interests are concerned, they will be dispossessed, I may tell you, without any compensation, because if you want this government to pay compensation, it will have to rob Peter to pay Paul, and that would be impossible."

On the same occasion, while he did not go to the length of advocating in full throat the state control of key industries, he had been seen to be moving slowly but steadily from his earlier position. Here we find a man growing, developing, moving and making the masses move with him for the realisation of a new society as he envisaged it free from exploitation. He clarified in the Round Table Conference, "The Congress conception is that if the key industries are not taken over by the state itself, the state will at least have a predominant say in the conduct and administration and development of key industries." [53]

In the wake of suspension of Civil Disobedience Movement in 1933, there emerged the Congress Socialist group. At the first Congress Socialist Conference, held at Patna in 1934, the programme of the party was formulated. After the publication of the programme an attempt was made by some of the leaders of CSP to ascertain Gandhi's views on it. In the course of the discussion, he admitted, "I call myself a socialist. I love the very word, but I will not preach the same socialism as most socialists do."[54]

He had his own picture of socialism. In 1934, he advocated, "The socialism that India can assimilate is the socialism of the spinning wheel."[55] In a speech delivered at the Exhibition ground of Faizpur Congress session he said on December 27, 1936, "Real socialism has been handed down to us by our ancestors who taught: 'All land belongs to Gopal, where then is the boundary line? Man is the maker of that line and he can, therefore, unmake it'. Gopal literally means shepherd; it also means God. In modern language it means the state, i.e. the people. That the land today does not belong to the people is too true. But the fault is not in the teaching. It is in us who has not lived upto it. I have no doubt that we can make as good an approach to it as is possible for any nation, not excluding Russia, and that without violence. The most effective substitute for violent dispossession is the wheel with all the implications. Land and all property is his who will work for it. Unfortunately, the workers are or have been kept ignorant of this simple fact."[56]

His concept of socialism was entirely his own in the sense that socialism did not represent itself to him as a necessary and logical stage in social evolution growing out of the technological basis and production relations of capitalism. As he said, "Socialism was not born with the discovery of the misuse of capital by capitalists. As I have contended socialism, even communism is explicit in the first verse of Ishopanishad.[57]

ईशा वास्यम इदं सर्व
यत किं च जगत्यां जगत।
तेन त्यक्तेन भुंजे या
मा गृधः कस्य स्विद धानम।।

Whatever life there is in this world is filled with God. Nothing exists without God. Speaking in terms of kingdom only He reigns. He alone is the master. Understanding this it is our duty to offer everything to Him and whatever we receive from Him, we must joyfully accept as His gracious gift. Nothing belongs to me everything belongs to Him. This must be our attitude. Whosoever lives in this way—considering nothing to be his own, everything God's—he will receive every thing. Whatsoever he receives he will be satisfied with. He will not envy others. He will not cover the wealth of others.[58]

In this brief mantra a great comprehensive axiom regarding life has been enunciated as also the way of expressing it through action. Dedication to God, the acceptance of whatever one gets, only as a token of his grace, freedom from envy, not coveting wealth and using it for the welfare of all—is the purest form of socialism. And this is what Gandhi meant by socialism.[59]

In 1946, when Louis Fischer put before him an interpolation that you are a socialist and so are they (who believed in violent overthrow) "I am, they are not", affirmed Gandhi. "I was socialist before many of them were born. I carried conviction to a rabid socialist in Johannesburg, but that is neither here nor there. My claim will live when their socialism is dead." To him, socialism is either a way of life or else it is an arm chair philosophy. He was obviously referring to his experiments at the Tolstoy farm in South Africa and in his different ashrams. Therefore, he called himself the foremost socialist. He believed in the equality of man. Even as the limbs of the individual body are equal so are the members of the society. Perhaps, he got this idea from his faith in the fatherhood of God and brotherhood of man. He had a rock like belief in God and unity of man. He wanted to bring equalization of status because he believed that all men are equal. He was pained to find that the working classes have all these centuries been isolated and relegated to a lower status. So he wanted "to allow no differentiation between the son of a weaver, of an agriculturist and of a bureaucrat. When he was asked to define his socialism, Gandhi said, "My socialism means 'even unto this last'. I do not want to rise on the ashes of the blind, the deaf and the dumb. In their socialism, probably, these have no place. Their one aim is material progress. For instance, America aims at having a car for every citizen. I do not. I want freedom for full expression of my personality. I must be free to build staircase to Sirius if I want to. That does not mean that I want to do any such thing. Under the other socialism, there is no individual freedom you own nothing, not even your body". He was of the firm view that man is superior to the system he propounded. Therefore, he could not compromise with individual freedom. But the present day socialism in various countries present a different picture. There is a dilemma! Make man free and they become unequal, make them equal and they cease to be free. This is fact that socialism and individual liberty do not go together, at least in the communist countries. They openly profess the doctrine of the dictatorship of the proletariat, and advocate the rule of one party, i.e., the Communist Party, which they call as the 'vanguard of the people'.

But Gandhi wanted to bring economic equality through non-violence, by the people to (his) point of view by harnessing the forces of love as against hatred. His way was to make the ruler a socialist through love. "If socialism means befriending one's enemies I should be treated as a true socialist. This conception of socialism is my own. The socialists should learn the socialism from me. Only, then we can establish a true workers' and peasants' raj."[60]

In an editorial in *Harijan* dated July 13, 1947, he wrote, "Socialism is a beautiful word and so far as I am aware in socialism all members are equal—none high. In the individual body, the head is not high because it is the top of the body, nor are the soles of the feet low because they touch the earth. Even as members of the individual body are equal so are the members of the society. This is socialism.

In it the princess and the peasants, the wealthy the poor, the employer employee are all on the same level. In terms of religion there is no duality in socialism. It is all unity....

Socialism begins with the first convert. If there is one such, you can add zeros to the one and the first zero will count for ten times the previous number. If, however, the beginner is zero, in other words no one makes the beginning, multiplicity of zeros will produce zero value. Time and paper occupied in writing zeros will be so much waste.

The socialism is as pure as crystal. It, therefore, requires crystal like means to achieve it. Impure means result in impure ends. Hence the prince and the peasant will not be equalized by cutting-off the prince's head, nor can the process at cutting of equalize the employer and the employed. One can not reach truth. Truthful conduct can alone reach truth.... Only truthful, non-violent, and pure hearted socialists will be able to establish a socialistic society in India and the world. To my knowledge there is no country in the world which is purely socialistic. Without the means described above the existence of such a society is impossible.[61]

Future of Gandhian Socialism

Communism has become out of date. To speak for it is fighting a loosing battle. Capitalism has developed contradictions both economic and socio-cultural. Modern testimony, has raised certain unavoidable questions of dehumanisation, pollution, centralisation and violence. And violence has proved its own bankruptcy. Violence and civilization can not co-exist today. Violence is not only overt, it is ingrained in the very system. Men must learn lessons from the absurdity of today's civilisation. We want peace but we plan for war. We want democracy, but we despise centralisation both in economics and politics and then we groan under dictatorship and militarism. We aspire socialism but we stick to individualism. Socialism has become a matter of slogan than practice. So, when a group of 15 students, who called themselves socialists, came to see Gandhi, he wrote on a slip of paper 'to shed sloth and aversion to physical labour is the first word socialism'. He then asked how many of them had servants in their homes? When told that there was atleast one servant in each house, he wrote—'And you call yourself socialists while you make others slave for you'. To him, socialism begins with the first convert. His socialism was socialism from within based on the idea of fellow—feeling, service and dignity of labour. Socialism to him was a way of life, a way of society and civilization. By basing on non-violence Gandhi has made a definite advance over the traditional socialist thought. Then, his socialism is not sectarian but for all-Sarvodaya. It is not a trade union affair but a more noble, something more universal, more radical where liberty and equality, good of the poor as well as of the rich have to be balanced to work out a harmonious society free from strife and conflict. His socialism is the socialism of future.

NOTES AND REFERENCES

1. *Harijan*, 31.3.1946, p. 63.
2. Vinoba Bhave's, Introduction in K.G. Mashruwala, Gandhi and Marx (Ahmedabad: Navajivan Publishing House, 1971), p. 29.
3. *Harijan*, 13.3.1937, p. 40.
4. 'Marx', 'On Rousseau' in D. Caute (ed.), Essential Writings of Marx (London: Panther, 1967), p. 18.
5. Frank Thakurdas, "In Defence of Social Equality" in *The Indian Journal of Political Science*, Vol. XXXVII, No. 1, 1976, p. 5.
6. *Harijan*, 31.3.1946, pp. 64-64.
7. Victor Afanasyeu, "Basis and Super Structure of Society" in USSR: Society, Life Today, Sept. 1963, p. 39.
8. Fundamental of Marxism Leninism (Moscow: F.L.P.M., 1975).
9. *Harijan*, 5.5.1946, p. 116.
10. *Young India*, 19.9.1929, p. 305.
11. Heinrich Gemkow, Karl Marx: A Biography (Dresden: Verlag Zeit in Bild, 1968), p. 384.
12. Wilhelm Liebknecht, Marx and Engels: Through The Eyes of Their Contemporaries (Moscow: Progress Publishers, 1972), p. 29.
13. Karl Marx, Thesis on Feurbach Karl Marx's Selected Writings (Oxford: Oxford University Press, 1977), p. 158.
14. M.K. Gandhi, An Autobiography, *op. cit.*, pp. 69-70.
15. *Ibid.*
16. Heinrich Gemkov, *op. cit.*
17. Karl Marx, Dos Capital, Vol. 1, *op. cit.*, p. 432.
18. Karl Marx, Economic and Philosophic Manuscripts of 1844 (Moscow: Progress Publishers, 1967).
19. *Young India*, 10.9.1931, p. 255.
20. K.G. Mashruwala, Gandhi and Marx, *op. cit.*, pp. 37-38.
21. *Ibid.*, pp. 16-17.
22. *Young India*, 26-12-1924, p. 3.
23. *Ibid.*, 17-7-1924, pp. 236-37.
24. Wihelm, Liebnecht, Marx in Reminscences of Marx and Engels, Moscow, p. 104.
25. William Ash, Marxism and Moral Concepts (New York: Monthly Review Press).
26. Reference to the "Manifesto of the Communist Party," Marx and Engels, Selected Works, FL-O.H., 1962), p. 55.
27. Karl Marx, Manifesto of the Communist Party (Moscow: Progress Publishers, 1978), pp. 40-41.
28. V.I. Lenin, Left Wing Communism: An Infantile Disorder (Moscow: Novosti Press, 1969), p. 5.
29. Rene Fulop Miller, Lenin and Gandhi (London: G.P. Putnam's Sons, 1927), p. XIII.
30. *Harijan*, 12.11.1938, p. 226.
31. *Young India*,, 5.3.1925, p. 81.
32. Karl Marx, Economic and Philosophic Manuscript, *op. cit.*, p. 71.

33. Marx and Engels, The German Ideology (New York: International Publishers, 1939), p. 172.
34. Lemin, Collected Works, Vol. XIV, (Moscow: F.L.P.H.), p. 130.
35. Karl Marx, Selected Works, Vol. I, pp. 330-31.
36. Engels, Selected Works, Vol. II, p. 143.
37. *Harijan*, 11.8.1940, p. 245.
38. *Ibid.*, 3.10.1936.
39. *Young India*, 3.4.1924, p. 112.
40. M.K. Gandhi, An Autobiography, *op. cit.*, p. 420.
41. James Collins, God in Modern Philosophy (London: Routledge and Kegan Paul, 1960), pp. 255-57.
42. K.G. Mashruwala, Gandhi and Marx, *op. cit.*, p. 20.
43. *Ibid.*
44. *Harijan*, 29.4.1933, p. 2.
45. *Ibid.*, 30.9.1939, p. 288.
46. *CWMG*, Vol. XV, p. 168.
47. *Harijan*, 11.12.1924, p. 406.
48. *Young India*, 15.11.1928, p. 381.
49. *CWMG*, Vol. LVIII, p. 248.
50. *Harijan*, 8.6.1940, p. 159.
51. *Ibid.*, 4.8.1946, p. 246.
52. Speeches and Writings of Mahatma Gandhi (Madras: G.A. Natesan and Co., 1962), p. 324.
53. *CWMG*, Vol. XLVIII, pp. 291-368.
54. M.K. Gandhi, My Socialism, Compiled by R.K. Prabhu (Ahmedabad: Navajivan Publishing House, 1959), pp. 645.
55. *CWMG*, Vol. LVIII, p. 306.
56. *Harijan*, 2.1.1937, p. 375.
57. *Ibid.*, 20.2.1957, p. 12.
58. Isawasya Upanishad 1, translated by Donald G. Groom (Varanasi: Sarva Seva Parkashan, 1981).
59. *Harijan*, 4.8.1946, p. 246.
60. *CWMG*, Vol. LXXXVIII, pp. 245.
61. *Harijan*, 13.7.1947, p. 232.

9

Doctrine of Swadeshi

Winners don't do different things. They do things differently. Many of the conceptions Gandhi used, developed and made popular were not new. Gandhi claimed no originality for himself. He said, "I have nothing new to teach the world. Truth and non-violence are as old as hills."[1] Originality does not always lie in inventing new ideas. It also lies in giving old ideas new meanings and in many ways they are made practical and are popularised. Swadeshi was one of the ideas, which was not new. It was earlier used by Indian patriots, liberals or nationalists.

Before Gandhi also, political reformers had talked of reviving indigenous industries. India had centuries-long traditions of Industries. As a matter of fact, the far-famed wealth of India which gave it the name of 'Golden Ind' in the west before the advent of the British was due to its industry rather than its agriculture. Prior to the steam age, it was rare that the agricultural produce of any country was exported. Almost all the countries had to be self-sufficient in food. What could be exported were the products of Industry because in comparison to their bulk they fetched more price than food-grains. When the East India Company came to trade in India they could bring nothing from there or from Europe that the people of India needed. They had therefore, necessarily to bring bullion to purchase Indian spices and the manufactured articles which Europe needed. In those days it was customary for countries to preserve their gold and silver and not to allow them to leave the country. This so even now. However, the British parliament passed a special Act by which East India Company was allowed to take away £ 75,000 in gold for their trade with India. Afterwards, as the political power of the company increased, they did not want to bring their ships empty from England to India but, instead, to load it with Cargo which would at least pay for the freight charges. It was on this account that the Company's Government here put an excise duty on salt manufactured in India. This enabled the British masters to fill their ships with British salts and sell it profitably in India to cover the cost of the journey of their ships to India. This was the origin of the salt tax. That is why Gandhi called this tax sinful. It killed the flourishing salt Industry in India.

Indian patriots had realized, long before Gandhi, that the poverty of India was principally due to the murder of their Industry at the hands of the British. Books were written about this; the most important of these was R.C. Dutt's 'Poverty of India—under British Rule,' about which Gandhi said that when he read it, he was so powerfully affected that he began to shed tears. They felt that unless there was a revival of Indigenous Industry the masses of India would remain poor. Along with the annual Congress sessions, it was customary to call an industrial conference. Resolutions were passed both in Congress and at the industrial conferences advising people to use Swadeshi instead of foreign goods. The fact was that India supplied raw material and got from England finished goods; for instance, England imported cheap cotton from India and turned it into cloth which was exported back to India. Till then, the British and other European countries produced only woollen cloth, their requirements of silk and cotton cloth were met by imports; mostly from India. The very names given to several varieties of cloth in England were used in India, such as mull and doria. When they started the textile industry and dumped its products in India, the profits of the Industry and the carrying trade went to the benefit to the English people. This was so in the case of many articles. If, therefore, any dent was to be made in the abject poverty of the Indian masses, it could only be done by the revival of Indigenous industries.

The Swadeshi movement received a great impetus during the agitations of the partition of Bengal (1905). The agitation was characterised by a great deal of emotion and sentiments. During the partition days patriots could weave beautiful words but they could not produce articles of use. The result was that merchants passed-off imported goods as India made. Early in 1919 a meeting was arranged between Gandhi and a patriotic mill-owner. The latter told Gandhi, "You are aware that in the days of partition (Bengal) the mill-owner fully exploited the Swadeshi movement. When it was at its height, I raised the price of cloth and did even worse things. We are not conducting our business out of philanthropy. We do it for profit."[2] Gandhi then understood why the Swadeshi movement of the partition days had fizzled out.

Gandhi was more practical. He saw that the Swadeshi and the boycott movement could not prosper without an increase in indigenous production which would be independent of the mills. He also realised that in olden days the agricultural masses in India had always some subsidiary industries to add to their meagre income. Gandhi thought that the only industry which could be universal was the textile industry. This was also the biggest item of import from England which was the main cause of prosperity not only of Manchester but also of Great Britain. For centuries there had been a tradition in India of hand spinning and hand weaving. The former had been given up in many parts of the country owing to the import of mill yarn from England for manufacture in Indian mills. But weaving was yet common in all parts of India; though the handloom industry was being progressively wiped out in competition with Indigenous and foreign mill cloth. Gandhi considered spinning and weaving to be the industries which could best provide subsidiary work to the agricultural masses of India. Therefore, he worked for the revival of this industry. Gandhi also believed that if India could organise this industry so as to make the import of cloth from abroad superfluous, it would greatly add not only to its economic but also its social and political strength.

Further Gandhi's conception of Swadeshi was very identical to that of Swadharma in the Gita. This Swadharma depends upon Swabhava, one's fundamental nature. People must follow in life such avocations as would not do violence to this nature. The Gita says: "One's own dharma though imperfect is better than the dharma of another well performed. The dharma of another is fraught and fear." Gandhi says of this: "Interpreted in terms of one's physical environment, this gives us the law of Swadeshi, for Swadeshi is Swadharma applied to one's immediate environment."[3]

In a speech delivered before the Missionary Conference, Madras, on 14 February 1916, he defined Swadeshi in the following terms: "After much thinking I have arrived at a definition of Swadeshi that, perhaps, best illustrate my meaning. Swadeshi is that spirit in us which restrict us to the use and service of our immediate surroundings to the exclusion of the more remote. Thus, as for religion, in order to satisfy the requirements of definition, I must restrict myself to ancestral religion. That is the use of my immediate surroundings. If I find it defective, I should serve it by purging it of its defects. In domain of politics, I should make use of the indigenous institutions and serve them by curing them of their proved defects. In that of economics, I should use only things that are produced by my immediate neighbours and serve those industries by making them efficient and complete where they might be found wanting."[4]

As has been noted by Dr. Gopi Nath Dhawan, Gandhi's views on Swadeshi seem to have undergone an evolution.[5] A study of his address delivered at the Missionary Conference, Madras, 1916 shows that he then stood for total self-sufficiency of the country and its economic isolation from the world. Referring to external trade he said: "Much of the deep poverty of the masses is due to the ruinous departure from Swadeshi in the economic and Industrial life. If not an article of commerce had been brought from outside, she would be today a land flowing with milk and honey." In the same conference he further said, "It has been argued that India can not adopt Swadeshi in the economic life at any rate. Those who advance this objection do not look upon Swadeshi as a rule of life. With them it is a patriotic effort not to be made if involved any self-denial. Swadeshi is a religious discipline to be undergone in utter disregard of the physical comfort it may cause to individuals. Under its spell the deprivation of a pin or needle, because these are not manufactured in India, need cause no terror. A Swadeshist will learn to do without hundreds of things which today he may consider necessary. Moreover, those who dismiss Swadeshi from their minds by arguing the impossible, forget that Swadeshi is the only doctrine consistent with the law of humility and tone.[6]

In 1926 he wrote, "I have never considered the exclusion of every thing foreign under every conceivable circumstances as a part of Swadeshi. The broad definition of Swadeshi is the use of all home made things to the exclusion of foreign things, insofar as such use is necessary for the protection of home industry, more especially those industries without which India will become pauperized. In my opinion, therefore, Swadeshi which exclude the use of everything foreign no matter how beneficent it may be, is a narrow interpretation of Swadeshi."[7]

In Yervada Mandir we read: "To reject foreign manufactures because they are foreign and go on wasting national time and money in promotion in one's country of manufacture for which it is not suited would be criminal folly, and a negation of Swadeshi spirit."[8]

This shows that he moved away from his earlier position. Now he has permitted international trade and exchange of commodities if this meant an exchange of equal advantage and did not involve injustice. However, if it was to be a question of choice, he would have preferred self-sufficiency. But as a matter of practical policy he did not think that India should stand aloof in the matter of trade. "I would not wish India to live a life of complete isolation whereby it would live in water-tight compartments and allow nobody to enter her borders or to trade within her border."[9]

He defined "Swadeshi articles as any article which subserves the interest of the millions even though the capital and talent are foreign but under effective Indian control."[10]

What was meant by effective control? What industry could satisfy Gandhi as being Indian? "An Industry to be Indian must be demonstrably in the interest of the masses. It must be manned by Indians both skilled and unskilled. Its capital and machinery should be Indian and the labour employed should have a living wage and be comfortably housed, while the welfare of the children of the labourers should be guaranteed by the employers. This is an ideal definition."[11]

Until 1931, Gandhi distinguished between the economic aspect of Swadeshi and the economic boycott of foreign goods. In 1920 he categorically stated: "To say that Boycott is the same as Swadeshi even in effect is not to understand either. Swadeshi is an eternal principle.... It means production and distribution of articles manufactured in one's own country. But boycott, on the other hand, is a temporary makeshift resorted to compel the hands of the British people by deliberately making an attempt to inflict monetary loss upon them. Boycott...operates as an undue influence brought into secure one's purpose. It may indirectly result, but not unless it is persistent and prolonged, in greater manufacture at home.... I swear by Swadeshi because it is an evolutionary process gaining strength as it goes forward. Any organisation can serve it. It is independent of the justice or the injustice of the rulers. It is its own reward....Swadeshi and Boycott are not the same but are at the opposite poles."[12] During the Civil Disobedience Movement (1931-33) he acquiesced in the Congress "vigorously undertaking the boycott of British good."[13]

Gandhi, it seems had come, to believe that economic boycott could and should be used as a weapon of non-violent non-cooperation. In 1939, in answer to a question by a Chinese visitor, he favoured the economic boycott of the aggressor nation.[14] The extract, given below, from Gandhi's writings will give an idea as to Gandhi's concept of Swadeshi *vis-a-vis* the Swadeshi of the earlier days:

Q. "How does this new Swadeshi differ from the old?

A. The old emphasized the indigenous nature of the products, irrespective of the products, irrespective of the method of production or the prospects of the products. I have ruled out organised industries, not because they are not Swadeshi, but because they do not need special support. They can stand on their own legs and, in the present state of our awakening, can easily command a market. According to the new orientation, if it is new, I would have our Swadeshi organisation to seek out all village industries and find how they are faring. We will have experts and chemists who will be prepared to place their knowledge at the disposal of villagers. We will, through our experts, offer to test the articles manufactured by village handicraftsmen and make them suggestions to improve their wares, and would sell them if they would accept our conditions."[15]

Though Gandhi did not ordinarily favour legislative interference, yet we find him as an ardent supporter of protectionism. He pleaded strongly for stiff protective duties upon foreign goods in order to nurture national interest." This may be cited as showing his allegiance to the Indian capitalists class. But a correct reading will be that he was not guided by any such definite interest, though objectively the Indian capitalists benefited by this demand. As P. Spratt reminds us, "His support is no doubt likely to benefit the capitalists rather than anybody else, but he does not advocate with that intention. His protection is a villagers' protection, designed to help the effort for self-sufficiently, not that for profits."[17]

Though some deviation from the old stand taken on Swadeshi is quite obvious but the very essence of the doctrine remain undiluted by and large. Like the photographs of a person taken at the different stages of his life (from childhood to old age) one notices changes in them but the person remains the same. Same is the case here. My main concern, however, is not with the history or evolution of the concept but rather with Swadeshi regarded as an instance of the principle of ethical preference, which Gandhi tried to establish and its contemporary relevance.

Gandhi himself stressed that Swadeshi was not to be seen simply as a political expedient designed to weaken the hold of Lancashire on the Indian market for textiles and thereby embarrass the British rulers. It had to be justified in terms of fundamental moral principles. The principle that he invoked most often for this purpose was that of neighbourhood (This is also very crucial to prove its contemporary relevance). Gandhi defined Swadeshi as a principle which is broken when one professes to serve those who are more remote in preference to those who are near. A teaching that is shared by all mankind, states Gandhi, and one that is common to all religions alike, is that one must be kind and attentive to one's neighbours. The duty of helping one's neighbours is the core of the ethics of Swadeshi.

While it is true, we have duties to all humankind, but the duties we owe to all segments of it are not of equal importance. There is a hierarchy of duties based on the degree of proximity. Proximity is the decisive element in forming ties in terms both of closeness of feelings and knowledge of circumstances; "Our capacity for service is limited by our knowledge of the world in which we live."[18] Accordingly, we must start with service to our neighbours. An individual's service to his country and humanity consisted in serving his neighbours. One should not strave one's neighbour and claim to serve one's distant cousin in Antarctica, for one must not serve one's distant neighbour at the expense of the nearest. This is not only the teaching of all the religions in the world but also the foundation of true and humane economics. Gandhi saw no contradiction between the principle of Swadeshi, interpreted in terms of neighbourhood, and that of rendering service to all humanity, which he also upheld.

Asked if a man can serve the immediate neighbours and yet serve the whole of humanity, Gandhi replied that he can, provided the service to neighbours was not itself exploitative of others. The neighbour himself would in turn serve his neighbours and in this way the chain of service would be expanded to include the world, rather than shut it out.[19] For the same reason, the principle of neighbourhood according to Gandhi was neither metaphysical nor too philosophical for comprehension but just good common sense, for 'If you love your neighbour as thyself, he will do likewise with you,[20] and both would gain thereby'.

The neighbourhood principle was not confined to the choice of commodity bundles but applied quite generally to choice of states of affairs. When you demand Swaraj, you do not want Swaraj for yourself alone but for your neighbours.[21] It was the choice of commodities however, that formed the primary concern of the Swadeshi Movement.

The neighbourhood principle has a direct consequence for the interpretation of ethical preferences in terms of Swadeshi, namely that whenever local products are available they should be preferred to their imported counterparts. Whether the latter were imports from foreign countries or from other regions of the same country made no difference. From around 1919 onwards Gandhi spelt out this moral imperative of local buying in much detail using numerous specific examples: "And so long as the Godhra farmers and weavers could supply the wants of Godhra citizens, the latter had no right to go outside Godhra and support (say) the Bombay farmers and weavers."[22] A few years later, addressing people of his own home town (Porbander); he is repeating this argument in almost identical words, but using another set of examples:

> "Is it right that instead of getting stone from Ranavan, you should order your requirements from Italy? How can you afford to order your cloth or ghee from Calcutta in preference to the cloth woven in your own villages and the ghee made from the milk of your own cows and buffaloes?"[23] By consuming cloth or ghee imported from Calcutta rather than those made locally, the people of Porbander were being exploited. Likewise "If Bengal will live her natural and free life without exploiting the rest of India or the world outside, she must manufacture her cloth in her own villages as she grows her corn there."[24]

As between countries the neighbourhood principle translates as patriotism. An individual's preference ordering over commodity-bundles should therefore be guided by patriotism. The law of each country's progress demands on the part of its inhabitants preference for their own products and manufacturers."[25] Accordingly, for Indians there is a moral obligation to use products made in India whenever they can get them, even though these may be inferior to their foreign counterparts.

"There are several Swadeshi things in the market which are in danger of disappearance for want of patronage. They may not be up to the mark. It is up to us to use them and require the makers to improve them whenever improvement is possible,"[26] he pleaded.

Gandhi does not, however, explain how consumers continuing to use a product could at the same time require the makers to improve them. He mentions a number of goods belonging to this category. India produces a sufficient quantity of leather. It is therefore a duty on the part of an Indian consumer to wear shoes made of Indian leather in preference to foreign leather shoes, even if they are comparatively dearer and of an inferior quality. For the same reason products of Indian textile, sugar or rice mills 'must be preferred to the corresponding foreign product.'[27] Swadeshi items should not be discarded in favour of better or cheaper foreign things, for comparisons of price or quality are not relevant for the kind of consumer's choice Gandhi is talking about, but patriotism is. "We attend flag-hoisting ceremonies and are proud of our national flag. Let me tell you that our pride has no meaning if you do not like things made in India and hanker after foreign ones."[28]

If on the other hand, a particular commodity is not, or can not easily be made in India, the argument ceases to apply. Accordingly, while Gandhi regards it as a sin to import wheat from Australia on the score of its superior quality, he would not rule out importing Oatmeal from Scotland, for Oats are not grown in India. "I buy useful healthy literature from every part of the world. I buy surgical instruments from England, pins and pencils from Austria and watches from Switzerland."[29] For the same reason, in his Presidential Address at Belgaum Congress on December 26, 1924, he asserts: "All British goods do not harm us. Some goods such as English books we need for our intellectual or spiritual benefit."[30]

While upholding the principle of 'patriotic preference', Gandhi was at pains to bring out that spirit of Swadeshi was not vindictive. Exclusion of foreign goods was not intended as a punishment, it was a necessity of natural existence.[31] Nor was it narrow or parochial, 'for I buy from every part of the world what is needed for my growth'. But by the same token, 'I refuse to buy from anybody anything, however nice or beautiful, if it interferes with my growth or causes injuries those whom nature has made my first care.'[32]

Not all foreign things, therefore, were to be excluded but only certain foreign things, especially cloth. Gandhi attached considerable moral importance to this distinction, "If the emphasis were on all foreign things, it would be racial, parochial and wicked. The emphasis is on all foreign cloth. The restriction makes all the difference in the world."[33] Equally, the ethics of Swadeshi required that the exclusion should not be targeted at British cloth only. It applied just as much, say to the import of cloth from Japan, which was rapidly increasing during the 1930s. 'How can I take a single yard of Japanese cloth however fine and artistic it may be? It is poison to us, for it means starvation of the poor people of India.'[34]

Gandhi's doctrine that buying local products was a moral imperative had protectionist implications, but Gandhi had no particular allegiance to free trade. In response to an interviewer's comment that no country was free from foreign competition, Gandhi observed that on contrary each sovereign nation tried to protect its infant industries by bounties and tariffs and pointed to the sugar industry in Germany which had developed under a prohibitive tarrif-wall.[35] However, the exercise of ethical preference by consumer was, he claimed, a better solution because it was voluntary and hence was in correspondence with the principle of non-violence and was more likely to benefit the poor. Consumption behaviour that corresponded to the principle of ethical references, far from destroying the economic benefits flowing from foreign trade would conduce to the healthy growth of nations and so promote both material and moral progress.

"That economics is untrue which ignores or disregards moral values. The extension of the law of non-violence in the domain of economics means nothing than introduction of moral values as a factor to be considered in regulating international trade,[36] he again emphasized in his Presidential Address at Belgaum Congress. This approach to foreign trade would not lead to anarchy. There will be nations that will want to interchange with others because they cannot produce certain things. They will certainly depend on other nations for them but the nations that will provide for them should not exploit them."[37]

While the argument applies in principles to all home grown products. Gandhi singled out the products of village industry for special attention. Within that category Khadi claims place of pride. Indeed, the Swadeshi movement come to be regarded primarily as a means of encouraging consumer to wear Khaddar. Accordingly, people, especially town people, were asked to buy Khaddar in preference to the mill-made cloth and to boycott foreign cloth altogether.

Gandhi's identification of the Swadeshi Movement with village industry, and with hand-spinning in particular was based on a two-fold argument, that the urban population of India owed a special moral duty towards the villages; and that this duty would be best discharged by providing a market for village products and above all for hand-spun cloth. The first part of the argument is a logical consequence of the principles of neighbourhood (there are few towns or cities in India that are not surrounded by villages) and patriotism (most Indians are villagers) Gandhi sought to strengthen it further by introducing yet another moral principle, that of historical justice. Both economic and moral standards in the villages had declined through long neglect. City people as a whole were partly to blame. "The poor villagers are exploited by the foreign government and also by their own countrymen, the city dwellers. They produce the food and go hungry. They produce milk and their children have to go without it."[38]

Reparation had to be made. "We are guilty of a grievous wrong against the villagers and the only way in which we expiate it is by encouraging them to revive their lost industries and arts by assuring them of a ready market."[39]

This solution was entirely feasible, provided, that city people come to accept their moral responsibility. 'We have to be rural-minded and think of our necessities and the necessities of our households in terms of rural mindedness—it is in consonance with the true economics of our country.'[40] Gandhi saw himself as an exponent of this 'true economics'. A link has been built to bridge the yawning gulf between the cities and villages. We have only to cross this bridge. Patronising village industries will constitute the crossing of the bridge. Gandhi emphasized that this was not a matter of charity. As he saw it, he was proposing a purely commercial proposition. All that was required was the exercise of ethical preferences when choosing one's consumption bundle.

The second part of the argument seeks to justify the use of hand-spun cloth as the appropriate means of repaying the debt that city people owe to the villagers, and is based on standard economic reasoning. Spinning was a solution for rural unemployment. The whole scheme of Khadi, according to Gandhi, rested upon the supposition that there were millions of poor people in India who had no work during at least four months of the year. On Gandhi's reckoning, around three-quarters of the population of India belonged to this category. Because agricultural work was seasonal, they remained idle for a third of the year or more. This, Gandhi believed, was the principal cause of their endemic poverty. Even in a normal year their life was lived on the border line of starvation. If there was crop-failure or famine, the extent of involuntary unemployment become much greater and many of them died of hunger and disease. For the semi-starved but partially employed millions, spinning provided a means of part time employment as well an insurance against famine. Thus, Gandhi saw spinning primarily as supplementary industry for agriculture rather than as a means of employment for village artisans.[41]

Why, one might ask, choose spinning rather than some other subsidiary occupation for agricultural workers? Gandhi's answer to this question was strictly pragmatic. Spinning had long been practiced by villagers in the past. It required a few simple and low cost implement and little technical knowledge and skill. It could be learnt easily, did not require too much attention, could be done at odd moments and, for these reasons, was suitable as part time employment for masses of rural people. Neither cattle breeding nor weaving, which has been suggested as possible alternatives to spinning as a supplement to agriculture, enjoyed these advantages even though they were more remunerative.[42]

Spinning was the easiest, the cheapest and the best. It was the most economic means of putting money into the pockets of the largest number of villagers with the minimum capital outlay and organizational efforts. The test of Swadeshi was not the universality of the use of an article which goes under the name of Swadeshi but the universality of participation in the production or manufacturing of such articles[43] judged by this test spinning had a potential unmatched by other contenders.[44]

But it was not recommended for universal adoption. It was not for example, meant for individuals who already had more remunerative employment, such as urban workers in textile mills. Gandhi neither contemplated nor advised the abandonment of a single, healthy life giving industrial activity for the sake of hand spinning. On one occasion, he found that a number of women had been spinning who were not without occupation or means of making a living. 'Perhaps they spin in response to our appeal and because they realize it is good for the country'.[45] Nevertheless, Gandhi remained firm in his resolve that their spinning should stop, for the Charkha movement had not been conceived with such people in mind but only for able bodied people who were idle for want of work. The operative principle was quite clear: if there were no crises of semi-unemployed people there would be no room for spinning wheel.[46]

But Khadi as viewed by Gandhi, was not only an economic but a political phenomenon also. He had an absolute belief in the conception that the universal adoption of Khaddar by Indians was equivalent to the acquisition of Swaraj. Daily spinning on the wheel was a symbolic offering of dedication to India. Khadi was also the symbol of unity of India. Hence, spinning was a daily sacrament and a concrete viable technique of participation in this yajna for the unification and revivification of India. Furthermore, Khadi was a potent instrument of mass uplift and mass-education. The spinning wheel therefore was divine instrument and one calculated to satisfy the needs of the meanest and humblest of human beings.

The essence of the concept of Swadeshi lies in the following propositions:[47]

1. An individual consumer, will reduce one's wants. In reducing one's wants, the utility function will depend upon the commodities that are, or can be produced locally by neighbours. In other words, one's utility function will not be made up of commodities imported in their entirety. In urban areas, particularly in developing countries, the utility functions of the affluent members of the society is entirely made up of important commodities. Such a utility function is

unswadeshi since it denies the local producers the necessary means to produce commodities and thereby earn a livelihood for themselves.

2. Not only will the consumer redesign his or her utility function such that it is made up of commodities produced, or producible, in the neighbourhood, but also the consumer will make an effort to obtain these commodities from the neighbourhood itself. In other words, the consumer will prefer the commodities produced by the immediate neighbour to the commodities produced by a distant neighbour except when either the immediate neighbour does not produce these goods or refuses to improve the efficiency of production. Only in such cases will the consumer obtain these goods from a distant neighbour.
3. The consumer will cooperate with the producer neighbour in the process of improving the efficiency of production. This translates into the idea that the utility function not only contains the commodities produced in the neighbourhood but also a variable reflecting cooperation with the producer. In this sense the consumer and producer do not generate antagonistic relationships; such as in the dictum that consumer is sovereign and the producer the willing slave. On the contrary, the consumer and the producer are jointly involved in a cooperative effort.
4. Translated in economic language Swadeshi involves two shifts: an upward shift in the demand curve and a downward shift in the cost curve for a commodity produced in the neighbourhood/locality. Both these shifts take place simultaneously. The effect of these two shifts is obvious. It ensures that the production of the needed goods producible in the neighbourhood is profitable and hence feasible. Swadeshi, thus, is opposite to the trend in the last sixty years where the demand curve has been shifting downwards and the cost curve upwards. This was exactly the policy of British colonialism in India. The people were encouraged to consume goods produced in England and high taxes were levied on the producer in India of

> competing goods. Neo-colonialism is also operating through this mechanism. As a result of these two movements, the village industries have become uneconomic and eventually have gone out of production.

Swadeshi, if revived, can provide the resurgence of village industries. In view of dynamic interactions between the consumers and producers, it can lead to a process of self-reliance.

SWADESHI : SOME MISUNDERSTANDINGS

As the idea of Swadeshi mingled with the national movement for independence, a number of even well meaning intellectuals equated Swadeshi, with the 'buy Indian' movement. This 'buy Indian' movement stood by itself and was, in a way, the economic dimension of the political movement. It involves an act of resistance. Various reasons were given. It was argued that the British colonialism was able to obtain resources through exports to India. Furthermore, the 'buy Indian' movement will generate production, employment and income of Indians. This will help the resistance. This idea of buy nationally produced goods has been refined into a new 'import substitution industrialization strategy of development'. In this strategy, the country attempt to produce goods that it imports and goods that are produced in other countries. Both these versions reflect a misunderstanding of the Gandhian concept of Swadeshi. In the 'buy Indian' idea the consumer should switch to production within India which is different from the idea of production, by the immediate neighbour. The 'buy Indian' idea does attempt to shift the demand curve for the goods in India upwards. However, it also pits the Indian manufacture against the foreign, it involves a concept of narrow national patriotism and generates a competitive struggle between the national and the international or foreign producer. In this sense, it goes against the Swadeshi spirit which is to serve the world via service to the immediate neighbour. The import substitution strategy, on the other hand, does not have any redeeming features. It is based on the proposition that the utility function of the consumer is based on commodities produced in foreign countries from which imports are obtained. Swadeshi involves changing these utility functions. Import substitution strategies work towards the satisfaction and further accentuation of such utility functions. Since import substitution is not necessarily based on the idea of local resources, the import substitution prices do not even ensure the reduction in the cost curves of the production of substitution goods. There is thus nothing Swadeshi about import substitution.

Some scholars have confined Swadeshi with autarky: Autarky is a state where a country produces everything within its borders. It is a state in which there is no trade. Autarky concerns itself only with production. The reason is that autarky poses no relationship between the consumer and the producer. Swadeshi, on the other hand, involves a dynamic relationship between the consumer and the producer where in cost curves are shifted downwards and curve upwards. In an autarky, demand curve remains independent of production and cost curves may be shifted upwards. Furthermore, autarky imposes a competitive relationship between foreign and domestic producers.

CONTEMPORARY RELEVANCE

During the freedom struggle most of the Congress leaders missed the comprehensive nature of Swadeshi as conceived by Gandhi. They merely concerned themselves with its economics. In the boycott of British goods they also found an effective weapon to fight the foreign government. Even from the point of economics, they did not fully grasp the meaning of Swadeshi, as enunciated by Gandhi in terms of Swadharma, which required people to give preferences to goods made by their neighbours over goods made at far-away places. Whether in India or outside, the educated Congressmen, and more especially the socialists and communists, conceived of Swadeshi in its limited aspect of patronizing Indian goods, whether made through village and cottage industry in the villages or factories in the cities. Gandhi did not deny this conception. But he said mill cloth need no encouragement from Indian patriots; it could stand on its own legs.

After independence, the political motive for boycott of British goods disappeared; unfortunately, along with it also disappeared the economic aspect of Swadeshi as providing work for the unemployed and semi-employed masses living in the villages. The spiritual side of it, unfortunately was never understood except by very few people.

Under the leadership of Pandit Jawaharlal Nehru, our first Prime Minister, free India was keen to industrialise itself as quickly as possible after the fashion of Europe, America and Russia, through centralized and mechanized big industries. This, it was thought, could be most quickly and effectively done through planning, and therefore had its successive five year plans. In this process the spirit of Swadeshi declined.

Acharya Kripalani brought this tendency to the notice of Panditji. His reply was very significant from the point of view of his philosophy. He asked: "Why do we need Swadeshi now, being a free country managing our own affairs? We could bring from abroad the things that we want. We could also prevent the import of things that we did not want."[48] Kripalani also pointed out to him the psychological effect of the cult of Swadeshi on the common people, but Pandit Nehru was convinced that the government could do the needful in this matter. When everything was to be decided by the Government, it was no wonder that the spirit of Swadeshi began to decline.[49] However, certain concessions were made to Khadi industry which cost the exchanger a pretty penny but could not check the grandiose schemes of the Government of speedily industrializing India.

The neglect of Swadeshi has progressively landed us in the economic and financial crisis. It has led to our enormous adverse balance of trade with almost every country in Europe, America and with Japan in Asia. It has obliged us to take to deficit financing which has progressively assumed the character of inflation. In the last quarter of the last century the country was neck deep in debt and the creditors were hovering around to extract their pound of flesh. Instead of becoming a land flowing with milk and honey, the country was heading towards near financial bankruptcy.

In the aftermath of the balance of payments crisis of the early 1990s, the nervous turn around in economic policy has not helped India develop enduring relations with the world through trade and investment. While dealing with global economic forces, an open door economic policy has been a rather timid and myopic response to external economic pressures and India has remained only a marginal player in the global market place.

The economics and business of India's globalisation of trade and investment flows have undermined its complex cultural and strategic policy perspective. India's trade and investment priorities have to be shaped within the emerging global power structure. In dealing with the world, India has to maintain internal socio-economic stability and defends its sovereignty and territorial integrity. But in order to walk on two legs and retain its status in the global community, it has to develop its complex capacity of unity of (and not in) diversity. Given our potential, we can stand alongside the five great powers of the post-cold war polycentric world—the U.S.A., Russia, China, Japan and European Union.

After the collapse of the Soviet Union and with the moves towards liberalization, privatization and globalisation the world has not become unipolar as expected by many. Rather, a new cold war has started, given the bitter economic rivalry between U.S.A. and Japan and the competing interests of the members of the European Union. This has provided an opportunity for a big market like India to attract investment through a conscious and sustained effort after ensuring internal politico-economic stability. But the Indian state took the plunge to liberalise and integrate with the global without an overall assessment of the global economic and strategic situation. The Asian continent is poised to become the global economic, political, and strategic centre of gravity as five (Russia, Israel, India and Pakistan) out of the eight (the other three being the U.S.A., British and France) nuclear powers or near nuclear powers are in Asia; major energy source (Russia, South-China, Middle East and Central Asia) are located here and 60 per cent of global population is in this continent.

In the 1950s and 1960s, India nursed a certain vision to emerge as a major global force in Asia along with and next only to Russia and China. In a changed and more skewed world, the vision had by the mid-1980s considerably shrunk to become the power only in South Asia. Now after the end of the Cold War, a more shriveled self-image is discernible, without any social consensus on the course India should take, a move towards internal economic liberalization notwithstanding. It is reflected in our foreign policy that has acquired defensive, diffident and unbalanced character.

Earlier, the Nehruvian foreign policy consensus was based on the principles of democracy, secularism, non-alignment and distributive justice within a regulated capitalist system. Nehruvian paradigm was favoured by Keynesian and development philosophies of early post-war period. It was also buttressed through such measures as the public sector, land reforms and affirmative action.

The Nehruvian consensus broke down with the end of one party dominance and the course kind of realism took over as Indira Gandhi moved towards a real politik-based approach. Under the Congress system, Indian society became increasingly dualistic with an unstated accent on elitist economic growth; the perspective of secularism and regulated capitalistic "socialism" was discarded.

In this context and, along with the collapse of USSR, a weak, confused, diffident, rudderless and disoriented political rule got established in India. Instead of a relatively possible autonomous development, it plumped for an uncritical pro-U.S. and western orientation and accepted, India's unequal integration in the global power structure led by the "Washington consensus" of new-liberalism. In the past decade, India has become a handmaiden of the predatory forces of global capitalism as is evident from its excessive non-action, preoccupation with Pakistan, overemphasis on foreign investment in the emerging market economy, acceptance of inequitable economic and trade terms, accommodation of the west in the UN and acquiescence in the dominance of multilateral institutions.

A pattern is discernible here of a compromise on sovereignty, lack of an independent move and a trade-off with the western-prescribed neo-liberal economic policy on human rights and nuclear issues. Because of the new policy perspective in the context of persistent poverty and domestic destitution, India's position is marginalized in the world. There must be alternative to inequality-enhancing capitalism. India's domestic and foreign orientation must change radically for securing sustainable political peace, economic prosperity and social justice, otherwise, marginalisation is the only alternative.

If India is to emerge as a nation whose global relevance is commensurate with itself image, it must establish its credentials by furthering productive multilateral economic and political relationship all round, and not remain hostage to the western global interests. In fact, the linkage of the India's economy with the global economy is such that India has no option but to grapple with the dynamics of globalisation. Whether to globalise India or not is not the question now because globalisation of the world financial system is a historical process. India is already hooked on to both the world financial economy and the ballooning flow of world information. It can not hope to remain half-pregnant, and its choice now is either to abort or to go all the way India should become capable of drawing on the economic and technological potential of the Indian diaspora world-wide, giving our continental economic dimension and civilizational cultural attributes. In seeking new linkage with the world, in an era of internal economic reform, India should strengthen its position in the global community through Non-Resident Indians (N.R.I.) in different parts of the world. To draw upon the strength and skills of the Indian diaspora in forging politico-economic relations with the world, the best way is to pursue cultural diplomacy.

The root of our difficulty is that we have constitutionally decreed freedom of expression and judicially sanctified freedom of the press but not the transparency; accountability and accessibility necessary to fix our priorities better in rapidly changing world. Because of persistent poverty, mass-illiteracy and dominant caste-religious hierarchy, an attitude of reverential acceptance of state dominance has become embedded in our collective psyche.

At present, we have to assess once again our relative position in the world. If we want to be present at the grand ball of the global financial and information economy; we have to revise our still abrasive attitude towards the rest of the world. But again we have to ask ourselves, "shall we dance." This is a dialectical question of political economy of development.

Notes and References

1. *Harijan*, 28.3.1936, p. 49.
2. J.B. Kripalani, "The Meaning of Swadeshi", *Gandhi Marg*, Vol. 11, No. 3, July 1967.
3. *Ibid*.
4. *CWMG*, Vol. 13, p. 219.
5. Gopi Nath Dhawan, The Political Philosophy of Mahatma Gandhi (Ahmedabad: Navajivan Publishing House, 1951), p. 106.
6. *CWMG*, Vol. 13, p. 222.
7. *Young India*, 17.2.1926, p. 213.
8. M.K. Gandhi, From Yervada Mandir (Ahmedabad: Navajivan Publishing House, 1957), p. 66.
9. C. Rajagopalachari, and J.C. Kumarappa, The Nation's Voice (Ahmedabad: Navajivan Publishing House, 1957), p. 51.
10. *Harijan*, 25.2.1939, p. 25.
11. *Ibid*., 23.10.1937, p. 311.
12. *Young India*, 14.1.1920, p. 3.
13. Pattabhi Sitaramayya, "History of Indian National Congress", (Delhi: S. Chand Company, 1969), Vol. I, pp. 398, 404-5.
14. *Harijan*, 23.1.1939, p. 441.
15. *Ibid*., 28.9.1934, p. 209.
16. *CWMG*, Vol. 13, pp. 217-25.
17. P. Spratt, Gandhism: An Analysis (Madras: The Huxley Press, 1939), p. 223.
18. *CWMG*, Vol. 63, p. 233.
19. *Ibid*., Vol. 87, p. 26.
20. *Ibid*., Vol. 60, p. 254.
21. *Ibid*.
22. *Ibid*., Vol. 16, p. 30.
23. *Ibid*., Vol. 26, p. 173.
24. *Ibid*., Vol. 28, p. 428.
25. *Ibid*., Vol. 40, p. 435.
26. *Ibid*.
27. *Ibid*., Vol. 58, p. 294.
28. *Ibid*., Vol. 62, p. 324.
29. *Ibid*., Vol. 26, p. 279.
30. *Ibid*., Vol. 25, p. 475.
31. *Ibid*.
32. *Young India*, 12.3.1925, p. 88.
33. *Young India*, 1.2.1921, p. 278.
34. *CWMG*, Vol. 68, p. 188.
35. *Ibid*., Vol. 36, p. 128.
36. *Ibid*., Vol. 35, p. 475.
37. *Harijan*, 12.2.1938, p. 5.
38. *CWMG*, Vol. 83, pp. 26-27.
39. *Ibid*., Vol. 60, p. 256.
40. *Ibid*.
41. *Ibid*., Vol. 61, p. 232.

42. *Ibid*., Vol. 32, p. 23-24.
43. *Ibid*., Vol. 31, p. 11.
44. *Ibid*., Vol. 30, p. 454.
45. *Ibid*., p. 386.
46. *Ibid*., p. 454.
47. *Ibid*., Vol. 70, p. 205.
48. J.B. Kripalani, *op. cit*., p. 288.
49. *Ibid*.

10

Gandhian Economic Order

Few people would deny that the world is in a grim state. Although many sparks of light are visible, much of the world appears to be deeply enmeshed in economic crisis. The rattling of nuclear sabres makes many of us wonder whether human civilisation will survive for another decade or two. Most observers would agree on many of the symptoms of malaise in the world, and agree that these have not appeared overnight, but rather have been accumulating for decades. Unemployment, alienation from work, cruelty and violence to others, self-abuse of many varieties, environmental degradation and a technology that seems to be out of control—these form only the beginning of a possible list of symptoms, symptoms which lead many to argue that a fundamental change in our ways of life is long overdue.

The ways of life to which we are accustomed are indeed liable to change drastically in coming years. In some cases, the problems associated with our current social and economic practices are building upto intolerable levels. In other cases, activists are promoting change in the belief that we can live more healthy and fulfilling lives. And now technologies seem to be reshapping our work and leisure alike. For Third World

Nations are seeking to change an international order which has fulfilled its promise of 'development' for so few of them. That a new stage in 'North-South' relations has been reached has been evident at least since OPEC increased petroleum prices in the early 1970s; thus demonstrating that developing countries could no longer rely on cheap resources from the rest of world to sustain their ways of life. There is a strong urgency to change this way of life. Such changes are also necessary in order to establish a more equitable world. With increasing global instability, this claim may become more than a moral plea: it may be enforced through political or economic action.

With equal urgency, theoretical assessments of what is wrong with our ways of life have to be accompanied by actions to change or preserve crucial features of our world. And we find here, too, divergences over the implications of the present period of crisis for such action. Many people believe that more economic growth is required as the necessary basis for restoring falling employment levels and satisfactory welfare services. But most of the people argue that economic growth atleast of the variety we have experienced in recent decades, is itself part of crisis. Simply rejuvenating past patterns of production and consumption is not enough. The economic crisis provides an opportunity for a wider public to be altered to the complex of problems characterising ways of life. With choices posed more starkly than ever alternative directions for our societies may be soon as not only desirable but realistic, and as capable of being realized.

Two concepts underpin two corresponding approaches. The first concept is that of Dominant Ways of Life (DML). This refers to the patterning of our relationships with each other and with nature. Within a society these relationships are given a structure which means that social and environmental interactions typically vary systematically across class, sex and age group, and that their main features are reproduced with few drastic changes. This brief definition should be sufficient to indicate that by calling attention to ways of life we are doing more then considering the life styles of particular groups. We also want to go beyond thinking of ways of life as the accidental outcome of millions of isolated individual choices to understand how our choices are channelled within political, economic and cultural institutions, and how this social structuring of choices and opportunities affects our quality of life and our possible futures.

The second concept which is used extensively, is that of Alternative Ways of Life (AWL). Agreeing that all is not well with our dominant ways of life, all right thinking persons are concerned with what alternatives might promote more satisfactory human and environmental relationships within countries, and a more just and peaceful international order. In part, this is done by considering what alternatives to our ways of life already exist within our societies, and in part by taking up questions of the strategies which can effect different sorts of change. At this point, it should be made clear that all aspects of our social life are not deteriorating, nor that every ominous trend necessarily signifies worsening conditions in dominating ways of life. Even over recent decades, many facets of life have improved. Much difficult and unpleasant work has been abolished; many lives have been saved that would once have been lost; we know more about conditions in other parts of the world; and so on. The problem that we seek to confront is that of explaining how such benefits can be produced along side new levels of disillusion, despair and destruction; and of determining how we can preserve such benefits while removing the causes of our social ills.

But still the point that some thing has gone wrong somewhere, is abundantly substantiated by general mass poverty among abundance, (India is a rich country inhabited by the poor) unemployment, widening gap between rich and poor, alienation, exploitation, etc. and there is a need for an alternative. That alternatives are possible, we have no doubt. The problem lies in realising them in going from the desire to overcome problems to concrete strategies for achieving change.

Before selecting an alternative, we can learn from what has already been ventured, from past failures and successes. Most importantly, we need to relate our actions to achieve alternative way of life to our explanations of what is wrong with the present way of life, so that each can inform the other. To put this point another way, we have to grasp both the processes which produce basic features of the present way of life, and those which continually tend to undermine them.

According to one view point, many of the problems currently confronting the world can only be alleviated by the creation and deployment of more wealth. It is argued that during the prosperity of last three or four decades, people became rather too interested in consumption at the expense of production. The welfare state has likewise grown into an unproductive bureaucratic monster: parasitic on, but interfering short-sightedly with economic growth, it has rapped enterprise by over-taxation and spawned inflation by printing money. Even the wealth that already exists is used most inefficiently. The necessary change according to this view point, centres around re-establishing efficiency and productivity as the motor forces of our economics. The ultimate aim is depicted as being the creation of societies in which the most modern technologies can be rapidly developed. This will enable an ever-increasing variety of social needs to be freely expressed and provided for through consumer sovereignty in the market.

Otherwise also, man has been quick in using to his immediate advantage the technological power he acquired so rapidly. In the last few decades, he has made more material progress than in many centuries before. For our generation, it has indeed been a thrilling experience to see mankind reach pinnacles of knowledge and performance, and then move on, each time to new conquests and ever greater heights. And this has created in many people that urge which is called the revolution of rising expectations.

Man is able to fight and vanquish many maladies, prolonging his average life span by one-half over that of his predecessors, to improve upon his home and his diet. He also perfected methods for producing goods and services on an incredible mass scale, and invented techniques for transporting himself and his wares at great speeds across continents and oceans, and communicating with any one, anywhere instantly. He has opened up roads, created dams, built settlements, dug mines everywhere literally conquering and subjecting the whole planet.

Having penetrated a number of erstwhile mysteries and being able to sway events massively, man is now vested with unprecedented, tremendous responsibilities and thrown into the new role of moderator of life on the earth—including his own life. There is no doubt that man is not yet fulfilling this role. He has not even started to realize that his responsibilities have changed. He still tends to attribute to technology high miraculous qualities, hoping that it can overcome any difficulty, solve practically any problem, pave the way to a shining future—automatically Trusting in its quasi omnipotence, he thus fails to consider that, however might technology is void of intelligence, lacks judgment, has no inherent sense of direction—and that it is incumbent on his, its master, to modulate and guide it.

Man actually does not know how to be a truly modern man. Other species do not have similar failings. A tiger knows how to be a tiger. A spider lives like a spider. A swallow has learned what it takes to be a swallow. By the use of natural wisdom, their species are continually readjusting and refining their survival, qualities, adapting them to the modifications of their environment. Their success is proved by their very existence, as the present day end-product of age long evolution. Now they are in a danger enemy-man moves ever more against them. Man has many things in common with these other creatures, but apparently, lacks their wisdom for survival. Already at the dawn of history he began to forsake his natural capacity to adapt and survive, finding it expedient to trust his lot more and more to his brain, that is, to his technological capacity and by it to modify the environment instead.

In recent decades, he has put on a spurt and made some quite exceptional jumps, but has not had the time to master them or to adjust to them. He has thus lost the sense of reality, is even unable to realize the place and role he occupies in it. The entire reference base which his ancestors had painstakingly constructed during the preceding ages to keep the human system together and regulate its intercourse with the ecosystem, is no longer valid. His traditional outlook of himself and of his fellow humans, of family, society and of life itself has to be profoundly revised.

The absence in modern man of a sense of responsibility consonant with his new status is all the graver the powerful he becomes. Might without wisdom has made him a modern barbarian possessing tremendous strength but little judgment on how to use it.

Mulling over these points time and again, one becomes progressively convinced that the present global crisis, in which every thing in human system seems to be out of balance with particularly everything else, is a direct consequence of man's inability to rise to the level of understanding and responsibility demanded by his new power role in world. The problem is within man, not outside him, and so is any possible solution. And this is precisely what Mahatma Gandhi preached. To quote his own words, "The world will live in peace only when the individuals composing it make up their mind to do so."[1] It means that the individual should attain a state 'when mind and body and speech are in proper co-ordination'.[2] It can be summed up in the axiom that the most important factor on which human destiny depends is human quality—not only the quality of certain elites but plainly the average quality of the billions of inhabitant of the planet.

Under these circumstances, when search for an alternative way of life has begun, the new Gandhian economic order deserves a fair trial. The first focal point of this Gandhian order is the establishment of a non-exploitative economy.

Gandhi formulated his economic order in the context of his design, of an ideal social order: a non-violent, non-exploitative, humanistic and egalitarian society: His approach to Economics is through the avenue of truth and non-violence. Its goal is not pure material benefit but the advancement of humanity on its road to progress by strengthening the character and the individual development of personality of every single person engaged in such activity. No one's gain should be anybody's loss—financial, physical, moral or spiritual. If there is to be a choice, the preference should fall on the eternal constituents of man rather than on the material. It is the first brick upon which the edifice of his entire economic philosophy stands. He denounced the concept of economic man because the mind of this industrial robot suffers an almost complete black out when it comes to freedom and responsibilities of a human person and it will not easily be quickened into a realisation of what has happened to it.

The problem is how to conduct economic affairs in a manner that is compatible with non-violence. The problem gains real urgency, from the strenuous attempt all over the world to develop the under-developed countries. This development is generally conceived along Western lines. Yet it is easy to see that the Western way of life can not be permanent and will be incompatible with peace if it spreads to all mankind. It is based on non-renewable resources and rejects any idea of voluntary self-limitation.

The western way of life, even in a much more modest form than its American model requires the annual use of several tons of 'fossil' fuel per person. But the worlds resources of fossil fuels, obtainable at a reasonable cost, are strictly limited. It follows that a civilisation based on fossil fuels can be only an episode in the history of man—and when measured against the life of nations a very short episode. By using coal and oil, we live on capital instead of income. This is quite legitimate under certain conditions. Many a young men has his education financed out of capital funds, but if he is wise he does two things: (a) he voluntarily limits his annual drafts on capital so that it will last atleast until he no longer needs it, and (b) he never losses sight of the fact that he must quickly learn to subsist an income, without further substantial drafts on capital. His principal task is to find a way of life that is self-supporting. And that precisely is also the major task of modern man.

A way of life that even more rapidly depletes the power of earth to sustain it and piles up ever more insoluble problems for each succeeding generation can only be called violent. It is not a way of life that one would like to see exported to countries not yet committed to it. Man's urgent task is to follow a non-violent way in his economic life. It is a concept that needs to be widened out, to combat not merely the violence of man against man, but also the violence of man in his dealings with living nature around him and with the limited and finite resources of the earth. Let us take the agricultural research the world over which still goes into method, of violence—insecticides, herbicides, fungicides, artificial fertilisers, etc.—so that modern agriculture has become a gigantic battle with nature instead of a careful devoted striving to gear in with her unbelievably gentle and efficient methods. If man should emerge as victor from this battle with nature, he would undoubtedly find himself on the losing side. Similarly, a civilization ruled almost exclusively by town-dwellers is always in danger of forgetting this basic truth, until the emergence of famine reminds it of its utter dependence on the health of country side.

As in agriculture so in industry and in every walk of life. We need to give our attention to the development and perfection of non-violent methods, so that answers will be found to the three-fold crisis of this modem world—the crisis of resources exhaustion, the ecological crisis, and the crisis of man's alienation and disorientation. All this require work with a new orientation.

Gandhi did not undermine the importance of economic aspect of life rather he gave it, its due importance. All men have material needs. It is neither wrong nor unworthy to devote thought and care to the satisfaction of those needs to the economic aspect of life. In view of the universality of the economic aspect it is not surprising that a systematic body of thought, should have grown up, commonly called Economics. But one thing is surprising that the science of Economic is based on one particular outlook on life, the outlook of the materialist. Every concept of Economics is rooted in this outlook. Even where Economics admits that man does not live by bread alone, it counts as cost any activity that fails to cater for material needs. Economics distinguishes between productive and unproductive activities, and only those are called productive which cater for material wants. Not that Economics had failed to concern itself with welfare. But even welfare is a term completely rooted in materialism.

The concept of 'economic man' is robbing the modern economics its moral character. Where Mammon is God, no one worships the true God. God lives only in the homes of the poor. Gandhi equated God with 'Daridranarayan' meaning God of the poor or God appearing in the hearts of the poor. He emphasized the divinity of man which is epitomised in the great maxim that 'a jive is always a Shiva', a man is by and large divine. And in this respect it is difficult to distinguish between a man and a man. It is on this deep feeling of spirituality and divinity of man that Gandhi based his economic order.

But economics today is simply the science of getting rich. Person who follow its precepts do become rich and person who disobey them become poor. Every capitalist has acquired his fortune by following the laws of our science. Every man of business knows by experience how money is made and how it is lost. But there are many different ways of getting rich. There was a time, when people sought to acquire wealth by poisoning owners of large estates and appropriating their possessions.

Now-a-days merchants adulterate the food, black marketeers, smugglers and other anti-social elements earn huge amount of wealth. This is on same level as getting rich by poisoning others. "Can we ask this either an art or a science of getting rich" asks Ruskin. He further argued that 'let us now, however, assume that by getting rich, economists merely means getting rich by robbing others.' They should point out that theirs' is a science of getting, rich by legal or just means. It happens these days that many things which are legal are not just. The only right way, therefore, to acquire wealth is to do so justly. And if this is true, we must know what is just. It is not enough to live by law of demand and supply. Fish, wolves and rats subsist in that manner. Bigger fish prey on smaller ones, rats swallow insects and wolves devour even human beings. That for them is the law of nature, they know no better. But God has endowed man with understanding, with a sense of justice. He must follow those and not think of growing rich by devouring others—by cheating others and reducing them to beggary."[3]

Economics as taught today throughout the world recognises no limit of any kind. It is therefore, the Economics of materialism and nothing else. There is implicit in it a purely materialist view of life, and it is inseparable from this view of life. When, then, shall we get a system of thought that could be called non-violent economics? When will people realize and understand that the economics of materialism is not of universal valid, that any ordering of life in accordance with its precepts will be utterly incompatible with, and inimical to the non-violent way of life? When will the teachers of Economics begin to be least objective enough to tell their students that the economics of present day teaching is the purest form of materialism and has no meaning for the hungry and semi-starved people outside? When will they take cognizance and admit that other systems of economics are possible and necessary and are even already available in rudimentary form?

Laying down the foundations of his non-violent economic order, Mahatma Gandhi said about Swadeshi, in your village you are bound to support your village barber to the exclusion of the finished barber who may come to you from Madras. If you find it necessary that your village barber should reach the attainments of barber from Madras you may train him to that. Send him to Madras by all means, if you wish, in order that he may learn his calling. Until that you are not justified in going to another barber. That is Swadeshi. So when we find that there are many things that we can not get in India we must be without them. We may have to do without many things... It has been urged that India can not adopt Swadeshi in the economic life. Those who advance this objection do not look upon Swadeshi as a rule of life. With them it is a more patriotic effort, not to be made if it involved any self-denial. But Swadeshi, as defined here, is a religious principle to be undergone in utter disregard of physical discomfort caused to individuals. Much of the deep poverty of India is due to the departure from Swadeshi in the economic life. If not a single article of commerce had been brought from outside India she would be today a land flowing with milk and honey.[4]

But he made it clear that under this plan of life, in seeing to serve India to the exclusion of every other country, 'I do not harm any other country. My patriotism is both exclusive and inclusive. It is exclusive in the sense that, in all humility, I confine my attention to the land of my birth, but is inclusive in the sense that my service is not of a competitive or antagonistic nature. *Sic utere lit alienum non laedas* is not merely a legal maxim, but it is grand doctrine of life. It is the key to a proper practice of non-violent economy."[5]

Drawing his picture of the ideal economy, he wrote in *Young India*, "According to me the economic constitution of India and for the matter of that, the world should be such that no one under it should suffer from the want of food and clothing. In other words, every body should be able to get sufficient work to enable him to make the two ends meet. And this ideal can be universally realized only if the means of production of the elementary necessaries of life remain in the control of masses. These should be freely available to all as God's air and water are or ought to be; they should not be made a vehicle of traffic for the exploitation of others. This monopolization by any country, nation or group of persons would be unjust. The neglect of this principle is the cause of destitution that we witness today not only in this unhappy land but in other parts of the world too."[6]

This takes us to the second focal point of his new economic order. The very idea of non-exploitative economy paves the way for decentralisation. A non-violent system such as he wished to see established in India was to him impossible so long as there was a wide gulf between the rich and poor. As a humanitarian it was the conditions of poverty prevailing in the country and the moral and material degradation that they spelt which claimed his attention when, from beyond India's shores he preached the gospel of self-sufficiency. It was the same humanitarian instincts which first prompted Gandhi, on his settling down in India, to turn to the production of cloth solely with the aid of the hands to provide employment for millions and thus to rid the country of its poverty. That poverty persisted despite the richness of the country's resources in men and material. Gandhi gave a new interpretation to the gospel of Swadeshi to redress the imbalance between agriculture and industries. The Swadeshi mentality, he averred, should denote a determination to find all the necessities of life in India. This was possible, he believed, with the aid of labour and intellect of the villagers. He had no doubt that if the proper atmosphere was created all our wants could be supplied from our villages.

Under the conditions of centralized production, economic power tended to be concentrated in fewer and fewer hands. This had instensified existing inequalities, to widen the gulf between the rich and the poor and to breed conflict between labour and capital. The adoption of decentralized methods of production would, he urged, ensure conditions of social justice, make it possible for producers to control their means of production and to enjoy in full measure the benefits accruing from their productive efforts.

But the protagonists of industrialization of the type that has developed particularly in the developed countries, have urged that the intensification and diversification of that form of industrialisation is the only means of enabling us to raise the standard of living of the people and of reducing unemployment. However, in such industries, the level of employment instead of going up has gone down. While labour engaged in some of the industries and in certain of the occupations in these industries may have received remuneration higher than what was available through cottage production, when the cost of living in towns and cities is taken into consideration, it is doubtful if everywhere the artisan who becomes a factory workers in a corresponding industry is better-off. Besides when account is taken of the large numbers who, in the process of industrialisation are thrown out of work or whose work has become intermittent, we find that the aggregate remuneration for a given number of individuals instead of rising has fallen. Even in terms of averages, the per capita income inspite of the tremendous contribution of industrial production of the national income has remained practically stationery because industrialisation of the centralized variety, increasingly dependent as it is on the use of steam, electricity or similar non-human power has the direct consequence of throwing out of employment the human beings who supplied the power. The corresponding non-mechanized industries find it more and more difficult to face competition of their well organized large scale rivals and gradually languish. A few lose all change of affording remunerative employment. Translated into economic terms, their enforced idleness must depress the per capita income and drag down the standard of living of the toilers by hand. What is more important to note is that large scale mechanized industries can not by any stretch of imagination, provide the additional employment needed to satisfy the demand for productive work by millions of our fellow citizens. Thus for employment generation, the pattern of our economic organisation must undergo a change, particularly in the matter of production of consumers' goods which the people in the countryside did in the past and can even now produce to meet their own requirements. Today, in several of these crafts and industries there is enormous idle capacity available, which can be put to productive use to add to the wealth of the nation and to supplement the pittance which the underemployed agricultural labourer and the small sized peasant or the artisan or cottage worker are able to earn. Our planners usually speak of the unused installed capacity of industrial plants. If we conduct a census of unutilised installed capacity of the modest appliances tools and implements of our artisans and other cottage workers, we would find that in the aggregate the latter represent a greater economic waste. The tools and appliances are simple, the processes are easy to learn, often the traditional skills and aptitudes are present and, besides, the pursuit of these crafts and industries can be fitted into the pattern of rural life. No centralised industries located in towns and cities and not even those established in rural surroundings can quite meet the requirements of a population large portions of which must work in the countryside for some hours almost throughout the year and occasionally during particular seasons. It is only the decentralised form of industrial organisation that can meet this peculiar need.

Small scale and cottage industries can also avoid the evils of industrialism. The heart of social reform today is to make the world acknowledge the central place in it of every man's work. In this mechanized age, most of us become merely cogs in a wheel. The environment provided by factory employment is not good enough to develop the basic qualities of manhood. It is for this reason that, if these evils of industrialism are to be avoided, wherever possible we should follow the road of decentralisation. It is only then that it will be possible for us in India still to preserve the dexterity, the skill and the art that our craftsmen engaged in various industrial pursuits possessed and still have not lost. There is no prospect that machine work will ever make anything like the demand or character from the ordinary workers that the old crafts used to make and some skilled work in some callings makes today, the craftsman who knows something of what beauty is because his own hands bring it into being, all get more from their work as well as giving more to it than the modern factory worker even can. "The dexterity, ingenuity, resourcefulness and above all a sense of beauty of her common people are" as Professor R.H. Tawney wrote about China, nearly half century ago, "a social and economic asset of inestimable value."[7] When we plan new social order let us ensure, wherever possible, and development of this asset which we also possess in India.

There is yet another aspect which should induce us as to prefer the decentralized form of industrial production wherever it is feasible. Planners should ensure that the operation of the economic system does not result in the concentration of wealth and means of production to the common detriment and that the ownership and control of the material resources of the community are so distributed as best to subserve the common good. The decentralised method of production has this to recommend it. But with mass production and mass-distribution go mass financing and three always conspire to expropriate ever increasing numbers of small owners of land and productive equipment, thus reducing the sum of freedom among the majority and increasing the economic power of minority to exercise a coercive control over the lives of their fellows. Hence, we have to eschew methods of economic organisation which lead to concentration of economic power in a few hands.

A few other considerations must also claim attention. All these justify concentration of efforts on cottage and small scale industries. The availability of raw materials, tools and implement, skill and markets are factors that have to be taken into account. The raw material needed for essential consumers' goods are ordinarily available in the rural areas. The tools and implements are already there or were there until recent times—or they are such as can be easily manufactured locally by skilled carpenters and blacksmiths. For most of the individual operations no great skill is needed; but undoubtedly, what little is required can be acquired without much difficulty. Providing for simple instruction in these crafts will not present much of a problem. In fact, the case with which the skill can be acquired is, itself, an argument in their favour. An additional advantage is that both men and women can ply these crafts and that the bulk of them can be carried on in their homes by the humblest of villagers. For most of the commodities the market they cater to will be the local ones. Transport should not add to the costs beyond what are incurred on the products of the centralized industries. Further, warehousing, handling, trading and other operations, instead of being centralized in growing trade centres and in metropolitan cities, will tend to get dispersed. That should count an additional advantage.

But the most important question that has to be answered is how decentralisation is to operate in practice. We have to seek for increase in production and the provision of additional employment in the traditional rural industries and crafts. These were parts of our economy in the past and met the local requirements of various consumers' goods with the surplus production passing on the towns and cities either for consumption or for export. It is mainly these industries and crafts that have to be reorganised. Reorganisation connotes effort for securing raw materials, supplying tools and implements, providing credit and arranging where necessary, for exchange of goods or marketing. Under the old economy, these operations were conducted in a particular manner. It may be that in the changed conditions of our economy the pattern of the operation may not be the same. This is particularly true of the occupations or crafts which during the past half of century went out of vogue and where the revival calls for some outside stimulus to be applied and for some facilities to be granted. Where new occupations are to be introduced in an area, similar organised effort will be necessary.

It is also likely that the unit of operation may not continue to be an individual or his family as in the past. A number of families may group themselves on trusteeship basis. The trust, according to the needs of the situation, may either be a village multipurpose agency or an institution for a specialized craft covering, if that is found necessary, an area larger than a village.

Integrated rural development is the next focal point of his economic order. This is closely related with the preceding one. Gandhi had sought to build India from the bottom, that is from the poorest and weakest and have followed the centrality of village. He was deeply pained to see the disintegration and ruin of the villages. "Our cities are not India. India lives in her seven and half lacs of villages. The city people are brokers and commission agents for the big houses of Europe, America and Japan." In the words of reminiscent of Dadabhai Naoroji's concept of drain the Mahatma referred to the suffering and exploitation of Indian villages as 'the bleeding process that has gone on for the past two hundred years'.[8] His heart bled to see the misery of the Indian villagers and he formulated his famous constructive programme a considerable number of whose categories are relevant to them.[9]

Gandhi felt that a strengthened and economically sound rural economy would revitalize Indian economy. He preached, hence the 'gospel of rural mindedness'. A rural economy of self-contained villages alone could be the basis of a non-violent economy. He stated, "You have therefore, to be rural-minded before you can be non-violent and to be rural-minded you have to faith in the spinning wheel".[10] He felt that the small communities moulding their lives on the basis of voluntary co-operation would be the best environment for the extinction of exploitation. The regeneration of India he felt to be impossible without village reconstruction. Hence he gave a slogan, 'Back to villages'. He gave a call to every body to go and work in villages, develop rural economy, rural industry and rural skill. In small self-sufficient villages producing mostly for their consumption, a peaceful life devoted to the pursuit of democratic values was possible. Big urban concentrations, on the other hand, result in the monopolisation and accumulation of wealth by a minority. Economic concentration is bound to lead to political centralisation. Centralisation in its turn, supports violence. He was of the definite view that non-violence could be realized not on the basis of a factory civilization but only on that of self-contained villages.

Pt. Jawaharlal Nehru expressed his doubt over this model and wrote: 'The whole question is how to achieve this (non-violent) society and what its contents should be. I do not understand why a village should necessarily embody truth and non-violence. A village normally speaking, is backward intellectually and culturally and no progress can be made from a backward environment. Narrow-minded people are much more likely to be untruthful and violent."[11] Gandhi himself acknowledged the abnoxious essential realities of Indian villages. Instead of having graceful hamlets dotting the land, we have dung heaps. The approach to many villages is not a refreshing experience. Often one would like to shut one's eyes and stuff one's nose; such is the surrounding dirt and offending smell.[12] However, he was not willing to accept this state of affair as *fait accompli*, as an irredeemable situation. He was confident that the prevailing situation would be transformed by the villagers themselves provided proper help and guidance are extended to them. But ever since we started planning our economic life most of our planners, conceive of national plans mainly in terms of industrialization. We have the slogan dinned into our ears, "Industrialise or Perish" and many of us have come to believe that industrialisation is the panacea for all our ills. What we need, essentially, is however, a better balanced economy under which the growing pressure of population on the land is reduced and those who are on the land are enabled to produce and earn more. The backwardness of the economy, or the unproductive employment of an increasing population or the non-utilisation of material resources locally can not be remedied by intensification of the process of industrialization. Besides the feasible rate of industrialisation is governed not merely by the problems associated with the erection of factories, it is a function of an organic type of growth in which the essential feature is the mutual dependence of the various sections involved. In any development these sectors must keep in pace.

Referring to the economic conditions of India, in a paper on 'The Human Dimension of Economic Growth: Challenge of Stagnation in Under Developed Countries' presented by him at Asia-assembly in New Delhi in 1973 Professor Gunnar Myrdal said:

> "Gandhi was certainly a planner, and a rationalistic planner but his planning was all embracing and laid main stress on sanitation and health, the raising of nutritional levels by mere intensive agriculture, a redirection and not only an expression of education so that it becomes basic and not merely literary and academic and a redistribution of land wealth to create greater equality."

He further said,

> "It is only in the latest years that we have more generally come back to Gandhi's ideas, when even some economists have moved to press for an integrated planning which is the modern term for what Gandhi was all the time teaching. My Indian friends will not be offended when I say that if Indian planning has not been more successful than it has actually been, the main explanation is that they have not kept as close as they should, to the fundamentals of the teachings of the Father of the Nation."[13]

The goals of Gandhian economic system are quite different from ones the country has been pursuing since independence.

Therefore, plans for economic development such as one envisaging a seven per cent or eight per cent rate of growth, which are some times presented as Gandhian alternatives, I am afraid must be outside the framework of the Gandhian Economic System taken seriously. My submission is that the Gandhian path is not an alternative path of reaching the same goal of economic development which the country is pursuing. It is a path leading to an alternative goal of human life and existence. The Gandhian alternative is Sarvodaya, a classless society based on destruction of the class but not on the destruction of the individuals who constitute the classes, a system of production that does not fail to make use of science and technology for creating an economy of abundance but does not in the process either kill individual initiative or freedom for development nor create a psychology of ceaseless striving for more and more of material goods, a system of distribution that will ensure a reasonable minimum income for all and, while not aiming at a universal equality of an arithmetical kind, will nevertheless ensure that all private property or talent beyond the minimum will be used as a trust for the public good and not for individual aggrandisement, a social order where all will work but there is no inequality either in status or in opportunity for any individual, and a political system where change is the result of persuasion, differences are resolved by discussion, and conflicts by love and recognition of mutuality of interest.

Gandhi's solution rested on the application of unadulterated non-violence to all aspects of life. Admitting that "it may fail," he asserted nevertheless that "if it does, it will be because of my ignorance of the technique of non-violence."[14] He conceded that while history has certainly recorded such changes in individual, one may not be able to point them in a whole society. There had been in history many individual votaries of non-violence, but society continued to be steeped in non-violence. There are many noble examples of voluntary poverty and dedicated service, but the social order continued to bristle with exploitation, inequality, and mass poverty. Religion was good but it was confined to one aspect of life with apparently no similar good effect on the other aspect of life. The individual stood apart from society and religion failed to bring about integrations between the two. Gandhi brooded over this paradox and the answer that he gave reminds one of the enlightenment that came to Buddha both in its suddenness and its startling simplicity. 'Somehow or other', he said, 'the wrong belief has taken possession of us that Ahimsa is preeminently a, weapon of individuals and its use should, therefore, be limited to that sphere. In fact, this is not the case. Ahimsa is definitely an attribute of society. To convince people of this truth is at once my effort and my experiment."[15] His experiment in Satyagraha non-violence or non-co-operation or the use of Ahimsa as a social or collective weapon are well known. Whether similar success will attend experiment in non-violence for bringing about economic change is still in the womb of future. The fact is that the experiment has not yet been attempted. And the great exponent of non-violence is no longer there either to conduct the experiment or give his personal guidance to those who may dare to make the attempt. But lessons of his experiments with truth and non-violence are there for who care to read them. What is required is their extension from the political to the social and economic field.

Thus, at a time when humanity is groaning under the crushing burden of a number of miseries and struggling with the nightmare of a terrifying future, the course indicated by the unerring fingers should come as a solace to all those who seek happiness, real prosperity, peace and goodwill for all.

Notes and References

1. M.K. Gandhi, Hindu Dharma (Ahmedabad: Navajivan Publishing House, 1950), p. 70.
2. *Young India*, 1.10.1931, p. 287.
3. John Ruskin, *supra*.
4. *CWMG*, Vol. XIII, p. 231.
5. *Young India*, 21.10.1926, p. 244.
6. *Ibid.*, 15.11.1929, p. 381.
7. R.H. Tawnev, Studies in Economic History: The Collected Papers of George Unwin (New York: Kelley and Millman Inc., 1927), pp. 72-73.
8. *Young India*, 13.10.1921, p. 325.
9. The Constituent categories of the Constructive Programme are: 1. Communal Unity, 2. Removal of Untouchability, 3. Prohibition, 4. Village Industries, 5. Village Sanitation, 6. New or Basic Education, 7. Adult Education, 8. Women, 9. Education in Health and Hygiene 10. Provincial Language, 11. National Language, 12. Kisans, 13. Labours, 14. Adiwasis, 15. Lepers, and 16. Students.

M.K. Gandhi, Constructive Programme, Its meaning and Place (Ahmedabad: Navajivan Publishing House, 1963).

10. *Harijan*, 1.11-1939, p. 331.
11. Pyare Lal, The Last Phase, Vol. II (Ahmedabad: Navajivan Publishing House, 1965), p. 545.
12. M.K Gandhi, Constructive Programme, *op. cit.*, p. 15.
13. The Nagpur Times, 16.2.1973.
14. *Harijan*, 20.2.1937, p. 12.
15. *Ibid.*, 25.8.1940, pp. 261-62.

Bibliography

Books

Anjaria, J.J., *An Essay on Gandhian Economics*, Bombay: Vora and Co., 1945.

Anstey, Vera, Economic Development of India, London: Longmans, 1952.

Bandyopadhyaya Jayantanuja, *Social and Political Thought of Gandhi*, Bombay: Allied Publishers, 1969.

Bepin Behari, *Gandhian Economic Philosophy*, Bombay: Vora and Co., 1963.

Bhatia, A.C., *The Gandhian Economy. What Gandhiji has done for India*, Lahore: Ilami Markay, 1946.

Bhattacharya, Bhabani, *Gandhi the Writer*, New Delhi: National Book Trust, 1969.

Bhattacharyya, Buddhadeva, *Evolution of Political Philosophy of Gandhi*, Calcutta: Calcutta Book House, 1969.

Bhattacharji, M.M. (ed.), *Speeches and Writings of Eminent Indians*, Calcutta: Macmillan, 1952.

Birla, G.D., *In the Shadow of the Mahatma*, Bombay: Orient Longmans Ltd., 1953.

Biswas, S.C. (ed.), *Gandhi, Theory and Practice, Social Impact and Contemporary Relevance*, Simla: Indian Institute of Advanced Study, 1969.

Bondurant, Joan V., *Conquest of Violence, The Gandhian Philosophy of Conflict*, Bombay: Oxford University Press, 1959.

Bose, Nirmal Kumar and Patwardhan, P.M., *Gandhi: In Indian Politics*, Bombay: Lalwani Publishing House, 1967.

Bose, Nirmal Kumar and Patwardhan, P.M., *Selections From Gandhi*, Ahmedabad: Navajivan Publishing House, 1959.

Bose, Nirmal Kumar, *Studies in Gandhism*, Calcutta: Indian Associated Publishing Co. Ltd., 1940.

Bose, Subhas Chandra, *The Indian Struggle, 1920-34*, Part 11, Calcutta: Published for Netaji Publishing Society, 1948.

Brailsford, H.N., *Rebel India*, London: Leonard Stein, 1931.

Brij Narain, *Economic Structure of Free Indian: Building from Below*, Bombay: All India Khadi and Village Industries Board, 1955.

Caute, D. (ed.), *Essential Writings of Marx*, London: Panther, 1967.

Chakrabarti, Atulananda, *The Mahatma and His Men*, G.D. Birla, New Delhi: Rupa and Co., 1968.

Chauhan, Sandip, *Demand for New International Order*, New Delhi: MD Publications, 1997.

———, GATT to WTO, Gandhian Alternative and NIEO, New Delhi, Deep and Deep Publications (P) Ltd., 2001.

Chandy, K.K., *The Attitude to Property, Christian, Marxist and Gandhi*, Kottayam, The Ashra Press, 1983.

Clark, J.M., Alternative to Serfdom, New York: Knopf, 1948.

———, Guideposts in Time of Change, New York: Harper, 1949.

Collins, James, *God in Modern Philosophy*, London: Routledge and Kegan Paul, 1960.

Dantwala, M.L., *Decentralised Economic Order*, Kashi: Sarva Seva Sangh Prakashan, 1961.

———, *Gandhism Reconsidered*, Bombay: Padma Publications, 1945.

Desai, Mahadev Haribhai, *A Righteous Struggle*, Ahmedabad: Navajivan Publishing House, 1951.

Deshmukh, C.D., *Economic Development in India, 1946-56, A Personal Retrospect*, Bombay: Asia, 1957.

Diwan, Romesh and Lutz, Mark, *Essays in Gandhian Economics*, Delhi: Gandhi Peace Foundation, 1985.

Dutt, R.P., *India Today*, Bombay: People Publishing House, 1949.

———, *Modern India*, London, 1927.

Edwin Seligman, R.A., *Encyclopaedia of the Social Sciences*, New York: The Macmillan Co., 1951.

Evans, Michael, *Karl Marx*, London: George Allen & Unwin, 1975.

Fischer, Louis, *The Life of Mahatma Gandhi,* Bombay, Bharatiya Vidya Bhawan, 1983.

———, *Fundamentals of Marxism and Leninism,* Moscow: F.L.P.M., 1975.

Gandhi, M.K., *An Autobiography or The Story of My Experiments with Truth,* Ahmedabad: Navajivan Publishing House, 1983.

———, *Ashram Observations in Action,* Ahmedabad: Navajivan Publishing House, 1955.

———, *Capital and Labour,* Bombay: Bhartiya Vidya Bhawan, 1970.

———, *Constructive Programme: Its Meaning and Place,* Ahmedabad: Navajivan Publishing House, 1970.

———, *From Yeravada Mandir,* Ahmedabad: Navajivan Publishing House, 1986.

———, *Hind Swaraj or Indian Home Rule,* Ahmedabad: Navajivan Publishing House, 1982.

———, *Hindu Dharma,* Ahmedabad: Navajivan Publishing House, 1950.

———, *Khadi Why and How,* Ahmedabad: Navajivan Publishing House, 1959.

———, *My Picture of Free India* (edited by A.T. Hingorani), Bombay: Bhartiya Vidya Bhawan, 1965.

———, *My Socialism,* Compiled by R.K. Prabhy, Ahmedabad: Navajivan Publishing House, 1949.

———, *Satyagraha in South Africa,* Ahmedabad: Navajivan Publishing House.

Ghosh, P.C., *Mahatma Gandhi: As I saw Him,* Delhi: Chand, 1968.

Gregg, Richard B., *A Philosophy of Economic Development,* Ahmedabad: Navajivan, 1959.

———, *To Which Way Lies Hope? Examination of Capitalism, Communism, Socialism and Gandhi's Programme,* Ahmedabad: Navajivan, 1959.

Hardiman, David, *Gandhi in His Time and Ours Delhi,* Permanent Back, 2003.

Hughes, E.R. (ed.), *The Individual in East and West,* London: Oxford University Press, 1937.

Ishwarya, *Upanishad, translated by Donald G. Groom,* Varanasi: Sarva Seva Sangh Prakashan, 1981.

Iyer, Raghavan N., *The Moral and Political Thought of Mahatma Gandhi,* Delhi: Oxford University Press, 1973.

Jai Narain and Dutta, Rakesh Kumar, *Economics of Defence: A Study of SAARC Countries*, New Delhi: Lancers, 1989.

Jai Narain, *Gandhi's View of Political Power*, New Delhi: Deep and Deep Publications, 1989.

Jha, S.N., *A Critical Study of Gandhi : An Economic Thought*, Agra: Lakshmi Narayan Aggarwal, 1961.

Kausika, Narayana, *Plea for a New World Order: A Scientific Approach in Truth and Non-violence*, Nemmana (Cahin) M.G.V. Aiyer, 1941.

Keynes, J.M., *The General Theory of Employment Interest and Money*, New York-Harcourt Book & Co., 1964.

Kripalani, J.B., *Gandhi: His Life and Thought*, New Delhi: Publication Division, Ministry of Information and Broadcasting, Government of India, 1971.

Kuhn, Alfred, *Labour: Institution and Economics*, New York: Rinchard and Co. Inc., 1957.

Kumarappa, Bharatan, *Capitalism, Socialism or Villagism*, Varanasi: Sarva Seva Sangh Prakashan, 1965.

Kumarappa, J.C., *Gandhian Economic Thought*, Bombay: Vora & Co., 1951, Varanasi Serva Seva Sangh, 1962.

———, *The Gandhian Way of Life*, Wardha: AIVIA, 1952.

———, The Economy of Peramnence: A Quest for Social Order based on Non-Violence, 2 Vol., Wardha: All India Village Industries Association, 1948.

———, *"A Non-Violent Way of Life, in, Gandhian Outlook and Techniques*, New Delhi: Ministry of Education: Government of India, 1953.

———, *Lessons From Europe*, Wardha: Sarva Seva Sangh, 1955.

———, *The Philosophy of Work and Other Essays*, Wardha: All India Village Industries Association, 1949.

———, *Present Economic Situation*, Wardha: AIVIA, 1949.

———, *Swaraj for the Masses*, Hind Kitabs, 1948.

———, *Why the Village Movement?*, Rajahmundry, Hindustan Publishing Co., 1936.

———, *"Gandhian Approach to Economics"*, in *Philosophy of Work and Other Essays*, Wardha: AIVIA, 1949.

———, and Mehta, V.L., *Economics of Non-Violence*, Bombay: Hamara Hindustan, 1944.

Lenin, VI, *Left Wing Communism: An Infantile Disorder,* Moscow: Novosti Press, 1969.

Lester, Richard, A., *Labour and Industrial Relations: A General Analysis,* New York: The Macmillan Co., 1951.

Lewis, John R., *Quest Crisis in India: Economic Development and American Policy,* Bombay: Asia, 1963.

Lewis, W.A., *The Theory of Economic Growth,* London: George Allen & Unwin, 1955.

Leibhnecht Wilhelm, *Marx and Engels Through the Eyes of Their Contemporaries,* Moscow: Progress Publishers, 1972.

Mahaprajna Acharya, Democracy: Social Revolution Through Individual Transformation, Ladnun, JVB, 1994.

———, Economics of Mahavira, New Delhi, Vikas, 2004.

Marshall, Alfred, *Principles of Economics,* London: Macmillan & Co., 1949.

Marx, Karl, *Das Capital* in three Volumes, Moscow: Progress Publishers, 1577.

———, *Economic and Philosophic Manuscripts of 1844,* Moscow: Progress Publishers, 1967.

———, Engels, E., *Manifesto of the Communist Party,* Moscow: Progress Publishers, 1973.

———, *The German Ideology,* New York: International Publishers, 1939.

Masani, M.R., *The Communist Party of India: A Short Story,* Bombay: Bhartiya Vidya Bhawan, 1967.

Mashruwala, K.G., *Gandhi and Marx,* Ahmedabad: Navajivan Publishing House, 1960.

Mathur, J.S., *Essays on Gandhian Economics,* Allahabad: Chaitanya Publishing House, 1959.

Mathur, J.S. and Mathur, A.S., *Economic Th.ought of Mahatma Gandhi,* Allahabad: Chaitanya Publishing House, 1962.

Mehta, J.K., *A Philosophical Interpretation of Economics,* London: George Allen & Unwin, 1962.

———, *Fundamentals of Economics,* Allal1abad: Pothshala Ltd., 1952.

———, *Gandhian Thought,* New Delhi: Ashish Publishing House, 1985.

Mehta, Vaikunth L., *Decentralised Economic Development,* Bombay: Khadi and Village Industries Commission, 1964.

Mehta, Ved, *Mahatma Gandhi and His Apostles,* New Delhi: Indian Book Company, 1977.

Mehta, Vrajendra Raj, *Beyond Marxism: Towards an Alternative Perspective,* New Delhi: Manohar, 1978.

Miliband, Ralph, *Marxism and Politics,* London: Oxford University Press, 1977.

Ming, Wang, *The Revolutionary Movement in Colonial Countries* New York: Workers Library Publishers, 1935.

Mishra, Vikas, *Hinduism and Economic Growth,* Oxford University Press, 1962.

Mukherji, D.P., *Diversities,* New Delhi: People Publishing House, 1958.

Mukerjee, Hiren: *Gandhi: A Study,* New Delhi: People Publishing House, 1960.

Munshi, K.M., *Reconstruction of Society Through Trusteeship,* Bombay: Bhartiya Vidhya Bhawan.

Myrdal, Gunnar, *Asian Drama: An Enquiry into the Poverty of Nations,* 3 Volumes, New York: Panteon, 1968.

Namboodiripad, E.M.S., *The Mahatma and the Ism,* New Delhi: People Publishing House, 1959.

Narayan, Jayaprakash, *Towards Total Revolution,* 4 Volumes, Bombay: Popular Prakashan, 1978.

Naoroji, Dadabhai, *Poverty and Un-British Rule in India,* New Delhi: Publications Division, Ministry of Information and Broadcasting, Government of India, 1961.

Nayar, Baldev Raj, *Globalisation and Nationalism,* New Delhi: Sage Publications, 2001.

Nehru, Jawahar Lal, *An Autobiography,* London: The Bodley Head, 1958.

———, *Mahatma Gandhi,* Calcutta: Signet Press, 1949.

Pani, Narendar, *Exclusive Economic,* New Delhi: Sage Publications, 2001.

Parekh, Bhikhu, *Gandhi's Political Philosophy,* Delhi, Ajanta, 1995.

Pasricha, Ashu, *Gandhian Approach to Integrated Rural Development,* New Delhi: Shipra, 2000.

Pavate, D.C., *Jamnalal Bajaj: A Brief Study of His Life and Character,* Ahmedabad: Navajivan Publishing House, 1962.

Paulox, VI., *The Indian Capitalist Class,* Delhi: People Publishing House, 1994.

Peccei, Aurelio, *The Human Quality*, Oxford: Pergoman Press, 1977.

Prabhu, R.K. and Rao, U.R., *The Mind of Mahatma Gandhi*, Ahmedabad: Navajivan Publishing House, 1967.

Pradhan, Benudhar, *The Socialism Thought of Mahatma Gandhi*, 2 Vols., Delhi: GDK Publications, 1980.

Pyare Lal, *Mahatma Gandhi: The Early Phase*, Vol. 1, Ahmedabad: Navajivan Publishing House, 1965.

———, *Mahatma Gandhi*, Vol. II, (The Early Phase), The Discovery of Satyagraha on the Threshold, Bombay: Sevak Prakashan, 1980.

———, *Mahatma Gandhi: The Last Phase*, in 2 Volumes, Ahmedabad: Navajivan Publishing House, 1956, 1958.

———, *Towards New Horizons*, Ahmedabad: Navajivan Publishing House, 1957.

Quennell, Peter (ed.), *Selected Writings of John Ruskin*, London: The Falleon Press, 1952.

Radhakrishan, S., *Speeches and Writings*, Third Series, New Delhi: The Publications Division, Ministry of Information and Broadcasting, Government of India.

———, (ed.), *Mahatma Gandhi: Essence and Reflection on His Life and Work*, Allahabad: Kitabistan, 1944.

Rajendra Prasad, *An Autobiography*, Bombay: Asia Publishing House, 1957.

———, *At the Feet of Mahatma Gandhi*, Bombay: Asia Publishing House, 1961.

Riven, Kenneth, *Economic Thought of Mahatma Gandhi*, Bombay: Allied Publishers, 1959.

Roy, M.N., *India in Transition*, Bombay: Nachiketa, 1971.

Rudolph, Llyod and Susanne H. Rudolph, New Delhi, Oxford University Press, 2006.

Ruskin, Unto This Last, A Paraphrase by M.K. Gandhi, Ahmedabad: Navajivan Publishing House, 1989.

Sankhdher, M.M., *Understanding Gandhi Today*, New Delhi: Deep and Deep Publications, 1996.

Say, J.B., *Trestise on Political Economy*, Translated by C.R. Prinsep, Boston: Wills and Lilly, 186 7.

Schumacher, E.F., *Future is Manageable*, New Delhi: Impex India, 1978.

Schumacher, E.F., *Roots of Economic Growth*, Varanasi: Gandhian Institute of Studies, 1962.

———, *Small is Beautiful: A Study of Economics if People Mattered*, London: Abacus, 1989.

Sengupta, Arjun, *Reforms, Equity and the IMF, An Economists World*, New Delhi: Har Anand, 2001.

Sethi, J.D., *Gandhi Today*, New Delhi: Vikas Publishing House Pvt. Ltd., 1976.

Sharma, Jai Narain and B.R. Dugar, Relative Economics, New Delhi: Deep and Deep Publications (P) Ltd., 2010.

———, *Human Resource Management*, New Delhi: Mittal, 2002.

Sharma, Rashmi, *Gandhian Economics: A Humane Approach*, New Delhi: Deep and Deep Publications, 1997.

Sinha, VB., *The Red Rebel in India*, New Delhi: Associated Publishing House, 1968.

Smith, Adam, *An Inquiry into the Nature and Causes of Wealth of Nations*, New York: The Modern Library, 1937.

Speeches and Writings of Gandhi, Madras: G.A. Natesan and Co., 1933.

Tawney, R.H., *Equality*, New York: Harcourt, Brace, 1931.

———, *Studies in Economic History: The Collected Paper of George Unwin*, New York: Kelley & Millman Inc., 1927.

Tendulkar, D.G. (ed.), *Mahatma*, Eight Volumes, Delhi: The Publications Division, Ministry of Information and Broadcasting, Government of India, 1962.

Tendulkar, D.G. and others, *Gandhiji—His Life and Work*, Bombay: Karnataka Publishing House, 1944.

Terchek, Ronald J. Gandhi : *Struggling for Autonomy*, New Delhi, Vistaar Publciations, 2000.

The Collected Works of Mahatma Gandhi, 100 Volumes, New Delhi: The Publications Division, Ministry of Information and Broadcasting, Government of India, 1961.

Toffler, Alvin, *Future Shocks*, New York: A National General Company, 1971.

Tolstoy, Leo, *What Then Must We Do*, London: Oxford University Press, 1950.

Toynbee, Arnold, *Study of History*, London: Thames and Hudson, 1977.

Varma, VP., *The Political Philosophy of Mahatma Gandhi and Sarvodaya*, Agra: Lakshmi Narain Aggarwal, 1981.

Wadia, PA., *The Gandhian Approach to Economics in Social and Political Ideas of Mahatma Gandhi*, Oxford University, 1949.

Weber, Max, *Theory of Social and Economic Organization*, (Translated by A.M. Handerson and T. Parson), New York: Oxford University Press, 1947.

Wellock, Wilfred, New Horizons, London: Houseman's Bookshop.

Journals, Newspapers and Reports

Amrit Bazar, Patrika, Calcutta.

Gandhi Marg : A Journal of Gandhi Peace Foudnation, New Delhi.

Harijan : A Journal of Applied Gandhism, 1933-55, New York, Garland Publishing Inc, 1973.

Inprecorr, Vol. XVI, February 29, 1936.

Journal of Gandhian Studies : A Journal of Indian Society of Gandhian Studies.

Nagpur Times, Nagpur.

Sarvodaya, Tamil Nadu Sarvodaya Sangh, Tirpur.

Seminar, 46, June 1963, New Delhi, Thaper.

The Hindu, Chennai.

The Tribune, Chandigarh.

The Indian Journal of Political Science, Vol. XXXVII, No. 1, 1976.

Young India, 1919-31, Ahmedabad: Navajivan Publishing House.

Index